BATMAN
Detective
No. 27

writer: **MICHAEL USLAN**

artist: **PETER SNEJBJERG**

letterer: **KURT HATHAWAY**

colorist & separator: **LEE LOUGHRIDGE**

BATMAN created by **BOB KANE**

BATMAN: DETECTIVE #27. PUBLISHED BY DC COMICS, 1700 BROADWAY, NEW YORK, NY 10019.
COPYRIGHT © 2003 DC COMICS. ALL RIGHTS RESERVED. ALL CHARACTERS FEATURED IN THIS
ISSUE, THE DISTINCTIVE LIKENESSES THEREOF AND RELATED INDICIA ARE TRADEMARKS OF
DC COMICS. THE STORIES, CHARACTERS AND INCIDENTS MENTIONED IN THIS MAGAZINE ARE
ENTIRELY FICTIONAL. DC COMICS DOES NOT READ OR ACCEPT UNSOLICITED SUBMISSIONS
OF IDEAS, STORIES OR ARTWORK. DC COMICS, A WARNER BROS. ENTERTAINMENT COMPANY.
PRINTED IN CANADA.
HARDCOVER ISBN: 1-4012-0185-7
SOFTCOVER ISBN: 1-4012-0107-5

COVER DESIGN: TERRY MARKS

ACT ONE

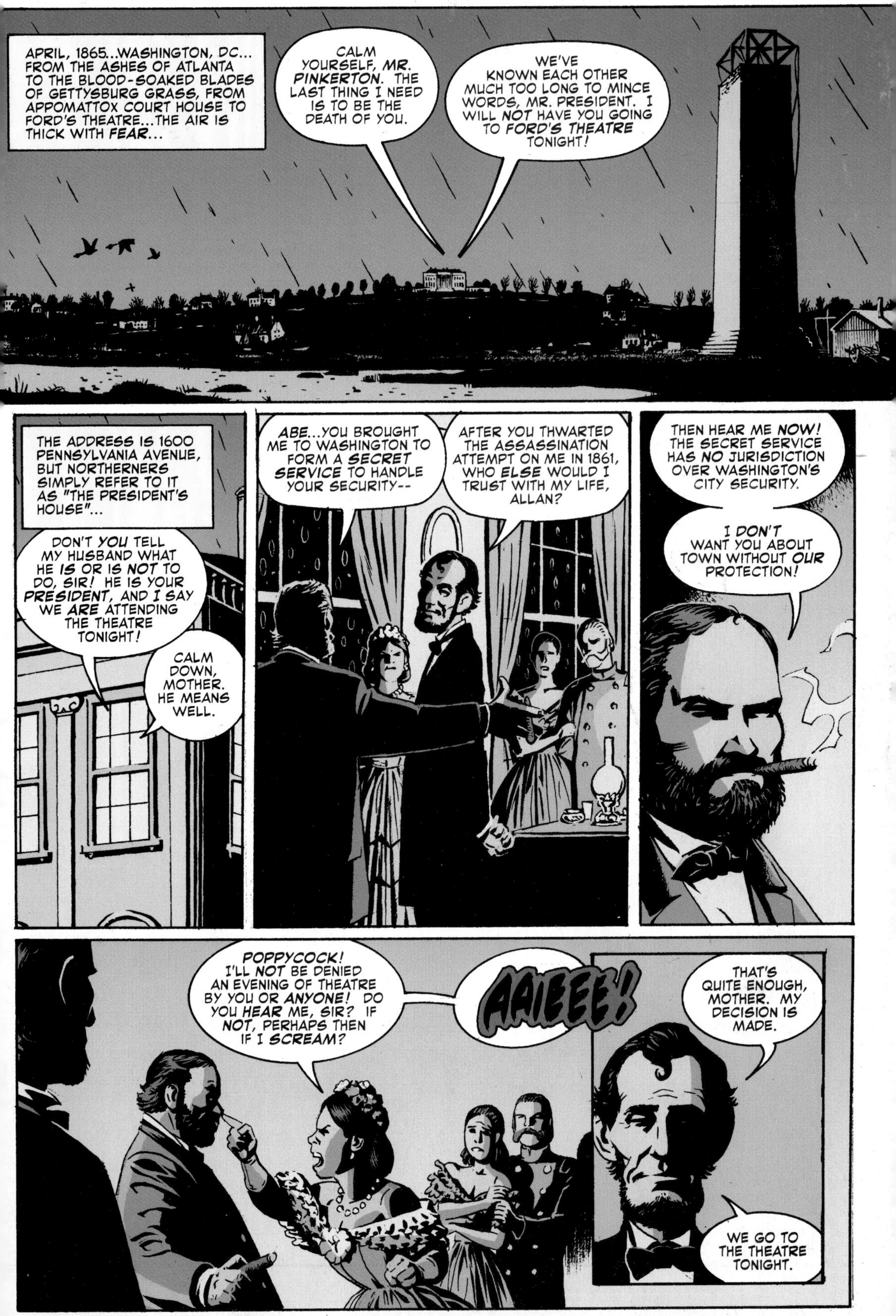

APRIL, 1865...WASHINGTON, DC... FROM THE ASHES OF ATLANTA TO THE BLOOD-SOAKED BLADES OF GETTYSBURG GRASS, FROM APPOMATTOX COURT HOUSE TO FORD'S THEATRE...THE AIR IS THICK WITH FEAR...
CALM YOURSELF, MR. PINKERTON. THE LAST THING I NEED IS TO BE THE DEATH OF YOU.
WE'VE KNOWN EACH OTHER MUCH TOO LONG TO MINCE WORDS, MR. PRESIDENT. I WILL NOT HAVE YOU GOING TO FORD'S THEATRE TONIGHT!
THE ADDRESS IS 1600 PENNSYLVANIA AVENUE, BUT NORTHERNERS SIMPLY REFER TO IT AS "THE PRESIDENT'S HOUSE"...
DON'T YOU TELL MY HUSBAND WHAT HE IS OR IS NOT TO DO, SIR! HE IS YOUR PRESIDENT, AND I SAY WE ARE ATTENDING THE THEATRE TONIGHT!
CALM DOWN, MOTHER. HE MEANS WELL.
ABE...YOU BROUGHT ME TO WASHINGTON TO FORM A SECRET SERVICE TO HANDLE YOUR SECURITY--
AFTER YOU THWARTED THE ASSASSINATION ATTEMPT ON ME IN 1861, WHO ELSE WOULD I TRUST WITH MY LIFE, ALLAN?
THEN HEAR ME NOW! THE SECRET SERVICE HAS NO JURISDICTION OVER WASHINGTON'S CITY SECURITY.
I DON'T WANT YOU ABOUT TOWN WITHOUT OUR PROTECTION!
POPPYCOCK! I'LL NOT BE DENIED AN EVENING OF THEATRE BY YOU OR ANYONE! DO YOU HEAR ME, SIR? IF NOT, PERHAPS THEN IF I SCREAM?
AAIEEE!
THAT'S QUITE ENOUGH, MOTHER. MY DECISION IS MADE.
WE GO TO THE THEATRE TONIGHT.

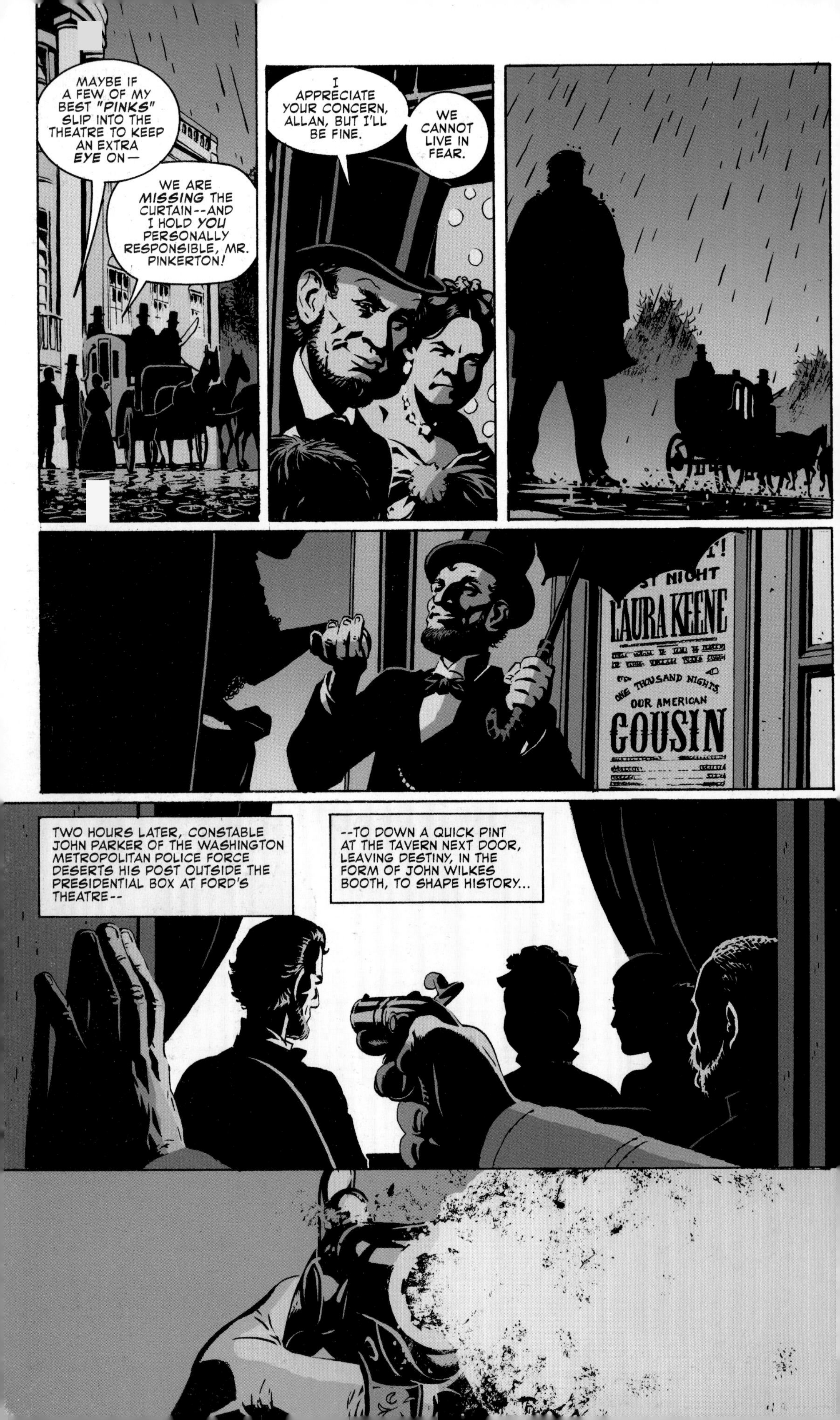
MAYBE IF A FEW OF MY BEST "PINKS" SLIP INTO THE THEATRE TO KEEP AN EXTRA EYE ON—
WE ARE MISSING THE CURTAIN--AND I HOLD YOU PERSONALLY RESPONSIBLE, MR. PINKERTON!
I APPRECIATE YOUR CONCERN, ALLAN, BUT I'LL BE FINE.
WE CANNOT LIVE IN FEAR.
LAURA KEENE
ONE THOUSAND NIGHTS
OUR AMERICAN COUSIN
TWO HOURS LATER, CONSTABLE JOHN PARKER OF THE WASHINGTON METROPOLITAN POLICE FORCE DESERTS HIS POST OUTSIDE THE PRESIDENTIAL BOX AT FORD'S THEATRE--
--TO DOWN A QUICK PINT AT THE TAVERN NEXT DOOR, LEAVING DESTINY, IN THE FORM OF JOHN WILKES BOOTH, TO SHAPE HISTORY...

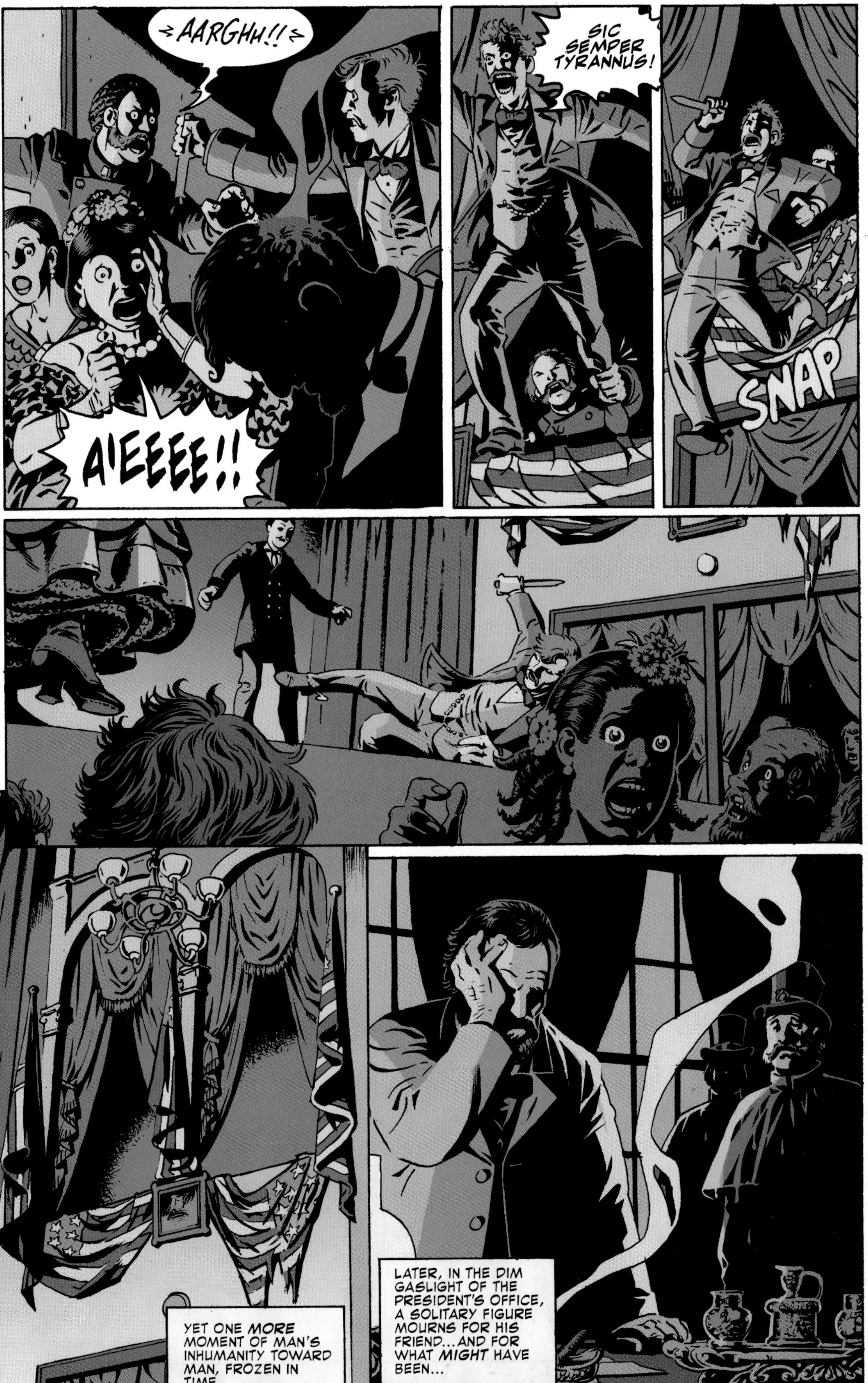
AARGHH!!
A'EEEE!!
SIC SEMPER TYRANNUS!
SNAP
YET ONE MORE MOMENT OF MAN'S INHUMANITY TOWARD MAN, FROZEN IN TIME...
LATER, IN THE DIM GASLIGHT OF THE PRESIDENT'S OFFICE, A SOLITARY FIGURE MOURNS FOR HIS FRIEND...AND FOR WHAT MIGHT HAVE BEEN...

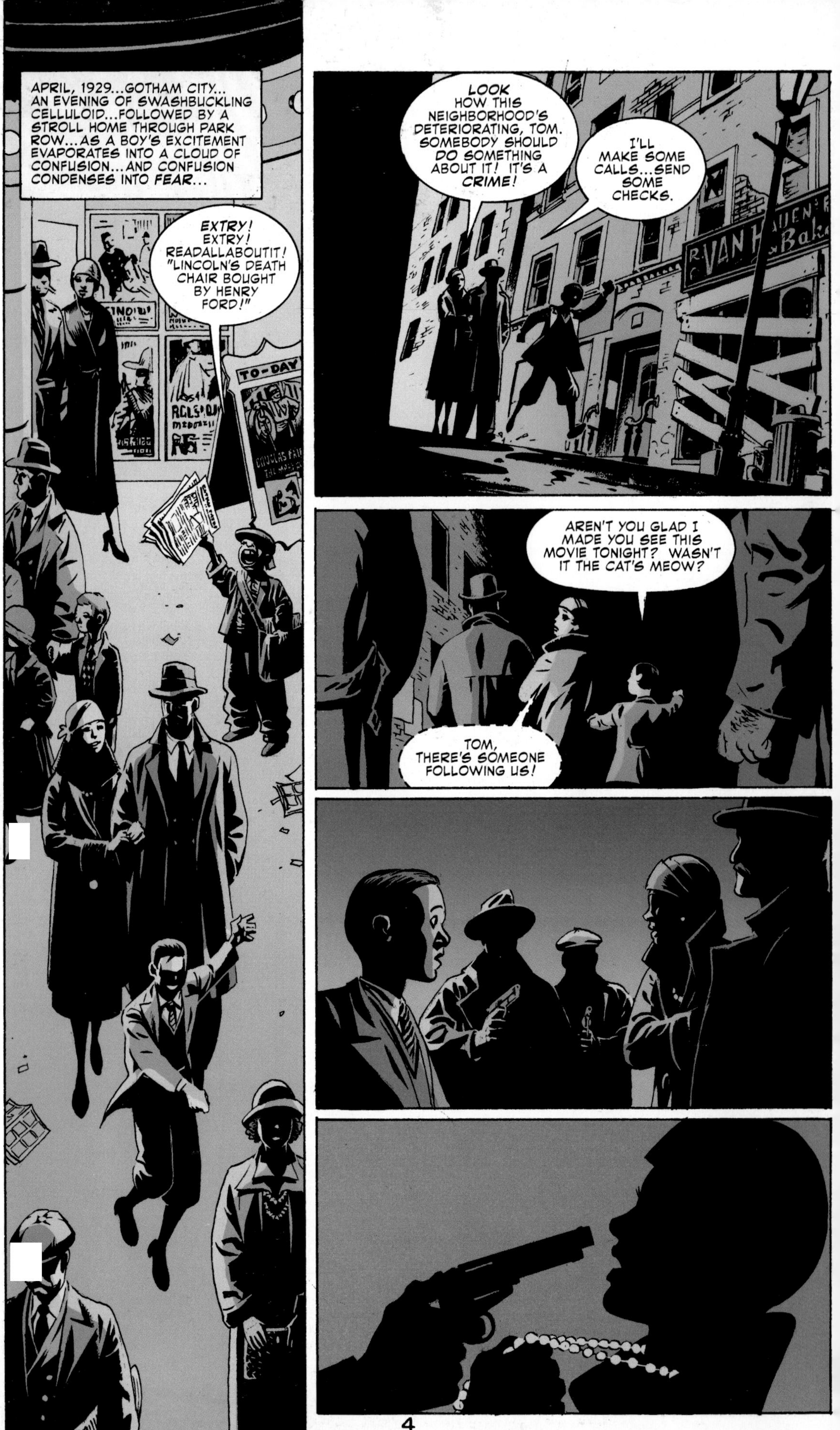
APRIL, 1929...GOTHAM CITY... AN EVENING OF SWASHBUCKLING CELLULOID...FOLLOWED BY A STROLL HOME THROUGH PARK ROW...AS A BOY'S EXCITEMENT EVAPORATES INTO A CLOUD OF CONFUSION...AND CONFUSION CONDENSES INTO FEAR...
EXTRY! EXTRY! READALLABOUTIT! "LINCOLN'S DEATH CHAIR BOUGHT BY HENRY FORD!"
TO-DAY
LOOK HOW THIS NEIGHBORHOOD'S DETERIORATING, TOM. SOMEBODY SHOULD DO SOMETHING ABOUT IT! IT'S A CRIME!
I'LL MAKE SOME CALLS...SEND SOME CHECKS.
AREN'T YOU GLAD I MADE YOU SEE THIS MOVIE TONIGHT? WASN'T IT THE CAT'S MEOW?
TOM, THERE'S SOMEONE FOLLOWING US!

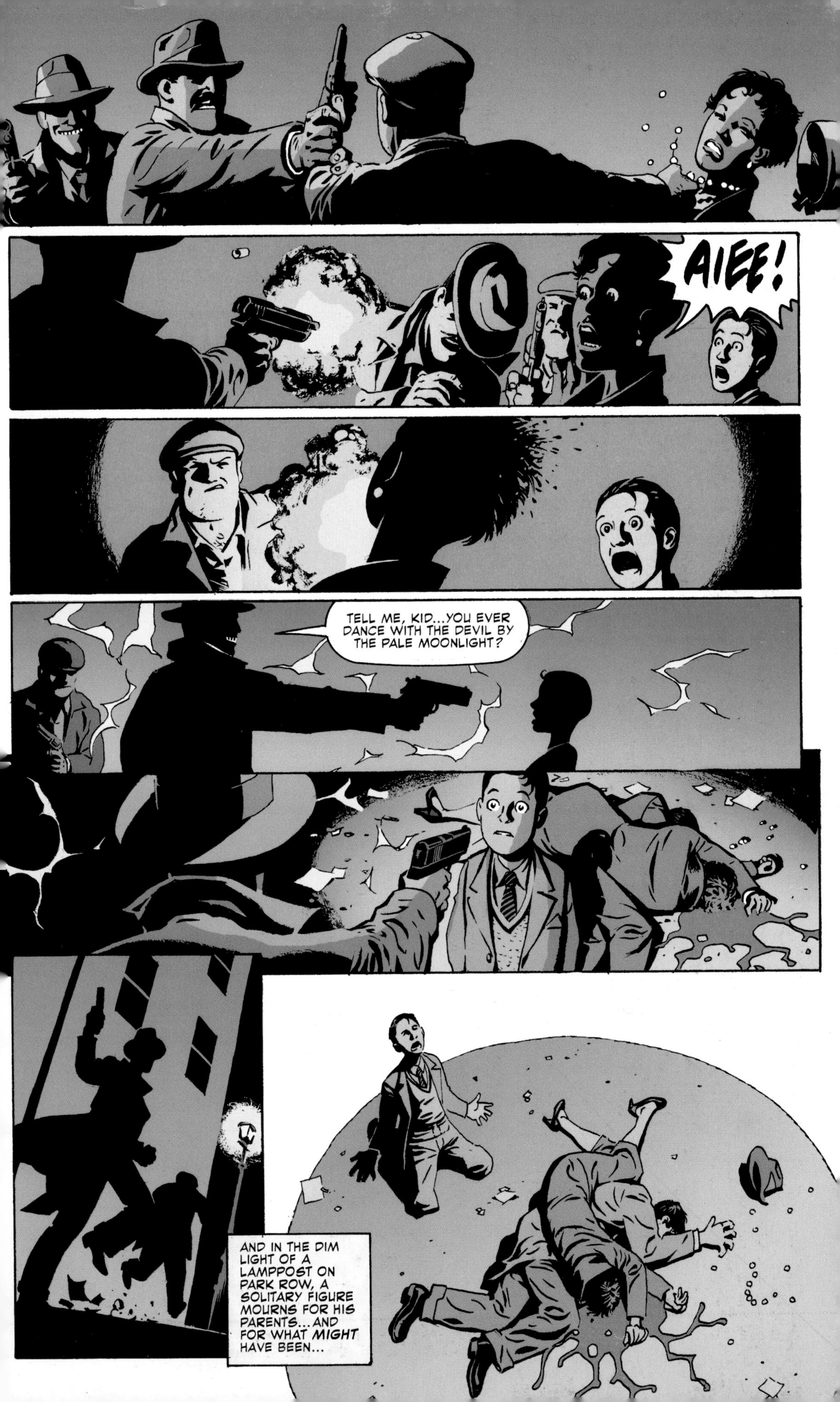
AIEE!
TELL ME, KID...YOU EVER DANCE WITH THE DEVIL BY THE PALE MOONLIGHT?
AND IN THE DIM LIGHT OF A LAMPPOST ON PARK ROW, A SOLITARY FIGURE MOURNS FOR HIS PARENTS... AND FOR WHAT *MIGHT* HAVE BEEN...

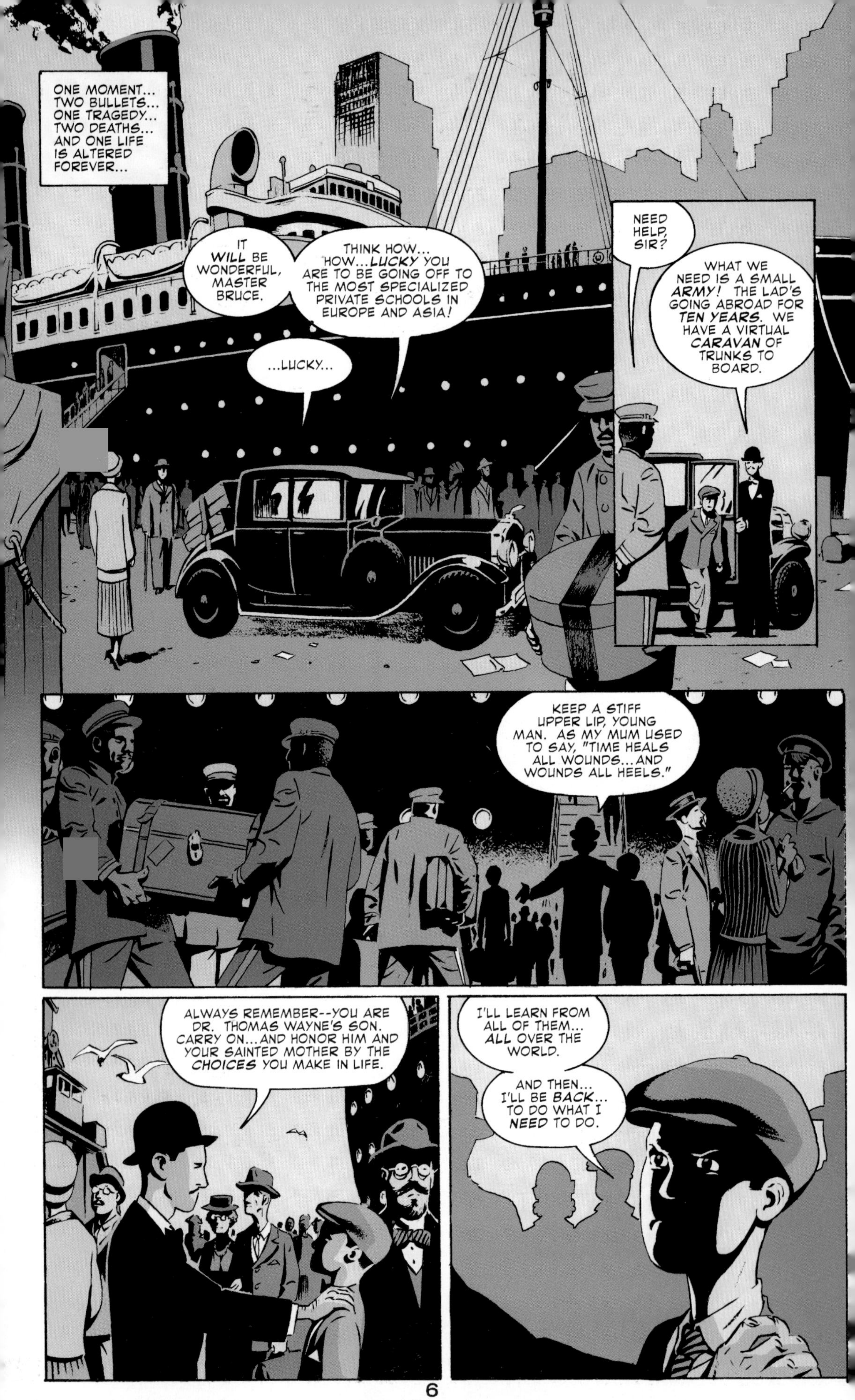

ONE MOMENT... TWO BULLETS... ONE TRAGEDY... TWO DEATHS... AND ONE LIFE IS ALTERED FOREVER...
IT WILL BE WONDERFUL, MASTER BRUCE.
THINK HOW... HOW...LUCKY YOU ARE TO BE GOING OFF TO THE MOST SPECIALIZED PRIVATE SCHOOLS IN EUROPE AND ASIA!
...LUCKY...
NEED HELP, SIR?
WHAT WE NEED IS A SMALL ARMY! THE LAD'S GOING ABROAD FOR TEN YEARS. WE HAVE A VIRTUAL CARAVAN OF TRUNKS TO BOARD.
KEEP A STIFF UPPER LIP, YOUNG MAN. AS MY MUM USED TO SAY, "TIME HEALS ALL WOUNDS...AND WOUNDS ALL HEELS."
ALWAYS REMEMBER--YOU ARE DR. THOMAS WAYNE'S SON. CARRY ON...AND HONOR HIM AND YOUR SAINTED MOTHER BY THE CHOICES YOU MAKE IN LIFE.
I'LL LEARN FROM ALL OF THEM... ALL OVER THE WORLD.
AND THEN... I'LL BE BACK... TO DO WHAT I NEED TO DO.

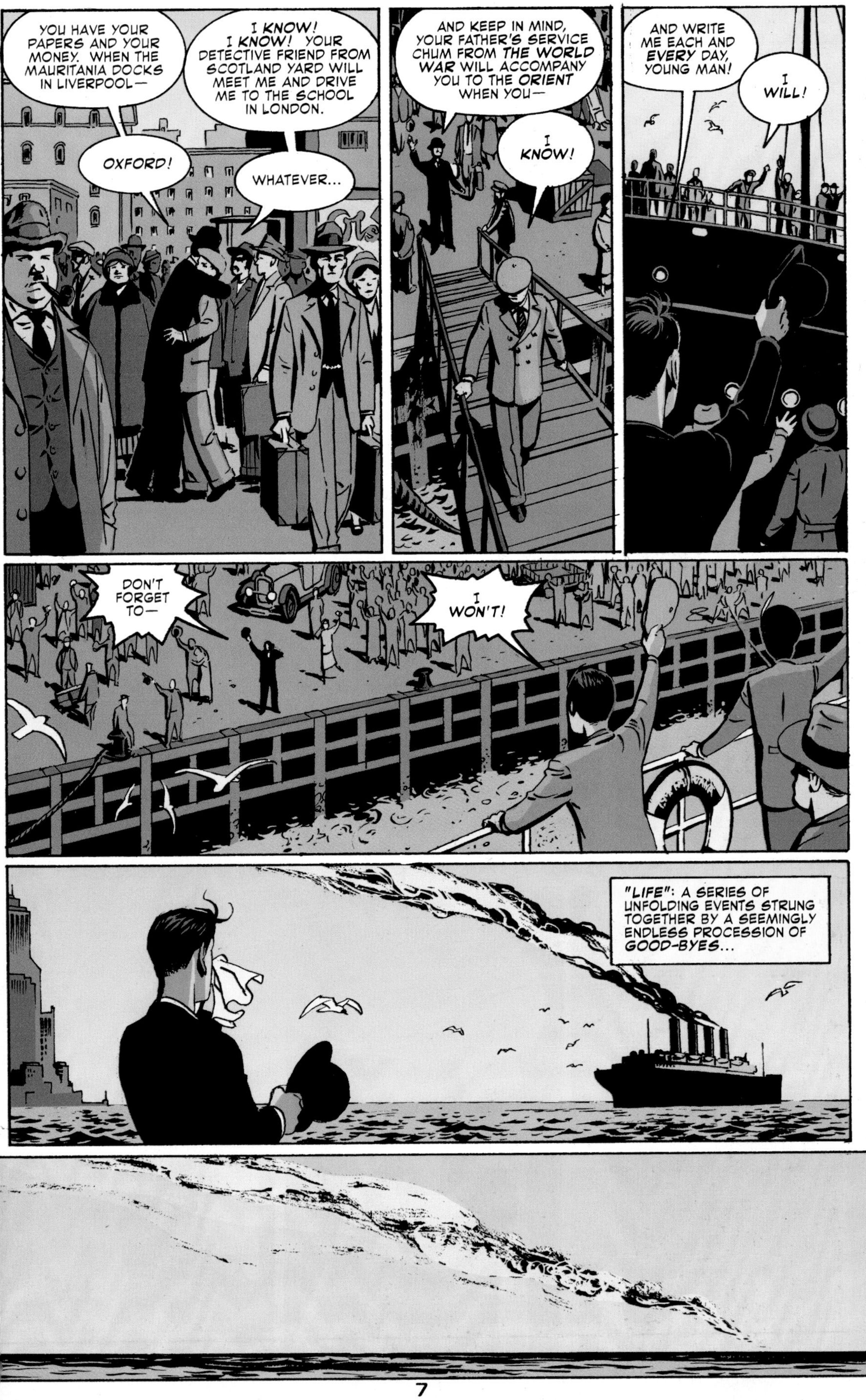
YOU HAVE YOUR PAPERS AND YOUR MONEY. WHEN THE MAURITANIA DOCKS IN LIVERPOOL—
OXFORD!
I KNOW! I KNOW! YOUR DETECTIVE FRIEND FROM SCOTLAND YARD WILL MEET ME AND DRIVE ME TO THE SCHOOL IN LONDON.
WHATEVER...
AND KEEP IN MIND, YOUR FATHER'S SERVICE CHUM FROM THE WORLD WAR WILL ACCOMPANY YOU TO THE ORIENT WHEN YOU—
I KNOW!
AND WRITE ME EACH AND EVERY DAY, YOUNG MAN!
I WILL!
DON'T FORGET TO—
I WON'T!
"LIFE": A SERIES OF UNFOLDING EVENTS STRUNG TOGETHER BY A SEEMINGLY ENDLESS PROCESSION OF GOOD-BYES...

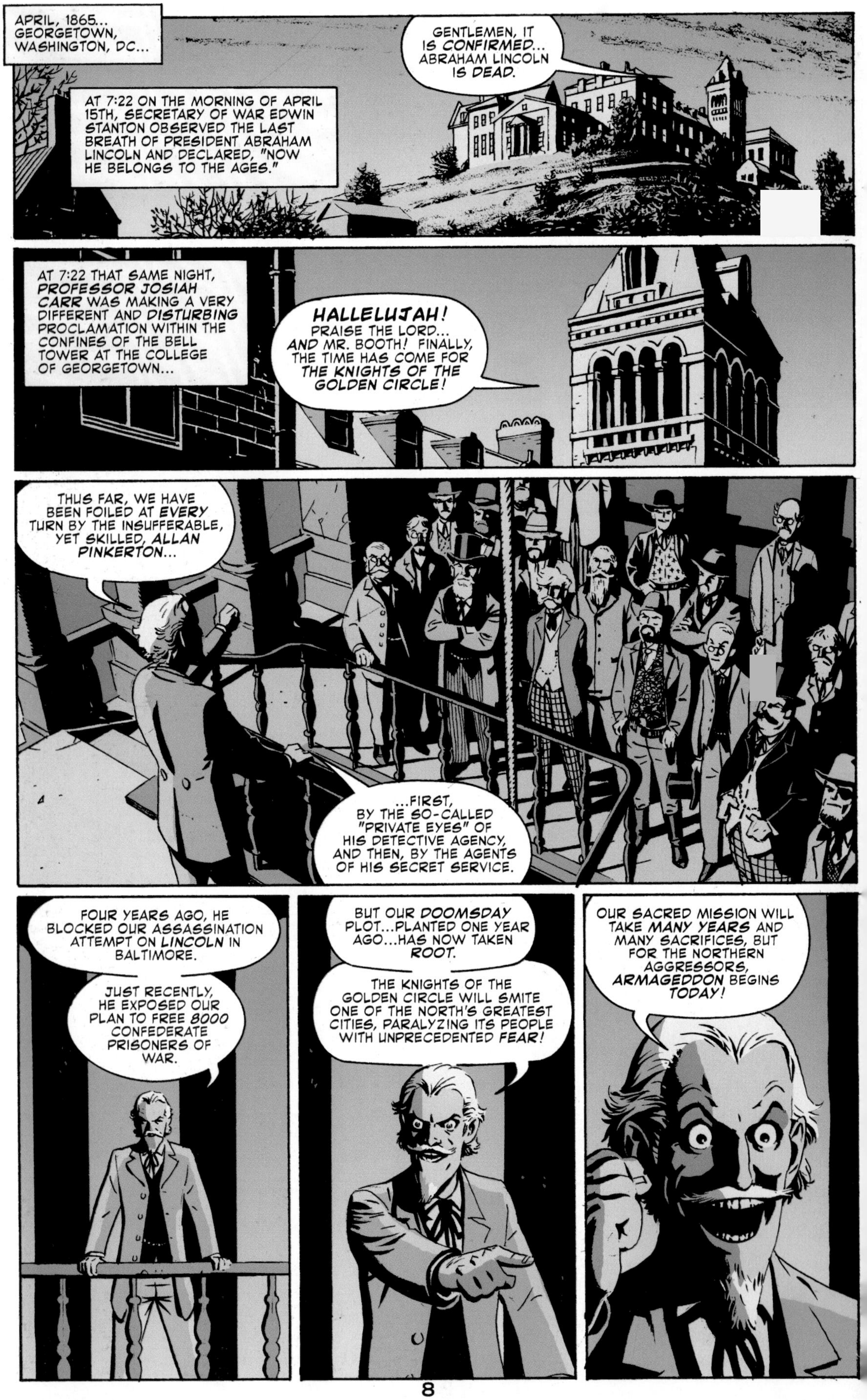
APRIL, 1865... GEORGETOWN, WASHINGTON, DC...
AT 7:22 ON THE MORNING OF APRIL 15TH, SECRETARY OF WAR EDWIN STANTON OBSERVED THE LAST BREATH OF PRESIDENT ABRAHAM LINCOLN AND DECLARED, "NOW HE BELONGS TO THE AGES."
GENTLEMEN, IT IS CONFIRMED... ABRAHAM LINCOLN IS DEAD.
AT 7:22 THAT SAME NIGHT, PROFESSOR JOSIAH CARR WAS MAKING A VERY DIFFERENT AND DISTURBING PROCLAMATION WITHIN THE CONFINES OF THE BELL TOWER AT THE COLLEGE OF GEORGETOWN...
HALLELUJAH! PRAISE THE LORD... AND MR. BOOTH! FINALLY, THE TIME HAS COME FOR THE KNIGHTS OF THE GOLDEN CIRCLE!
THUS FAR, WE HAVE BEEN FOILED AT EVERY TURN BY THE INSUFFERABLE, YET SKILLED, ALLAN PINKERTON...
...FIRST, BY THE SO-CALLED "PRIVATE EYES" OF HIS DETECTIVE AGENCY, AND THEN, BY THE AGENTS OF HIS SECRET SERVICE.
FOUR YEARS AGO, HE BLOCKED OUR ASSASSINATION ATTEMPT ON LINCOLN IN BALTIMORE.
JUST RECENTLY, HE EXPOSED OUR PLAN TO FREE 8000 CONFEDERATE PRISONERS OF WAR.
BUT OUR DOOMSDAY PLOT...PLANTED ONE YEAR AGO...HAS NOW TAKEN ROOT.
THE KNIGHTS OF THE GOLDEN CIRCLE WILL SMITE ONE OF THE NORTH'S GREATEST CITIES, PARALYZING ITS PEOPLE WITH UNPRECEDENTED FEAR!
OUR SACRED MISSION WILL TAKE MANY YEARS AND MANY SACRIFICES, BUT FOR THE NORTHERN AGGRESSORS, ARMAGEDDON BEGINS TODAY!

THIS *MANUSCRIPT* IS THE REASON I HAVE POURED OUR FINANCIAL RESOURCES INTO SECURING THE LOYALTY AND SERVICES OF THE SOUTH'S MOST BRILLIANT *BOTANISTS.* RESEARCH SCIENTISTS, AND *DOCTORS.*

WITH CONFEDERATE MONEY HAVING BECOME *VALUELESS,* MEN HAVE BECOME *DESPERATE.* DESPERATION SUPPLANTS PRINCIPLE AND HONOR.

WITHOUT PRINCIPLE AND HONOR, THE HEARTS AND MINDS OF MEN MAY BE BOUGHT BY GOLD...

...*OUR* GOLD!

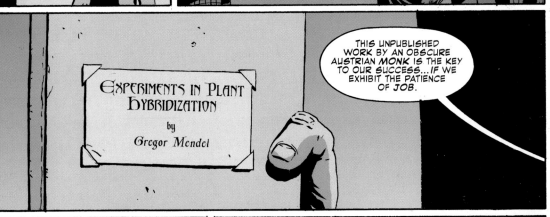

EXPERIMENTS IN PLANT HYBRIDIZATION

by

Gregor Mendel

THIS UNPUBLISHED WORK BY AN OBSCURE AUSTRIAN *MONK* IS THE KEY TO OUR *SUCCESS...IF* WE EXHIBIT THE PATIENCE OF *JOB.*

OUR LATE PRESIDENT'S *FAVORITE BOOK...*

...TONIGHT, WITH A DELICIOUS DASH OF IRONY, IT BECOMES YET ANOTHER *WEAPON* IN OUR REIGN OF *TERROR* AGAINST THE ENEMY!

JOE MILLER'S JOKE BOOK

AND SO, INSPIRED BY *JOE MILLER,* THE KING OF JOKERS AND RIDDLERS, I POSE THE QUESTION *THE NORTH* WILL ONE DAY BE *FORCED* TO ANSWER...

HAVE YOU EVER DANCED WITH THE DEVIL BY THE PALE MOONLIGHT?

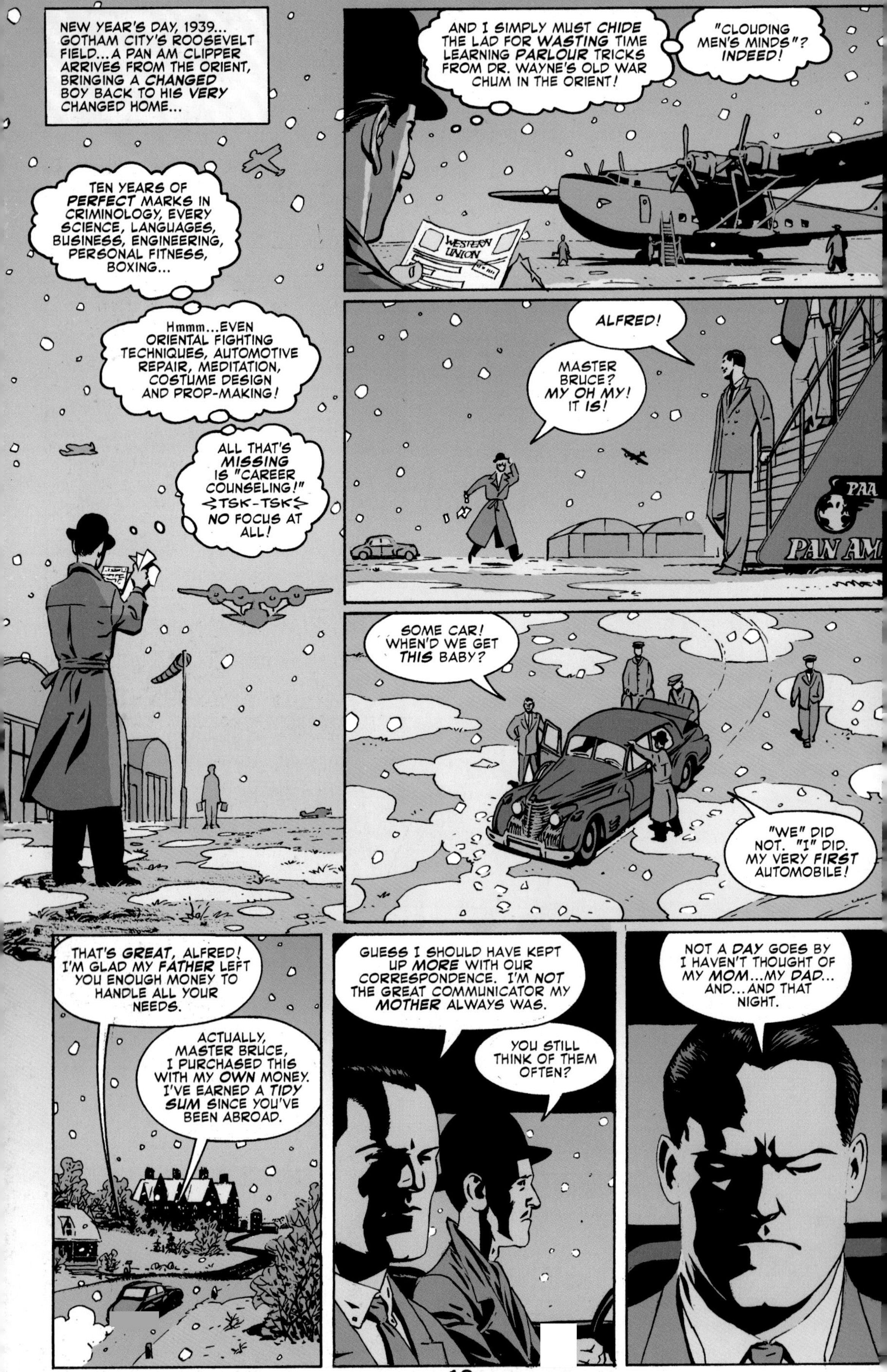

NEW YEAR'S DAY, 1939... GOTHAM CITY'S ROOSEVELT FIELD...A PAN AM CLIPPER ARRIVES FROM THE ORIENT, BRINGING A CHANGED BOY BACK TO HIS VERY CHANGED HOME...
TEN YEARS OF PERFECT MARKS IN CRIMINOLOGY, EVERY SCIENCE, LANGUAGES, BUSINESS, ENGINEERING, PERSONAL FITNESS, BOXING...
Hmmm...EVEN ORIENTAL FIGHTING TECHNIQUES, AUTOMOTIVE REPAIR, MEDITATION, COSTUME DESIGN AND PROP-MAKING!
ALL THAT'S MISSING IS "CAREER COUNSELING!" TSK-TSK NO FOCUS AT ALL!
AND I SIMPLY MUST CHIDE THE LAD FOR WASTING TIME LEARNING PARLOUR TRICKS FROM DR. WAYNE'S OLD WAR CHUM IN THE ORIENT!
"CLOUDING MEN'S MINDS"? INDEED!
WESTERN UNION
ALFRED!
MASTER BRUCE? MY OH MY! IT IS!
PAA
PAN AM
SOME CAR! WHEN'D WE GET THIS BABY?
"WE" DID NOT. "I" DID. MY VERY FIRST AUTOMOBILE!
THAT'S GREAT, ALFRED! I'M GLAD MY FATHER LEFT YOU ENOUGH MONEY TO HANDLE ALL YOUR NEEDS.
ACTUALLY, MASTER BRUCE, I PURCHASED THIS WITH MY OWN MONEY. I'VE EARNED A TIDY SUM SINCE YOU'VE BEEN ABROAD.
GUESS I SHOULD HAVE KEPT UP MORE WITH OUR CORRESPONDENCE. I'M NOT THE GREAT COMMUNICATOR MY MOTHER ALWAYS WAS.
YOU STILL THINK OF THEM OFTEN?
NOT A DAY GOES BY I HAVEN'T THOUGHT OF MY MOM...MY DAD... AND...AND THAT NIGHT.

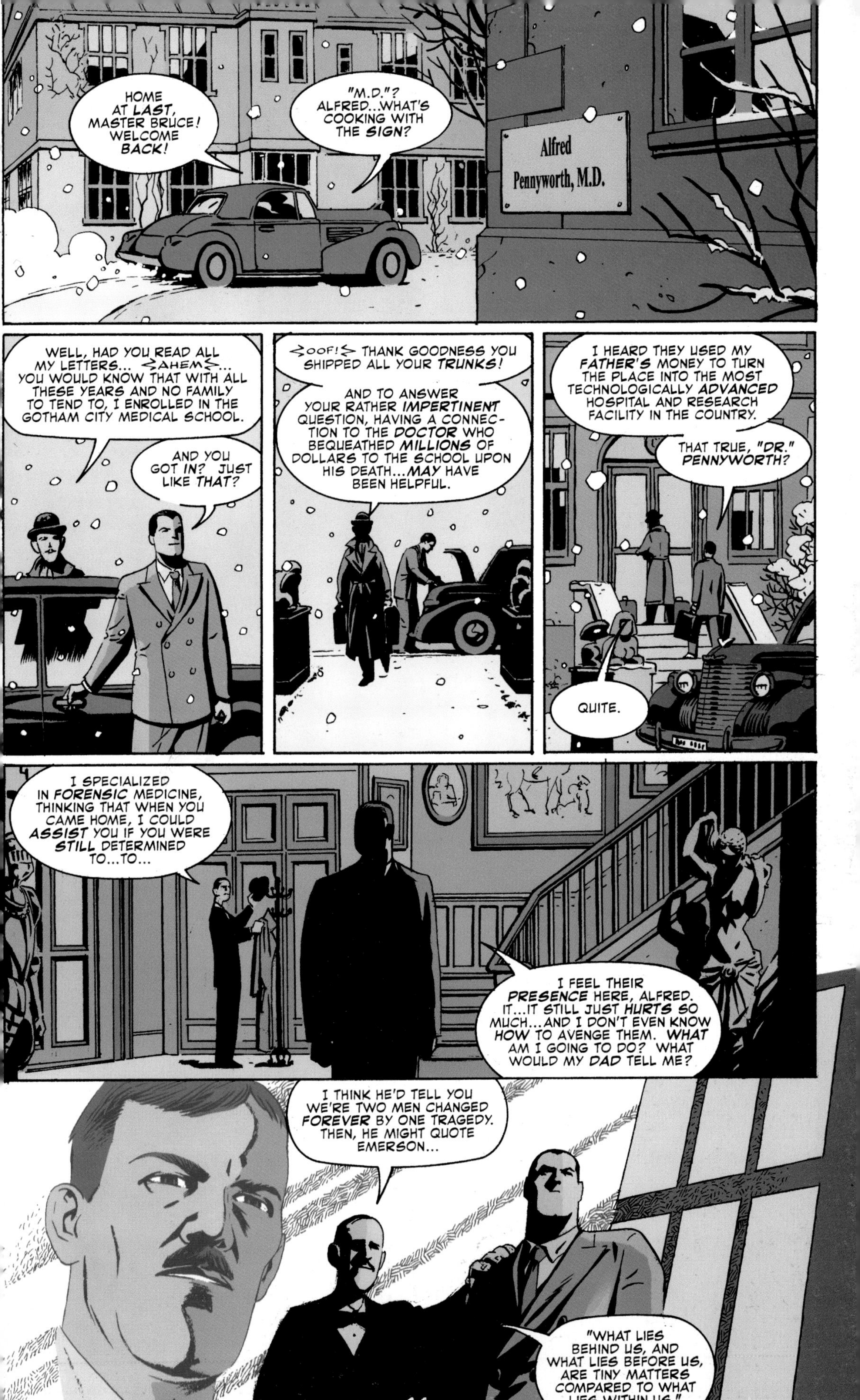

HOME AT LAST, MASTER BRUCE! WELCOME BACK!
"M.D."? ALFRED...WHAT'S COOKING WITH THE SIGN?
Alfred Pennyworth, M.D.
WELL, HAD YOU READ ALL MY LETTERS... <AHEM>... YOU WOULD KNOW THAT WITH ALL THESE YEARS AND NO FAMILY TO TEND TO, I ENROLLED IN THE GOTHAM CITY MEDICAL SCHOOL.
AND YOU GOT IN? JUST LIKE THAT?
<OOF!> THANK GOODNESS YOU SHIPPED ALL YOUR TRUNKS!
AND TO ANSWER YOUR RATHER IMPERTINENT QUESTION, HAVING A CONNECTION TO THE DOCTOR WHO BEQUEATHED MILLIONS OF DOLLARS TO THE SCHOOL UPON HIS DEATH...MAY HAVE BEEN HELPFUL.
I HEARD THEY USED MY FATHER'S MONEY TO TURN THE PLACE INTO THE MOST TECHNOLOGICALLY ADVANCED HOSPITAL AND RESEARCH FACILITY IN THE COUNTRY.
THAT TRUE, "DR." PENNYWORTH?
QUITE.
I SPECIALIZED IN FORENSIC MEDICINE, THINKING THAT WHEN YOU CAME HOME, I COULD ASSIST YOU IF YOU WERE STILL DETERMINED TO...TO...
I FEEL THEIR PRESENCE HERE, ALFRED. IT...IT STILL JUST HURTS SO MUCH...AND I DON'T EVEN KNOW HOW TO AVENGE THEM. WHAT AM I GOING TO DO? WHAT WOULD MY DAD TELL ME?
I THINK HE'D TELL YOU WE'RE TWO MEN CHANGED FOREVER BY ONE TRAGEDY. THEN, HE MIGHT QUOTE EMERSON...
"WHAT LIES BEHIND US, AND WHAT LIES BEFORE US, ARE TINY MATTERS COMPARED TO WHAT LIES WITHIN US."

APRIL, 1865...WHAT LIES WITHIN THE BELL TOWER OF THE COLLEGE OF GEORGETOWN IS FESTERING *HATRED*...

TODAY IS *LOST*. BUT IN *74 YEARS*, WE WILL EMERGE THE *VICTORS*! "SURVIVAL OF THE FITTEST."

AND IN THE YEAR *1939* THE KNIGHTS OF THE GOLDEN CIRCLE *WILL* BE THE FITTEST! THE *SOUTH* WILL RISE *AGAIN*!

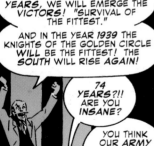

74 YEARS?!! ARE YOU *INSANE*?

YOU THINK OUR *ARMY* CAN RISE AGAIN ANY *FASTER*?

GENTLEMEN, OUR *GOLD* HAS BOUGHT US THE SERVICES OF THE *UNDER APPRECIATED* GENIUS WHO FIRST REALIZED THE CONCEPT OF "SURVIVAL OF THE FITTEST," THE BRITISH NATURALIST *CHARLES DARWIN*!

AND NOW ONE *MORE* SURPRISE...

THIS EVENING, I RECEIVED *PROOF* THAT CHARLES DARWIN IS, AS WE SPEAK, ENSCONCED IN A DEBATE IN LONDON OVER "NATURAL SELECTION."

APPARENTLY, THERE ARE *TWO* CHARLES DARWINS...

...AND I HAVE, NATURALLY, SELECTED *THIS* ONE TO DIE!

AND WHO *ELSE* COULD INFILTRATE OUR ORGANIZATION TIME AND AGAIN BUT...

ALLAN PINKERTON!

...WHO SHALL *NOW* JOIN HIS FRIEND, MR. LINCOLN, IN *HELL*!

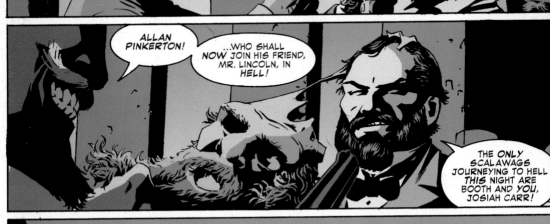

THE *ONLY* SCALAWAGS JOURNEYING TO HELL *THIS* NIGHT ARE BOOTH AND *YOU*, JOSIAH CARR!

K-CHAK!

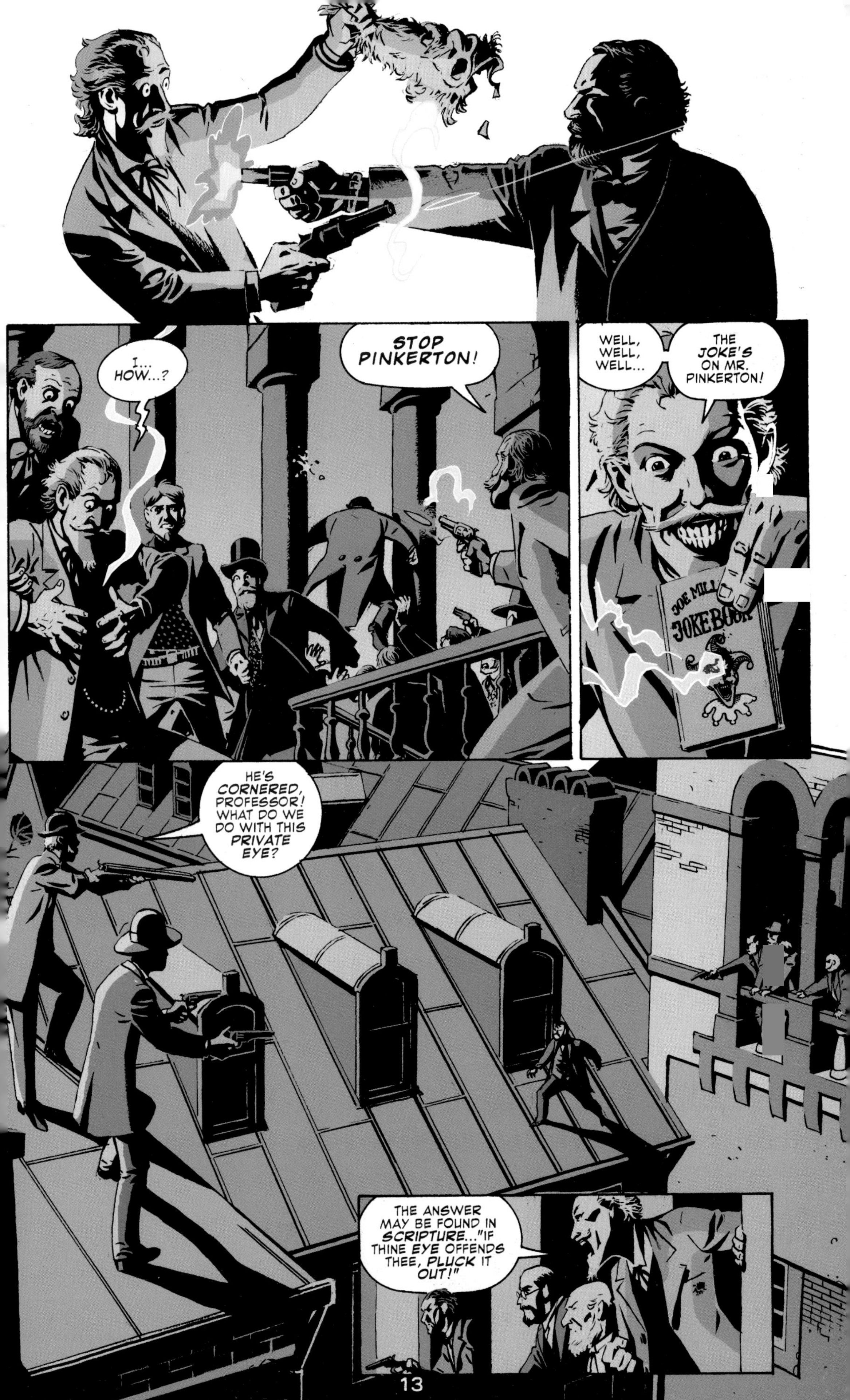
I... HOW...?
STOP PINKERTON!
WELL, WELL, WELL...
THE JOKE'S ON MR. PINKERTON!
JOE MILL
JOKEBOOK
HE'S CORNERED, PROFESSOR! WHAT DO WE DO WITH THIS PRIVATE EYE?
THE ANSWER MAY BE FOUND IN SCRIPTURE..."IF THINE EYE OFFENDS THEE, PLUCK IT OUT!"

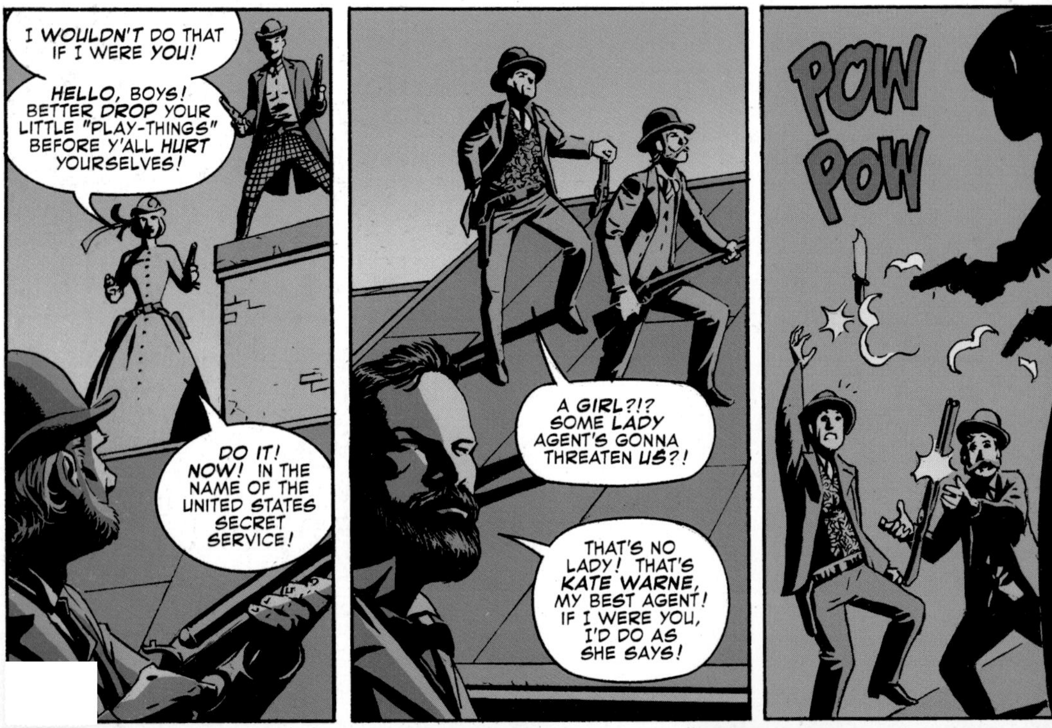
I WOULDN'T DO THAT IF I WERE YOU!
HELLO, BOYS! BETTER DROP YOUR LITTLE "PLAY-THINGS" BEFORE Y'ALL HURT YOURSELVES!
DO IT! NOW! IN THE NAME OF THE UNITED STATES SECRET SERVICE!
A GIRL?!? SOME LADY AGENT'S GONNA THREATEN US?!
THAT'S NO LADY! THAT'S KATE WARNE, MY BEST AGENT! IF I WERE YOU, I'D DO AS SHE SAYS!
POW
POW

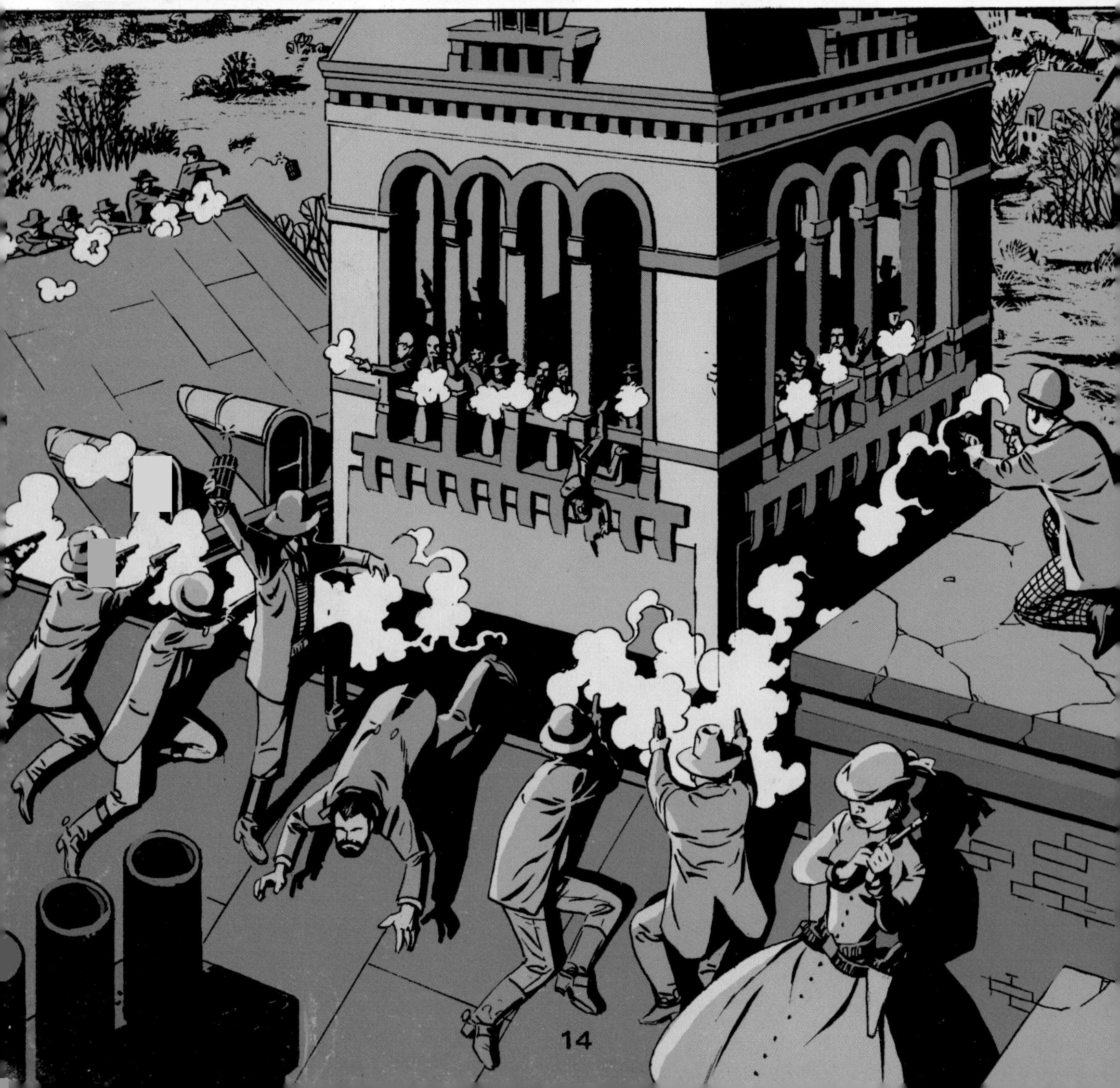

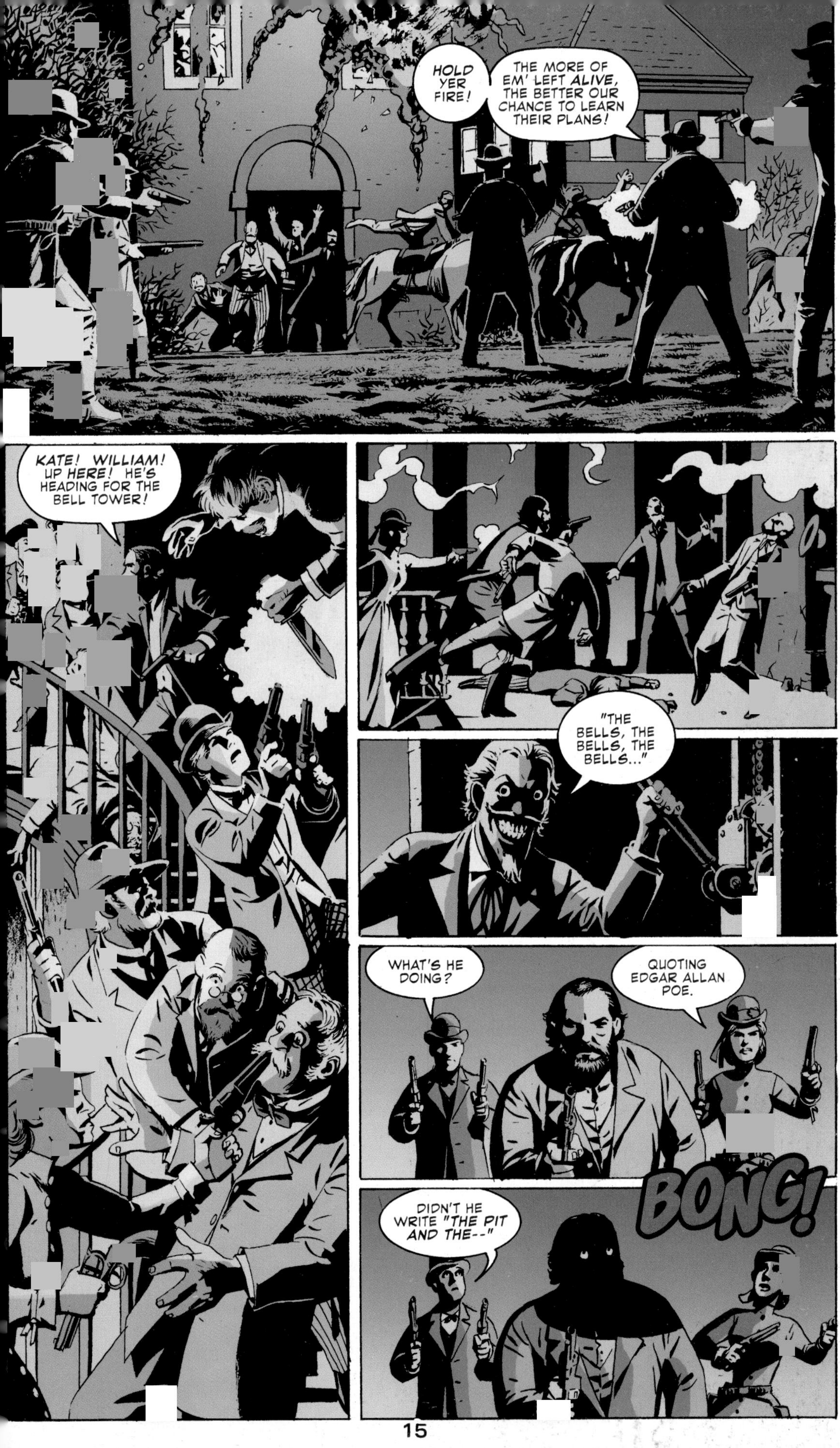

HOLD YER FIRE!
THE MORE OF EM' LEFT ALIVE, THE BETTER OUR CHANCE TO LEARN THEIR PLANS!
KATE! WILLIAM! UP HERE! HE'S HEADING FOR THE BELL TOWER!
"THE BELLS, THE BELLS, THE BELLS..."
WHAT'S HE DOING?
QUOTING EDGAR ALLAN POE.
BONG!
DIDN'T HE WRITE "THE PIT AND THE--"

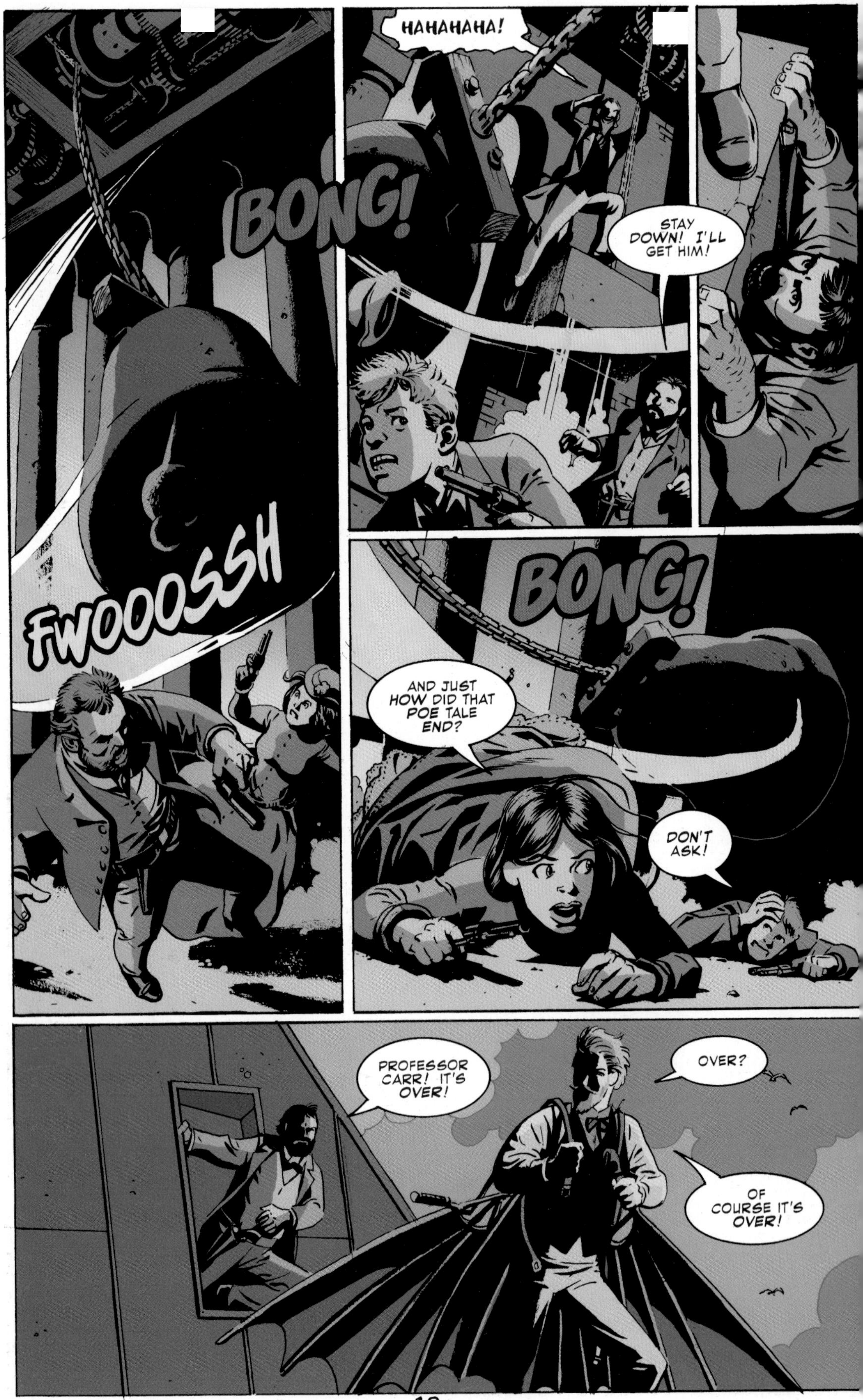
BONG!
FWOOOSSH
HAHAHAHA!
STAY DOWN! I'LL GET HIM!
BONG!
AND JUST HOW DID THAT POE TALE END?
DON'T ASK!
PROFESSOR CARR! IT'S OVER!
OVER?
OF COURSE IT'S OVER!

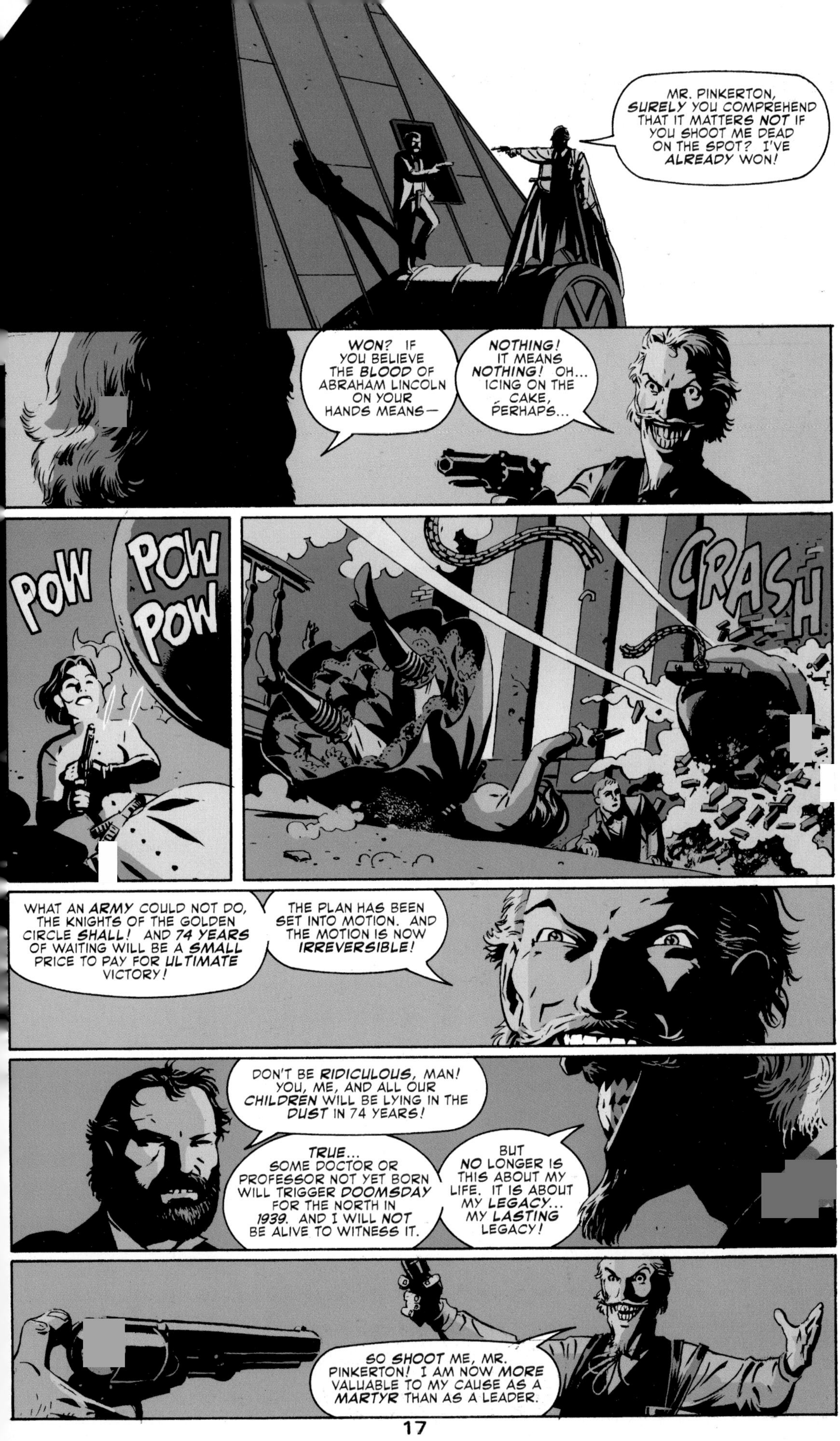
MR. PINKERTON, SURELY YOU COMPREHEND THAT IT MATTERS NOT IF YOU SHOOT ME DEAD ON THE SPOT? I'VE ALREADY WON!
WON? IF YOU BELIEVE THE BLOOD OF ABRAHAM LINCOLN ON YOUR HANDS MEANS—
NOTHING! IT MEANS NOTHING! OH... ICING ON THE CAKE, PERHAPS...
POW
POW POW
POW
CRASH
WHAT AN ARMY COULD NOT DO, THE KNIGHTS OF THE GOLDEN CIRCLE SHALL! AND 74 YEARS OF WAITING WILL BE A SMALL PRICE TO PAY FOR ULTIMATE VICTORY!
THE PLAN HAS BEEN SET INTO MOTION. AND THE MOTION IS NOW IRREVERSIBLE!
DON'T BE RIDICULOUS, MAN! YOU, ME, AND ALL OUR CHILDREN WILL BE LYING IN THE DUST IN 74 YEARS!
TRUE... SOME DOCTOR OR PROFESSOR NOT YET BORN WILL TRIGGER DOOMSDAY FOR THE NORTH IN 1939. AND I WILL NOT BE ALIVE TO WITNESS IT.
BUT NO LONGER IS THIS ABOUT MY LIFE. IT IS ABOUT MY LEGACY... MY LASTING LEGACY!
SO SHOOT ME, MR. PINKERTON! I AM NOW MORE VALUABLE TO MY CAUSE AS A MARTYR THAN AS A LEADER.

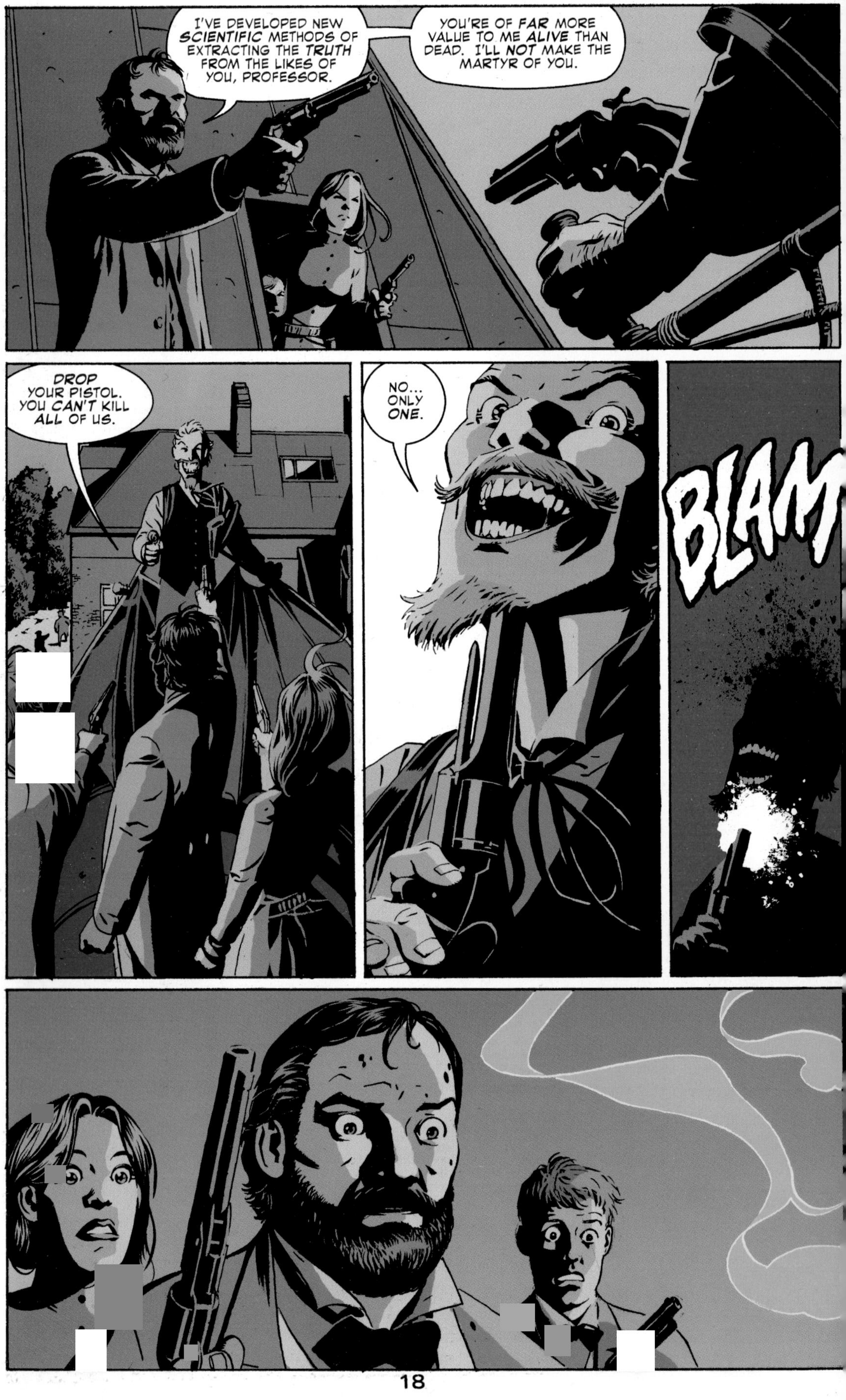
I'VE DEVELOPED NEW SCIENTIFIC METHODS OF EXTRACTING THE TRUTH FROM THE LIKES OF YOU, PROFESSOR.
YOU'RE OF FAR MORE VALUE TO ME ALIVE THAN DEAD. I'LL NOT MAKE THE MARTYR OF YOU.
DROP YOUR PISTOL. YOU CAN'T KILL ALL OF US.
NO... ONLY ONE.
BLAM

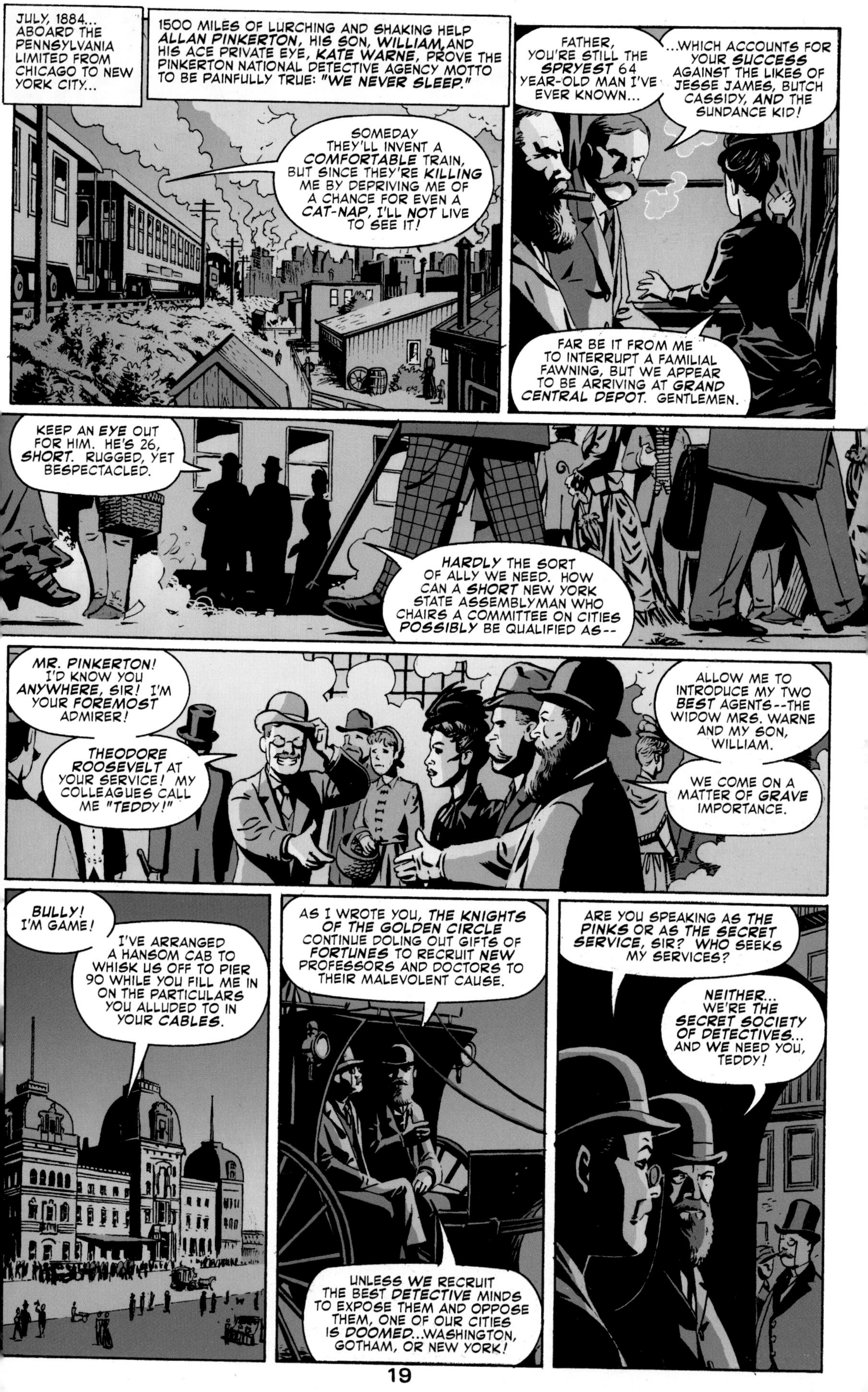

JULY, 1884... ABOARD THE PENNSYLVANIA LIMITED FROM CHICAGO TO NEW YORK CITY...
1500 MILES OF LURCHING AND SHAKING HELP ALLAN PINKERTON, HIS SON, WILLIAM, AND HIS ACE PRIVATE EYE, KATE WARNE, PROVE THE PINKERTON NATIONAL DETECTIVE AGENCY MOTTO TO BE PAINFULLY TRUE: "WE NEVER SLEEP."
SOMEDAY THEY'LL INVENT A COMFORTABLE TRAIN, BUT SINCE THEY'RE KILLING ME BY DEPRIVING ME OF A CHANCE FOR EVEN A CAT-NAP, I'LL NOT LIVE TO SEE IT!
FATHER, YOU'RE STILL THE SPRYEST 64 YEAR-OLD MAN I'VE EVER KNOWN...
...WHICH ACCOUNTS FOR YOUR SUCCESS AGAINST THE LIKES OF JESSE JAMES, BUTCH CASSIDY, AND THE SUNDANCE KID!
FAR BE IT FROM ME TO INTERRUPT A FAMILIAL FAWNING, BUT WE APPEAR TO BE ARRIVING AT GRAND CENTRAL DEPOT. GENTLEMEN.
KEEP AN EYE OUT FOR HIM. HE'S 26, SHORT. RUGGED, YET BESPECTACLED.
HARDLY THE SORT OF ALLY WE NEED. HOW CAN A SHORT NEW YORK STATE ASSEMBLYMAN WHO CHAIRS A COMMITTEE ON CITIES POSSIBLY BE QUALIFIED AS--
MR. PINKERTON! I'D KNOW YOU ANYWHERE, SIR! I'M YOUR FOREMOST ADMIRER!
THEODORE ROOSEVELT AT YOUR SERVICE! MY COLLEAGUES CALL ME "TEDDY!"
ALLOW ME TO INTRODUCE MY TWO BEST AGENTS--THE WIDOW MRS. WARNE AND MY SON, WILLIAM.
WE COME ON A MATTER OF GRAVE IMPORTANCE.
BULLY! I'M GAME!
I'VE ARRANGED A HANSOM CAB TO WHISK US OFF TO PIER 90 WHILE YOU FILL ME IN ON THE PARTICULARS YOU ALLUDED TO IN YOUR CABLES.
AS I WROTE YOU, THE KNIGHTS OF THE GOLDEN CIRCLE CONTINUE DOLING OUT GIFTS OF FORTUNES TO RECRUIT NEW PROFESSORS AND DOCTORS TO THEIR MALEVOLENT CAUSE.
UNLESS WE RECRUIT THE BEST DETECTIVE MINDS TO EXPOSE THEM AND OPPOSE THEM, ONE OF OUR CITIES IS DOOMED...WASHINGTON, GOTHAM, OR NEW YORK!
ARE YOU SPEAKING AS THE PINKS OR AS THE SECRET SERVICE, SIR? WHO SEEKS MY SERVICES?
NEITHER... WE'RE THE SECRET SOCIETY OF DETECTIVES... AND WE NEED YOU, TEDDY!

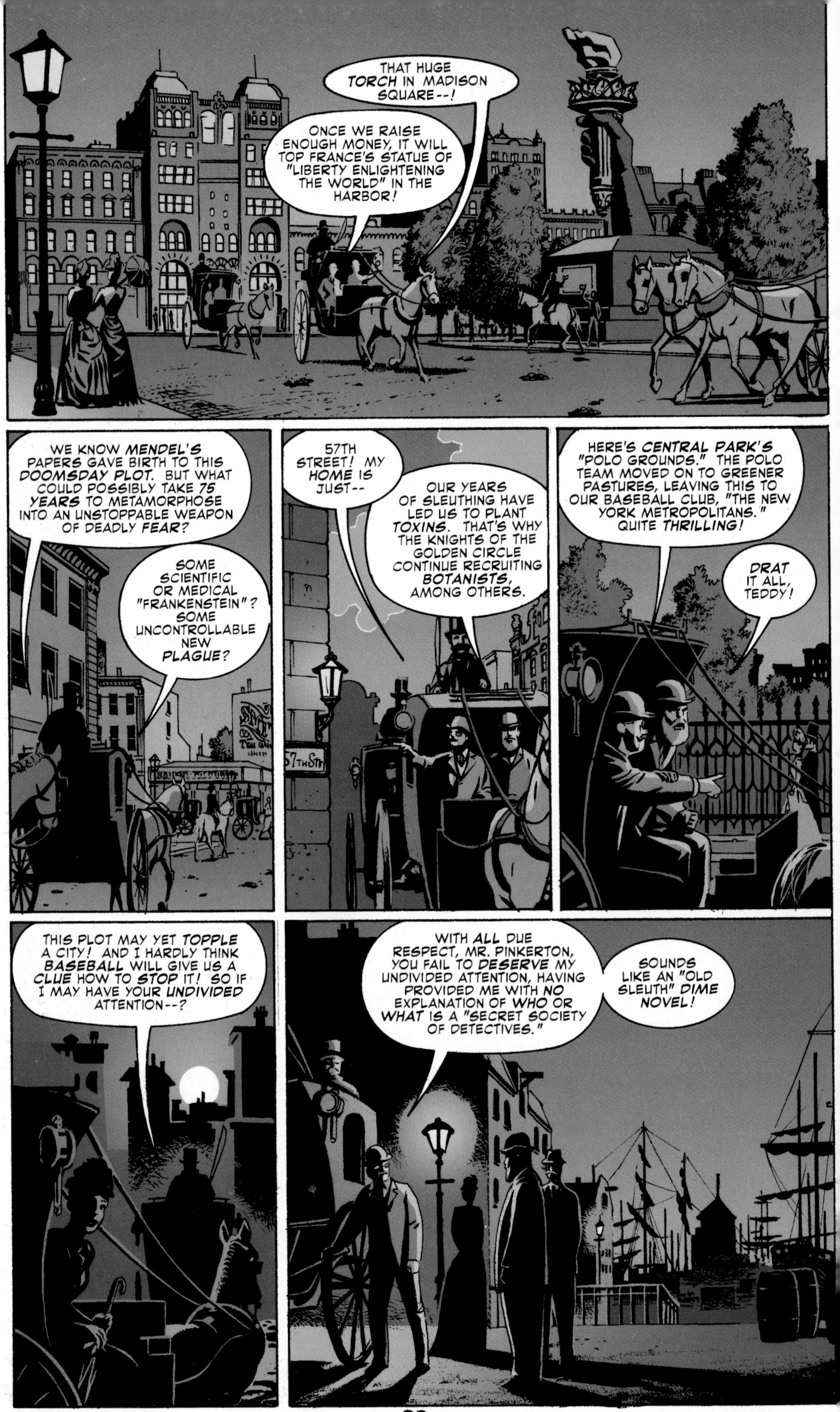
THAT HUGE TORCH IN MADISON SQUARE--!
ONCE WE RAISE ENOUGH MONEY, IT WILL TOP FRANCE'S STATUE OF "LIBERTY ENLIGHTENING THE WORLD" IN THE HARBOR!
WE KNOW MENDEL'S PAPERS GAVE BIRTH TO THIS DOOMSDAY PLOT. BUT WHAT COULD POSSIBLY TAKE 75 YEARS TO METAMORPHOSE INTO AN UNSTOPPABLE WEAPON OF DEADLY FEAR?
SOME SCIENTIFIC OR MEDICAL "FRANKENSTEIN"? SOME UNCONTROLLABLE NEW PLAGUE?
57TH STREET! MY HOME IS JUST--
OUR YEARS OF SLEUTHING HAVE LED US TO PLANT TOXINS. THAT'S WHY THE KNIGHTS OF THE GOLDEN CIRCLE CONTINUE RECRUITING BOTANISTS, AMONG OTHERS.
57TH St
HERE'S CENTRAL PARK'S "POLO GROUNDS." THE POLO TEAM MOVED ON TO GREENER PASTURES, LEAVING THIS TO OUR BASEBALL CLUB, "THE NEW YORK METROPOLITANS." QUITE THRILLING!
DRAT IT ALL, TEDDY!
THIS PLOT MAY YET TOPPLE A CITY! AND I HARDLY THINK BASEBALL WILL GIVE US A CLUE HOW TO STOP IT! SO IF I MAY HAVE YOUR UNDIVIDED ATTENTION--?
WITH ALL DUE RESPECT, MR. PINKERTON, YOU FAIL TO DESERVE MY UNDIVIDED ATTENTION, HAVING PROVIDED ME WITH NO EXPLANATION OF WHO OR WHAT IS A "SECRET SOCIETY OF DETECTIVES."
SOUNDS LIKE AN "OLD SLEUTH" DIME NOVEL!

TO PROTECT ITS MEMBERSHIP AND PRESERVE ITS ANONYMITY, THE SECRET SOCIETY OF DETECTIVES GIVES EACH INITIATE A NUMBER AND TAKES AWAY HIS NAME.

AND SO, IN ALL SOCIETY CORRESPONDENCE AND CONTACT, I'M SIMPLY "DETECTIVE #1: KATE--"DETECTIVE #2" AND WILLIAM-- "DETECTIVE #3."

WELL, IF IT'S SECRECY YOU DESIRE, YOU MIGHT WANT TO LOWER YOUR VOICE. IN THIS PART OF THE CITY, BETTER FOR A MAN OF NOTABLE MEANS TO WALK SOFTLY AND KEEP HIS WALLET.

I FORMED THIS UNIT TO COUNTER THE KNIGHTS OF THE GOLDEN CIRCLE...EVEN SHOULD IT TAKE THE FULL 75 YEARS TO EXPOSE ITS PLOT AND CORRAL ITS GROWING MEMBERSHIP.

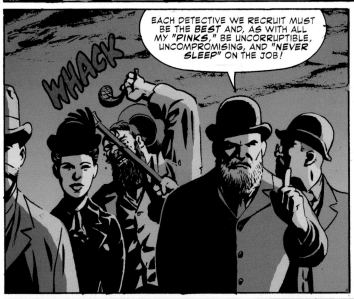

EACH DETECTIVE WE RECRUIT MUST BE THE BEST AND, AS WITH ALL MY "PINKS," BE UNCORRUPTIBLE, UNCOMPROMISING, AND "NEVER SLEEP" ON THE JOB!

WHACK

"WALK SOFTLY," EH?

WHACK WHACK

...Er... AND CARRY A BIG STICK! HA!

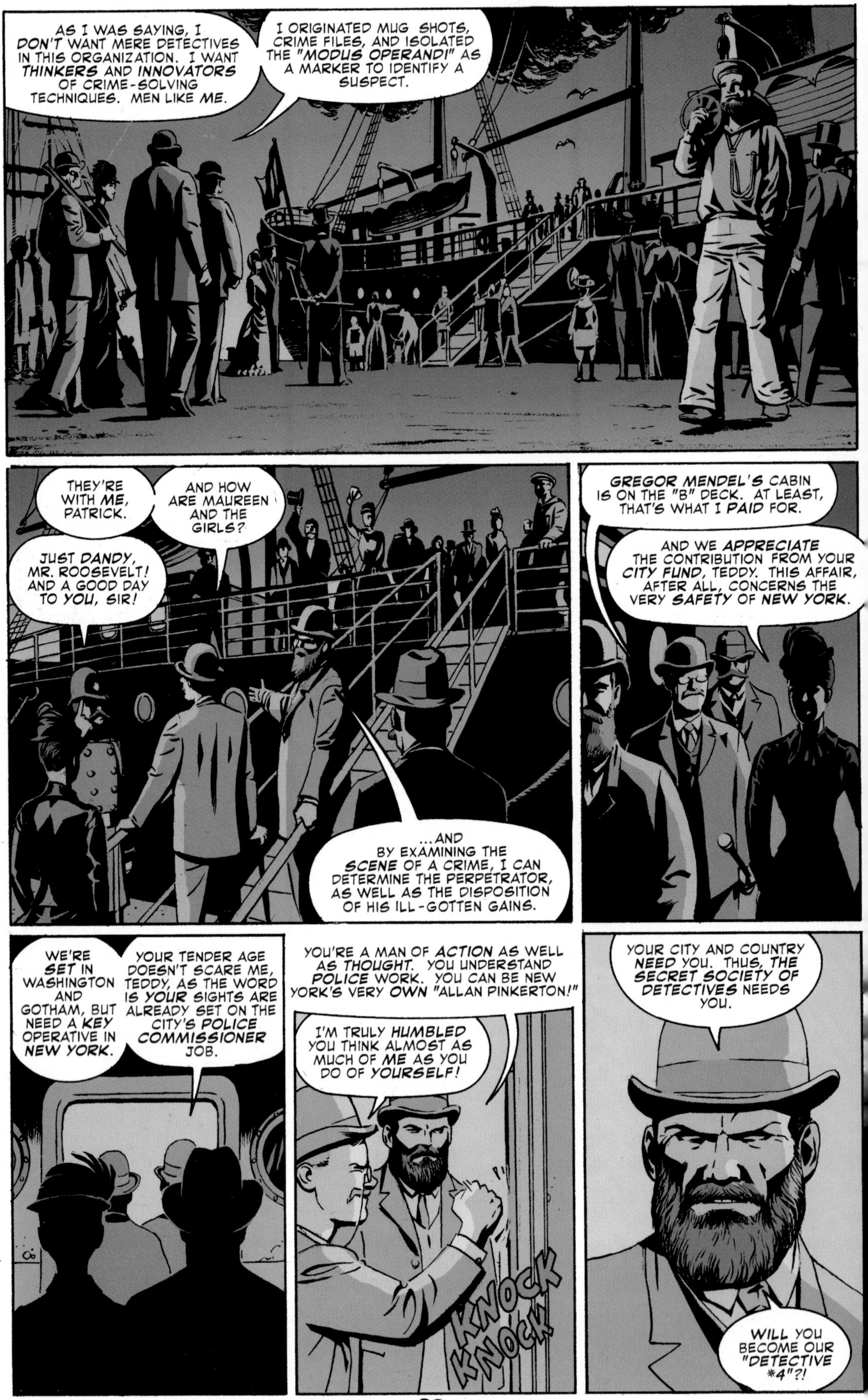
AS I WAS SAYING, I DON'T WANT MERE DETECTIVES IN THIS ORGANIZATION. I WANT THINKERS AND INNOVATORS OF CRIME-SOLVING TECHNIQUES. MEN LIKE ME.
I ORIGINATED MUG SHOTS, CRIME FILES, AND ISOLATED THE "MODUS OPERANDI" AS A MARKER TO IDENTIFY A SUSPECT.
THEY'RE WITH ME, PATRICK.
AND HOW ARE MAUREEN AND THE GIRLS?
JUST DANDY, MR. ROOSEVELT! AND A GOOD DAY TO YOU, SIR!
...AND BY EXAMINING THE SCENE OF A CRIME, I CAN DETERMINE THE PERPETRATOR, AS WELL AS THE DISPOSITION OF HIS ILL-GOTTEN GAINS.
GREGOR MENDEL'S CABIN IS ON THE "B" DECK. AT LEAST, THAT'S WHAT I PAID FOR.
AND WE APPRECIATE THE CONTRIBUTION FROM YOUR CITY FUND, TEDDY. THIS AFFAIR, AFTER ALL, CONCERNS THE VERY SAFETY OF NEW YORK.
WE'RE SET IN WASHINGTON AND GOTHAM, BUT NEED A KEY OPERATIVE IN NEW YORK.
YOUR TENDER AGE DOESN'T SCARE ME, TEDDY, AS THE WORD IS YOUR SIGHTS ARE ALREADY SET ON THE CITY'S POLICE COMMISSIONER JOB.
YOU'RE A MAN OF ACTION AS WELL AS THOUGHT. YOU UNDERSTAND POLICE WORK. YOU CAN BE NEW YORK'S VERY OWN "ALLAN PINKERTON!"
I'M TRULY HUMBLED YOU THINK ALMOST AS MUCH OF ME AS YOU DO OF YOURSELF!
KNOCK KNOCK
YOUR CITY AND COUNTRY NEED YOU. THUS, THE SECRET SOCIETY OF DETECTIVES NEEDS YOU.
WILL YOU BECOME OUR "DETECTIVE #4"?!

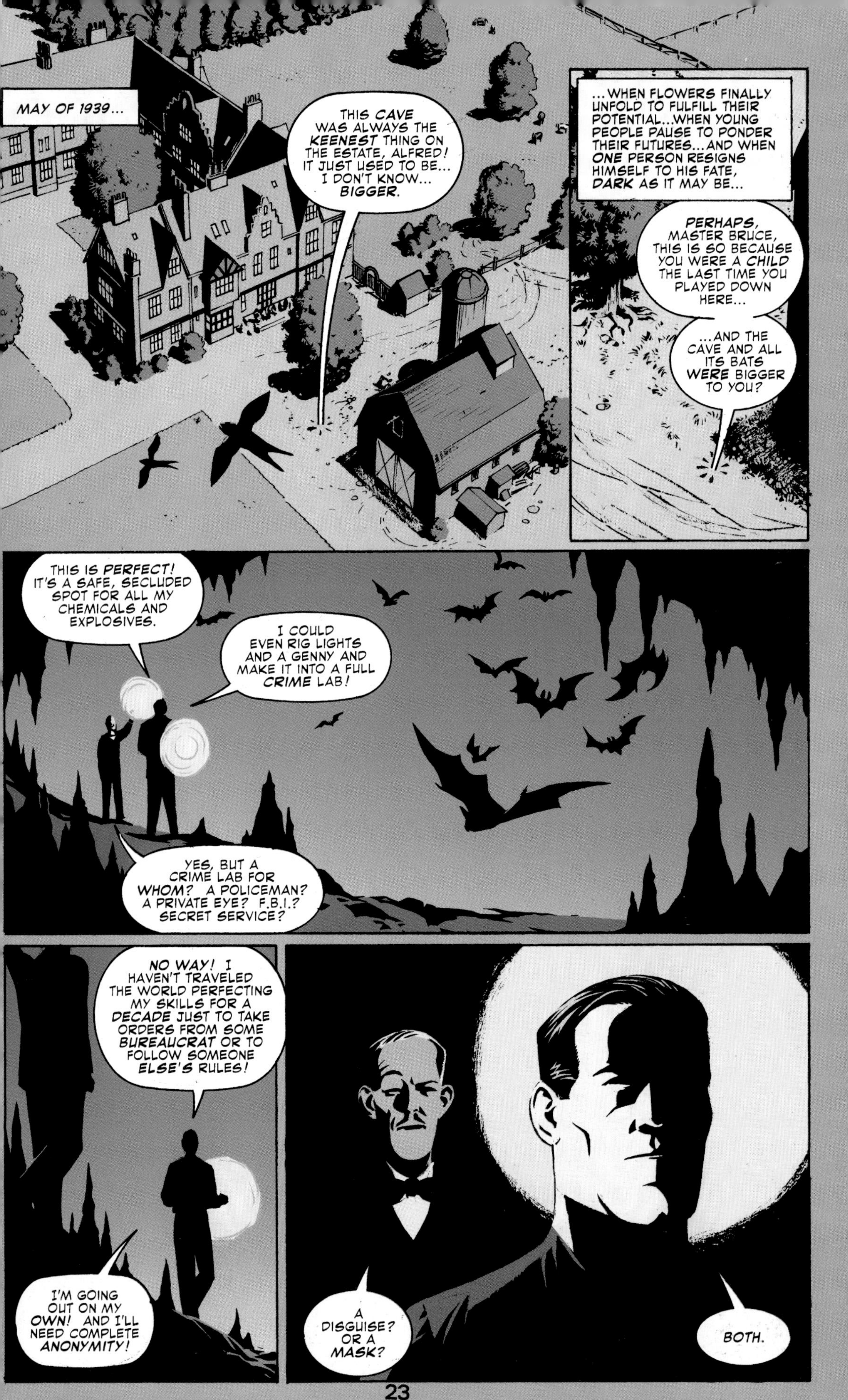

MAY OF 1939...
THIS CAVE WAS ALWAYS THE KEENEST THING ON THE ESTATE, ALFRED! IT JUST USED TO BE... I DON'T KNOW... BIGGER.
...WHEN FLOWERS FINALLY UNFOLD TO FULFILL THEIR POTENTIAL...WHEN YOUNG PEOPLE PAUSE TO PONDER THEIR FUTURES...AND WHEN ONE PERSON RESIGNS HIMSELF TO HIS FATE, DARK AS IT MAY BE...
PERHAPS, MASTER BRUCE, THIS IS SO BECAUSE YOU WERE A CHILD THE LAST TIME YOU PLAYED DOWN HERE...
...AND THE CAVE AND ALL ITS BATS WERE BIGGER TO YOU?
THIS IS PERFECT! IT'S A SAFE, SECLUDED SPOT FOR ALL MY CHEMICALS AND EXPLOSIVES.
I COULD EVEN RIG LIGHTS AND A GENNY AND MAKE IT INTO A FULL CRIME LAB!
YES, BUT A CRIME LAB FOR WHOM? A POLICEMAN? A PRIVATE EYE? F.B.I.? SECRET SERVICE?
NO WAY! I HAVEN'T TRAVELED THE WORLD PERFECTING MY SKILLS FOR A DECADE JUST TO TAKE ORDERS FROM SOME BUREAUCRAT OR TO FOLLOW SOMEONE ELSE'S RULES!
I'M GOING OUT ON MY OWN! AND I'LL NEED COMPLETE ANONYMITY!
A DISGUISE? OR A MASK?
BOTH.

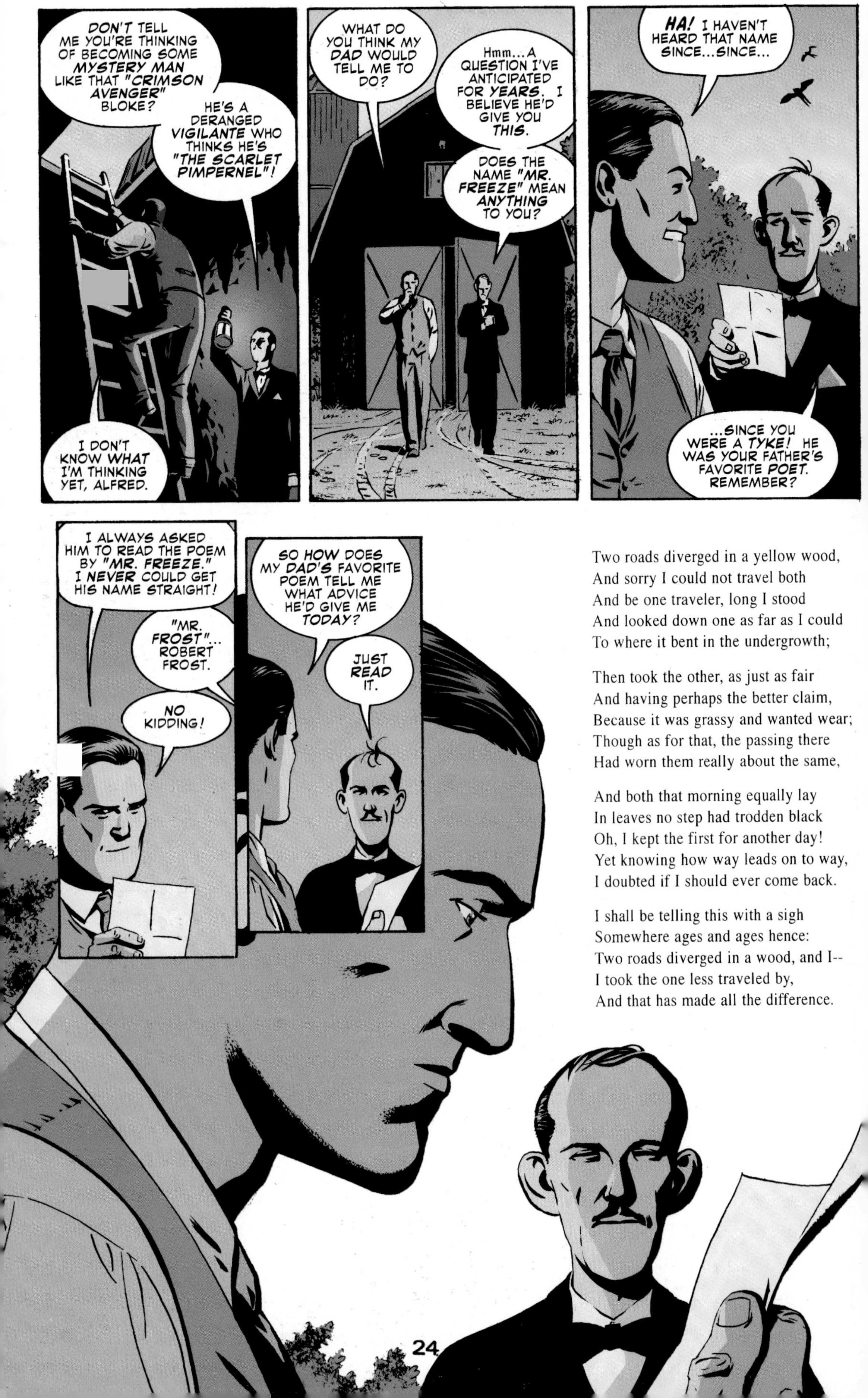
DON'T TELL ME YOU'RE THINKING OF BECOMING SOME MYSTERY MAN LIKE THAT "CRIMSON AVENGER" BLOKE?
HE'S A DERANGED VIGILANTE WHO THINKS HE'S "THE SCARLET PIMPERNEL"!
I DON'T KNOW WHAT I'M THINKING YET, ALFRED.
WHAT DO YOU THINK MY DAD WOULD TELL ME TO DO?
Hmm...A QUESTION I'VE ANTICIPATED FOR YEARS. I BELIEVE HE'D GIVE YOU THIS.
DOES THE NAME "MR. FREEZE" MEAN ANYTHING TO YOU?
HA! I HAVEN'T HEARD THAT NAME SINCE...SINCE...
...SINCE YOU WERE A TYKE! HE WAS YOUR FATHER'S FAVORITE POET. REMEMBER?
I ALWAYS ASKED HIM TO READ THE POEM BY "MR. FREEZE." I NEVER COULD GET HIS NAME STRAIGHT!
"MR. FROST"... ROBERT FROST.
NO KIDDING!
SO HOW DOES MY DAD'S FAVORITE POEM TELL ME WHAT ADVICE HE'D GIVE ME TODAY?
JUST READ IT.
Two roads diverged in a yellow wood,
And sorry I could not travel both
And be one traveler, long I stood
And looked down one as far as I could
To where it bent in the undergrowth;
Then took the other, as just as fair
And having perhaps the better claim,
Because it was grassy and wanted wear;
Though as for that, the passing there
Had worn them really about the same,
And both that morning equally lay
In leaves no step had trodden black
Oh, I kept the first for another day!
Yet knowing how way leads on to way,
I doubted if I should ever come back.
I shall be telling this with a sigh
Somewhere ages and ages hence:
Two roads diverged in a wood, and I--
I took the one less traveled by,
And that has made all the difference.

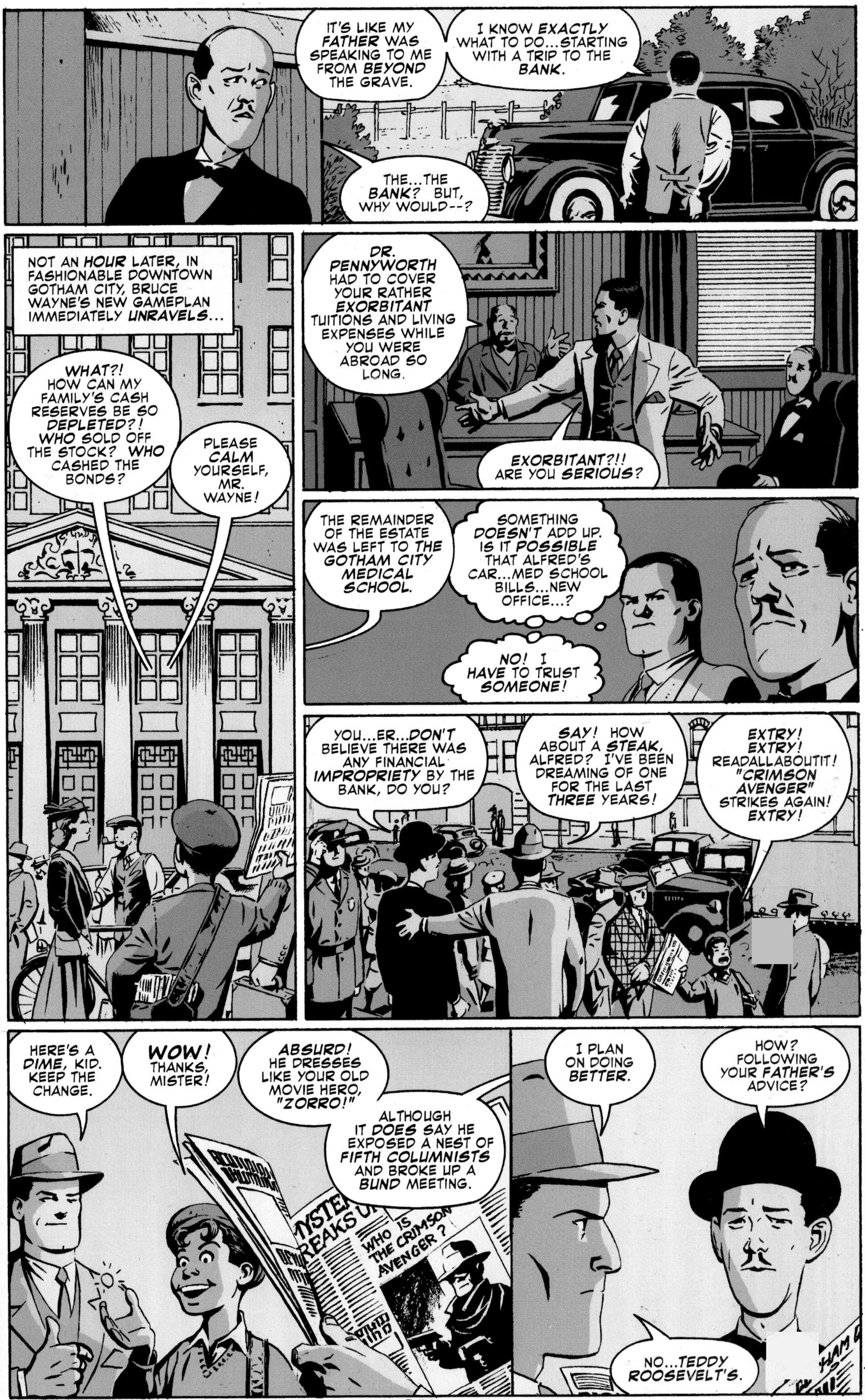
IT'S LIKE MY FATHER WAS SPEAKING TO ME FROM BEYOND THE GRAVE.
I KNOW EXACTLY WHAT TO DO...STARTING WITH A TRIP TO THE BANK.
THE...THE BANK? BUT, WHY WOULD--?
NOT AN HOUR LATER, IN FASHIONABLE DOWNTOWN GOTHAM CITY, BRUCE WAYNE'S NEW GAMEPLAN IMMEDIATELY UNRAVELS...
WHAT?! HOW CAN MY FAMILY'S CASH RESERVES BE SO DEPLETED?! WHO SOLD OFF THE STOCK? WHO CASHED THE BONDS?
PLEASE CALM YOURSELF, MR. WAYNE!
DR. PENNYWORTH HAD TO COVER YOUR RATHER EXORBITANT TUITIONS AND LIVING EXPENSES WHILE YOU WERE ABROAD SO LONG.
EXORBITANT?!! ARE YOU SERIOUS?
THE REMAINDER OF THE ESTATE WAS LEFT TO THE GOTHAM CITY MEDICAL SCHOOL.
SOMETHING DOESN'T ADD UP. IS IT POSSIBLE THAT ALFRED'S CAR...MED SCHOOL BILLS...NEW OFFICE...?
NO! I HAVE TO TRUST SOMEONE!
YOU...ER...DON'T BELIEVE THERE WAS ANY FINANCIAL IMPROPRIETY BY THE BANK, DO YOU?
SAY! HOW ABOUT A STEAK, ALFRED? I'VE BEEN DREAMING OF ONE FOR THE LAST THREE YEARS!
EXTRY! EXTRY! READALLABOUTIT! "CRIMSON AVENGER" STRIKES AGAIN! EXTRY!
HERE'S A DIME, KID. KEEP THE CHANGE.
WOW! THANKS, MISTER!
ABSURD! HE DRESSES LIKE YOUR OLD MOVIE HERO, "ZORRO!"
ALTHOUGH IT DOES SAY HE EXPOSED A NEST OF FIFTH COLUMNISTS AND BROKE UP A BUND MEETING.
MYSTER... BREAKS U...
WHO IS THE CRIMSON AVENGER?
I PLAN ON DOING BETTER.
HOW? FOLLOWING YOUR FATHER'S ADVICE?
NO...TEDDY ROOSEVELT'S.

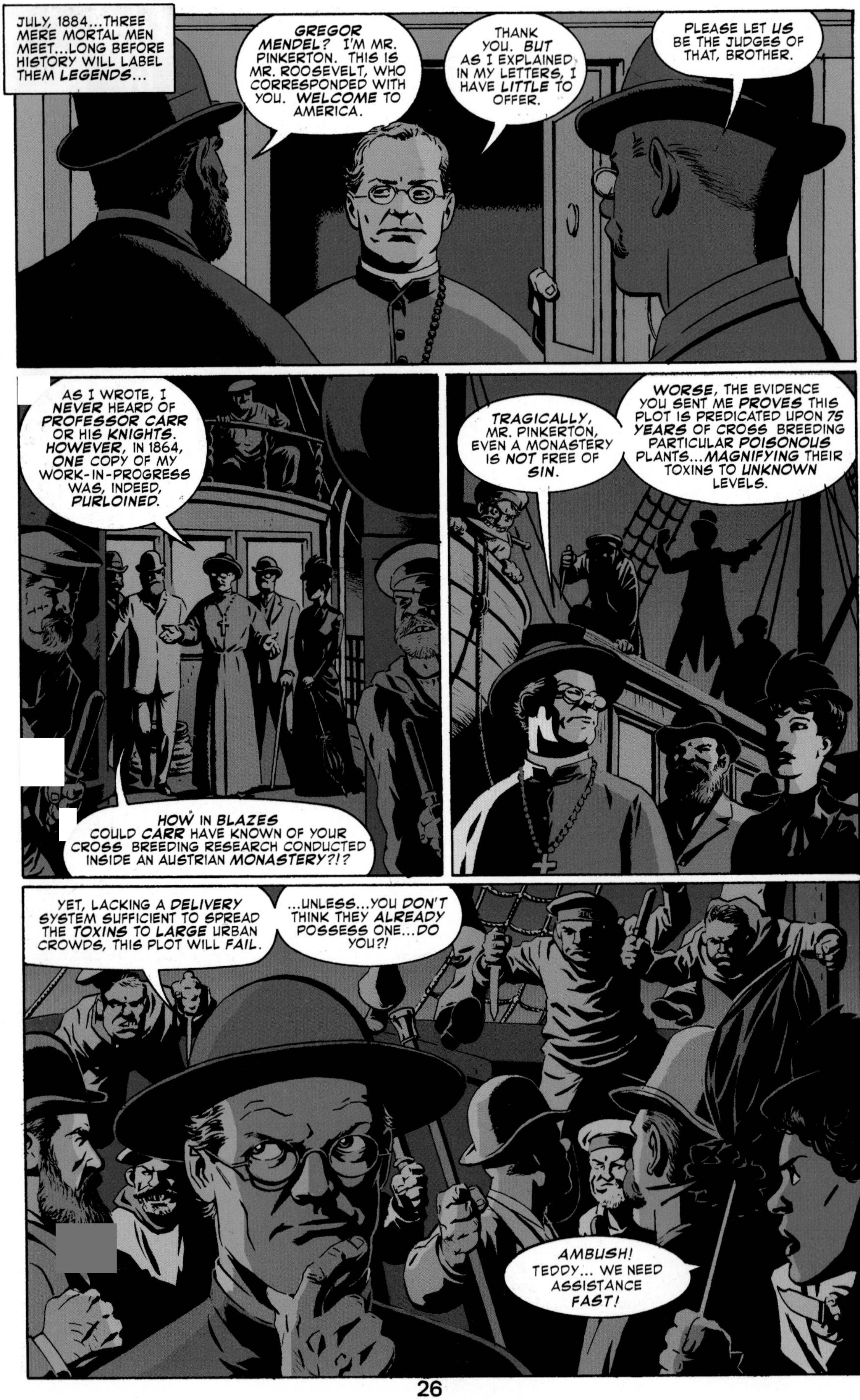

JULY, 1884...THREE MERE MORTAL MEN MEET...LONG BEFORE HISTORY WILL LABEL THEM LEGENDS...
GREGOR MENDEL? I'M MR. PINKERTON. THIS IS MR. ROOSEVELT, WHO CORRESPONDED WITH YOU. WELCOME TO AMERICA.
THANK YOU. BUT AS I EXPLAINED IN MY LETTERS, I HAVE LITTLE TO OFFER.
PLEASE LET US BE THE JUDGES OF THAT, BROTHER.
AS I WROTE, I NEVER HEARD OF PROFESSOR CARR OR HIS KNIGHTS. HOWEVER, IN 1864, ONE COPY OF MY WORK-IN-PROGRESS WAS, INDEED, PURLOINED.
HOW IN BLAZES COULD CARR HAVE KNOWN OF YOUR CROSS BREEDING RESEARCH CONDUCTED INSIDE AN AUSTRIAN MONASTERY?!?
TRAGICALLY, MR. PINKERTON, EVEN A MONASTERY IS NOT FREE OF SIN.
WORSE, THE EVIDENCE YOU SENT ME PROVES THIS PLOT IS PREDICATED UPON 75 YEARS OF CROSS BREEDING PARTICULAR POISONOUS PLANTS...MAGNIFYING THEIR TOXINS TO UNKNOWN LEVELS.
YET, LACKING A DELIVERY SYSTEM SUFFICIENT TO SPREAD THE TOXINS TO LARGE URBAN CROWDS, THIS PLOT WILL FAIL.
...UNLESS...YOU DON'T THINK THEY ALREADY POSSESS ONE...DO YOU?!
AMBUSH! TEDDY... WE NEED ASSISTANCE FAST!

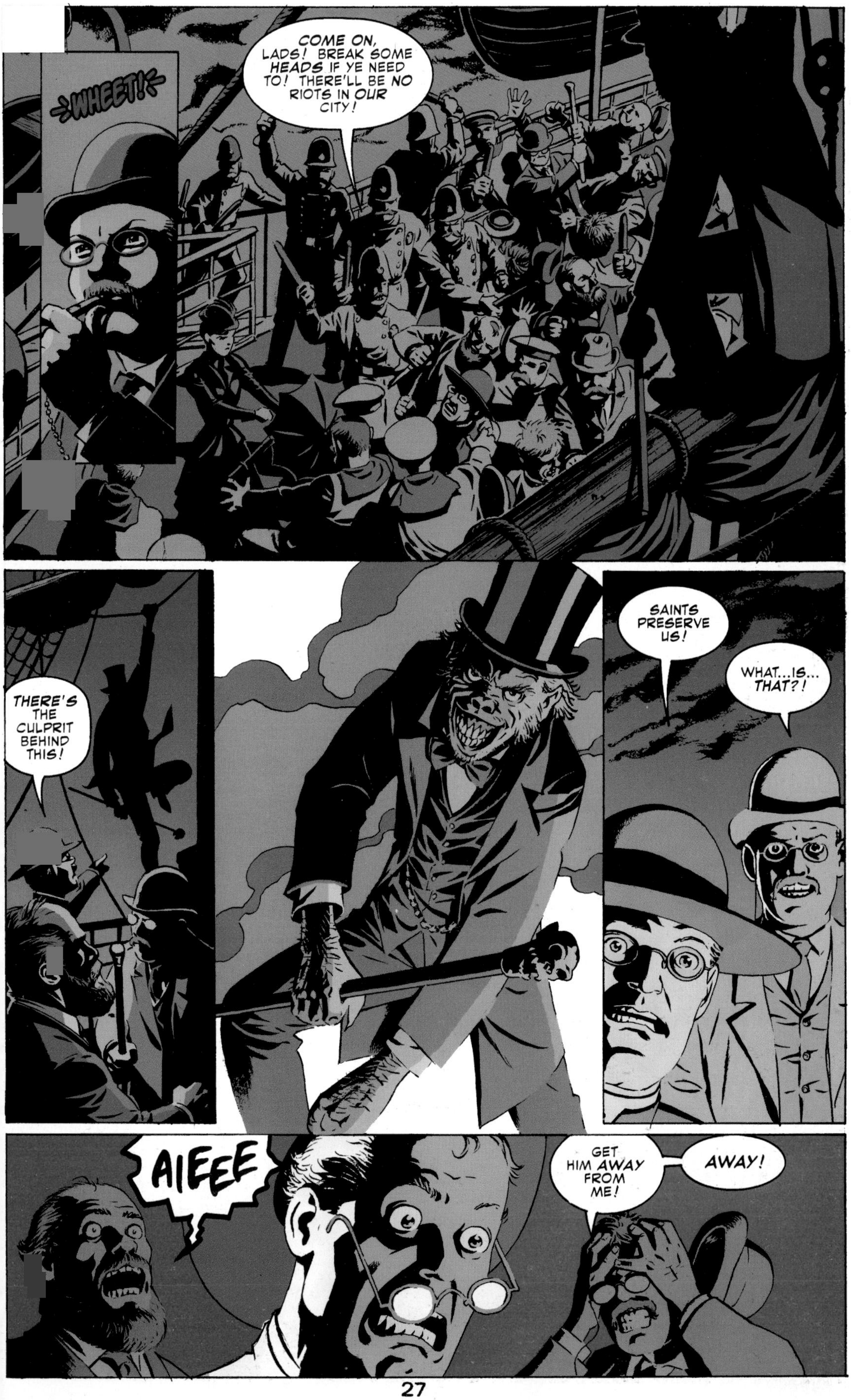
WHEET!
COME ON, LADS! BREAK SOME HEADS IF YE NEED TO! THERE'LL BE NO RIOTS IN OUR CITY!
THERE'S THE CULPRIT BEHIND THIS!
SAINTS PRESERVE US!
WHAT...IS... THAT?!
AIEEE
GET HIM AWAY FROM ME!
AWAY!

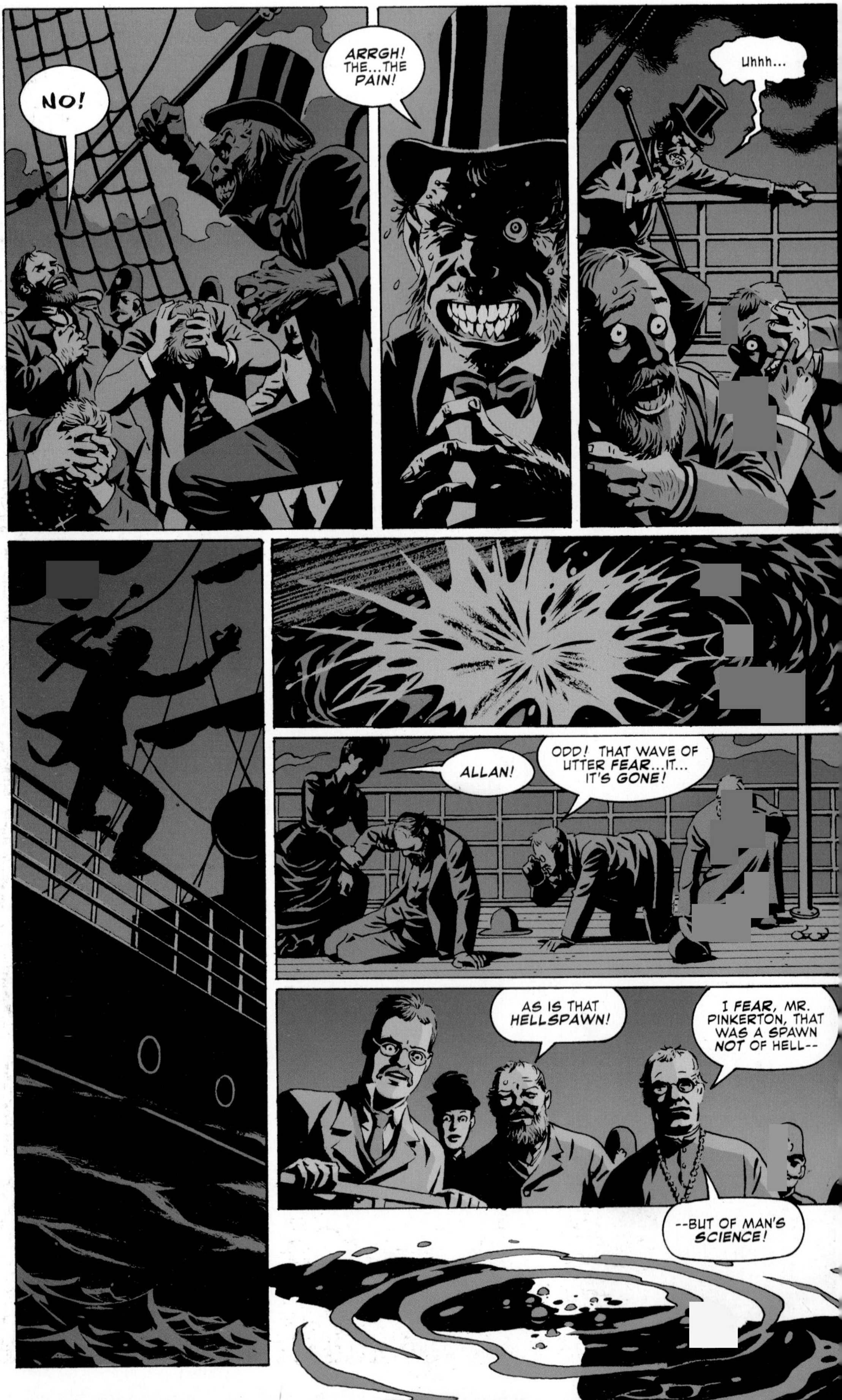
NO!
ARRGH! THE...THE PAIN!
Uhhh...
ALLAN!
ODD! THAT WAVE OF UTTER FEAR...IT... IT'S GONE!
AS IS THAT HELLSPAWN!
I FEAR, MR. PINKERTON, THAT WAS A SPAWN NOT OF HELL--
--BUT OF MAN'S SCIENCE!

DARKNESS FALLS AS TEDDY ROOSEVELT, ALLAN PINKERTON, AND GREGOR MENDEL CONDUCT A POSTMORTEM ON THE DAY'S HARROWING EVENTS...

THE POLICE QUESTIONED YOUR ASSAILANTS, BROTHER GREGOR.

THEIR LEADER WAS A "MR. HYDE," WHO HAS POSSIBLE CONNECTIONS TO A "DR. HENRY JEKYLL." DOES EITHER NAME MEAN *ANYTHING* TO YOU?

BOTH ARE *UNFAMILIAR*, MR. ROOSEVELT.

AH! I HAVEN'T HAD A STEAK IN *13 YEARS!*

AND I CAN GUARANTEE YOU'VE *NEVER* HAD A STEAK LIKE *THIS* ONE! YOU, *TOO*, PINKERTON! THEY'RE A *DOLLAR* EACH!

YOUR *LOBSTER WENBURGH* LOOKS SCRUMPTIOUS AS WELL, TEDDY.

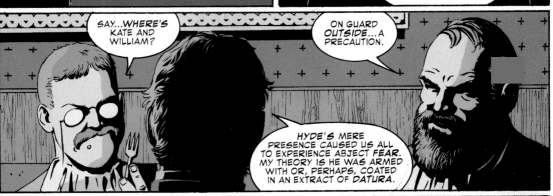

SAY...WHERE'S KATE AND WILLIAM?

ON GUARD *OUTSIDE*...A PRECAUTION.

HYDE'S MERE PRESENCE CAUSED US ALL TO EXPERIENCE ABJECT *FEAR*. MY THEORY IS HE WAS ARMED WITH OR, PERHAPS, COATED IN AN EXTRACT OF *DATURA*.

DATURA? IN CHICAGO, WE CALL THAT *"DEVIL'S THORN."*

VERY GOOD, MR. PINKERTON. THE PLANT BLOSSOMS ONLY AT *NIGHT* AND IS POLLINATED BY *BATS*. ITS FLOWERS, LEAVES, AND SEED ARE ALL POISONOUS TO HUMANS.

THAT MAY EXPLAIN HYDE'S *BIZARRE* APPEARANCE.

THIS *"DOOMSDAY PLOT"* YOU SENT ME A FILE ON...IF *DATURA* WAS CROSS BRED FOR *75* GENERATIONS WITH AN AIRBORNE *SPORE* FROM EMEX SPINOSA POLYGONACEAE--

ENGLISH, *PLEASE!*

"DEVIL'S BACKBONE."

AHA! GO ON, BROTHER...

...ITS *TOXICITY* WOULD REACH A LEVEL OF COMPLETE *PURITY*.

UNLEASHED ON AN URBAN POPULATION SOMEHOW, THE *DEATH* TOLL WOULD BE *STAGGERING* AND THE CITYWIDE SIDE EFFECTS WOULD BE *CRIPPLING!*

HOLY MOTHER OF GOD! SO THIS WAS *JOSIAH CARR'S* PLAN ALL ALONG!

THIS STEAK IS *DELICIOUS!*

THE HALLUCINOGENIC EFFECTS OF THE COMBINED "DEVILS" WOULD INCLUDE *EXTREME* PARANOIA AND PANIC, INDUCING UNCONTROLLABLE *FEAR* IN THE POPULACE.

END OF CIVILIZED LIVING.

END OF A *CITY.*

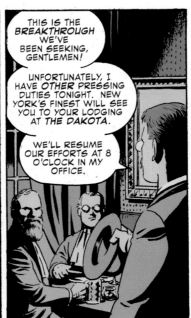

THIS IS THE *BREAKTHROUGH* WE'VE BEEN SEEKING, GENTLEMEN!

UNFORTUNATELY, I HAVE *OTHER* PRESSING DUTIES TONIGHT. NEW YORK'S FINEST WILL SEE YOU TO YOUR LODGING AT *THE DAKOTA.*

WE'LL RESUME OUR EFFORTS AT 8 O'CLOCK IN MY OFFICE.

BY *THEN,* I HOPE THE POLICE WILL HAVE *BOTH* HYDE AND DR. JEKYLL IN CUSTODY.

ANY PROGRESS?

I THINK BETWEEN BROTHER GREGOR AND YOUR BOSS, THIS CASE MAY BE *CRACKED* BY *TOMORROW!*

DID YOU TWO HAVE DINNER? YOU *DON'T* WANT TO MISS THE FOOD HERE!

THE CHEF, *JOHNNY,* CAME OUT AND OFFERED TO COOK US *STEAKS.*

MY MOUTH'S ALREADY WATERING!

THE CHEF IS *CHARLES,* NOT *JOHNNY!* 260? GRAYING HAIR?

150...BLOND...SOUTHERN ACCENT...?

THE *KITCHEN!* QUICKLY!

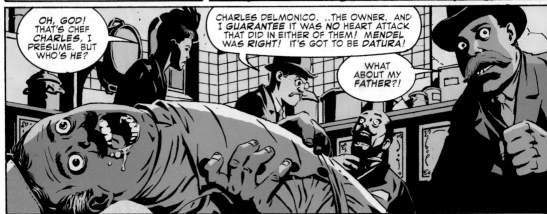

OH, GOD! THAT'S CHEF *CHARLES,* I PRESUME. BUT WHO'S HE?

CHARLES DELMONICO. ..THE OWNER. AND I *GUARANTEE* IT WAS *NO* HEART ATTACK THAT DID IN EITHER OF THEM! MENDEL WAS *RIGHT!* IT'S GOT TO BE *DATURA!*

WHAT ABOUT MY *FATHER?!*

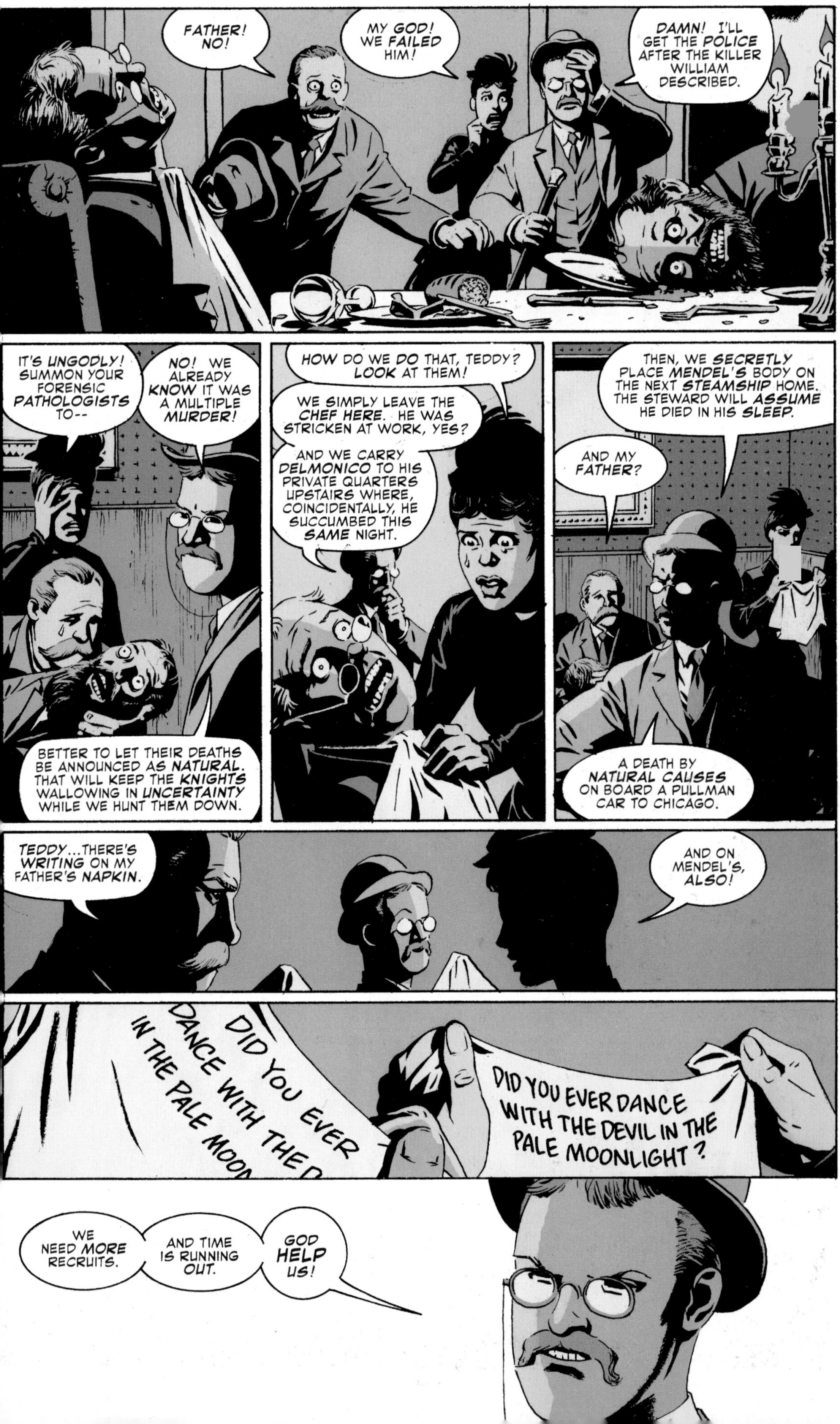
FATHER! NO!
MY GOD! WE FAILED HIM!
DAMN! I'LL GET THE POLICE AFTER THE KILLER WILLIAM DESCRIBED.
IT'S UNGODLY! SUMMON YOUR FORENSIC PATHOLOGISTS TO--
NO! WE ALREADY KNOW IT WAS A MULTIPLE MURDER!
BETTER TO LET THEIR DEATHS BE ANNOUNCED AS NATURAL. THAT WILL KEEP THE KNIGHTS WALLOWING IN UNCERTAINTY WHILE WE HUNT THEM DOWN.
HOW DO WE DO THAT, TEDDY? LOOK AT THEM!
WE SIMPLY LEAVE THE CHEF HERE. HE WAS STRICKEN AT WORK, YES?
AND WE CARRY DELMONICO TO HIS PRIVATE QUARTERS UPSTAIRS WHERE, COINCIDENTALLY, HE SUCCUMBED THIS SAME NIGHT.
THEN, WE SECRETLY PLACE MENDEL'S BODY ON THE NEXT STEAMSHIP HOME. THE STEWARD WILL ASSUME HE DIED IN HIS SLEEP.
AND MY FATHER?
A DEATH BY NATURAL CAUSES ON BOARD A PULLMAN CAR TO CHICAGO.
TEDDY...THERE'S WRITING ON MY FATHER'S NAPKIN.
AND ON MENDEL'S, ALSO!
DID YOU EVER DANCE WITH THE
IN THE PALE
DID YOU EVER DANCE WITH THE DEVIL IN THE PALE MOONLIGHT?
WE NEED MORE RECRUITS.
AND TIME IS RUNNING OUT.
GOD HELP US!

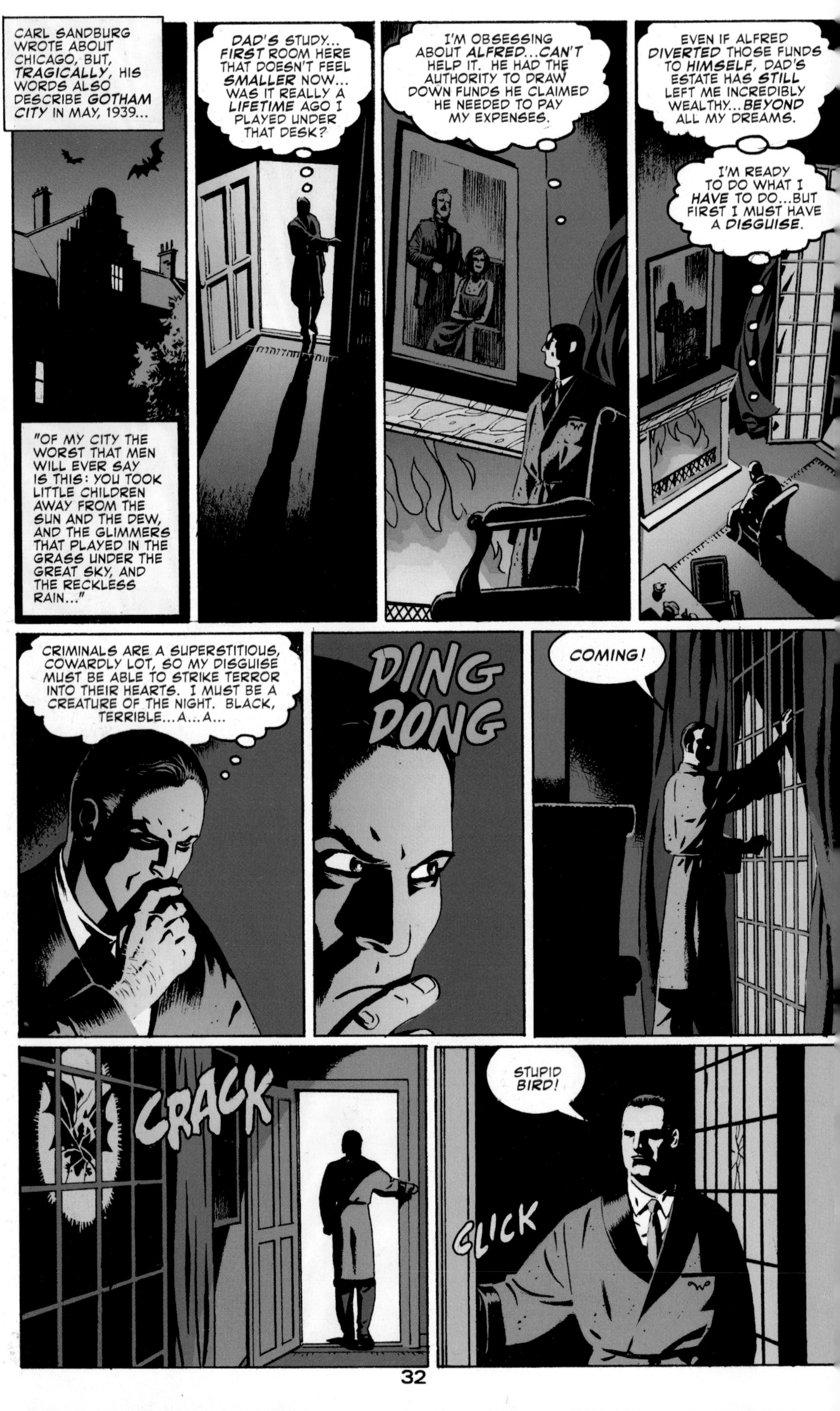
CARL SANDBURG WROTE ABOUT CHICAGO, BUT, TRAGICALLY, HIS WORDS ALSO DESCRIBE GOTHAM CITY IN MAY, 1939...
"OF MY CITY THE WORST THAT MEN WILL EVER SAY IS THIS: YOU TOOK LITTLE CHILDREN AWAY FROM THE SUN AND THE DEW, AND THE GLIMMERS THAT PLAYED IN THE GRASS UNDER THE GREAT SKY, AND THE RECKLESS RAIN..."
DAD'S STUDY... FIRST ROOM HERE THAT DOESN'T FEEL SMALLER NOW... WAS IT REALLY A LIFETIME AGO I PLAYED UNDER THAT DESK?
I'M OBSESSING ABOUT ALFRED...CAN'T HELP IT. HE HAD THE AUTHORITY TO DRAW DOWN FUNDS HE CLAIMED HE NEEDED TO PAY MY EXPENSES.
EVEN IF ALFRED DIVERTED THOSE FUNDS TO HIMSELF, DAD'S ESTATE HAS STILL LEFT ME INCREDIBLY WEALTHY...BEYOND ALL MY DREAMS.
I'M READY TO DO WHAT I HAVE TO DO...BUT FIRST I MUST HAVE A DISGUISE.
CRIMINALS ARE A SUPERSTITIOUS, COWARDLY LOT, SO MY DISGUISE MUST BE ABLE TO STRIKE TERROR INTO THEIR HEARTS. I MUST BE A CREATURE OF THE NIGHT. BLACK, TERRIBLE...A...A...
DING DONG
COMING!
CRACK
STUPID BIRD!
CLICK

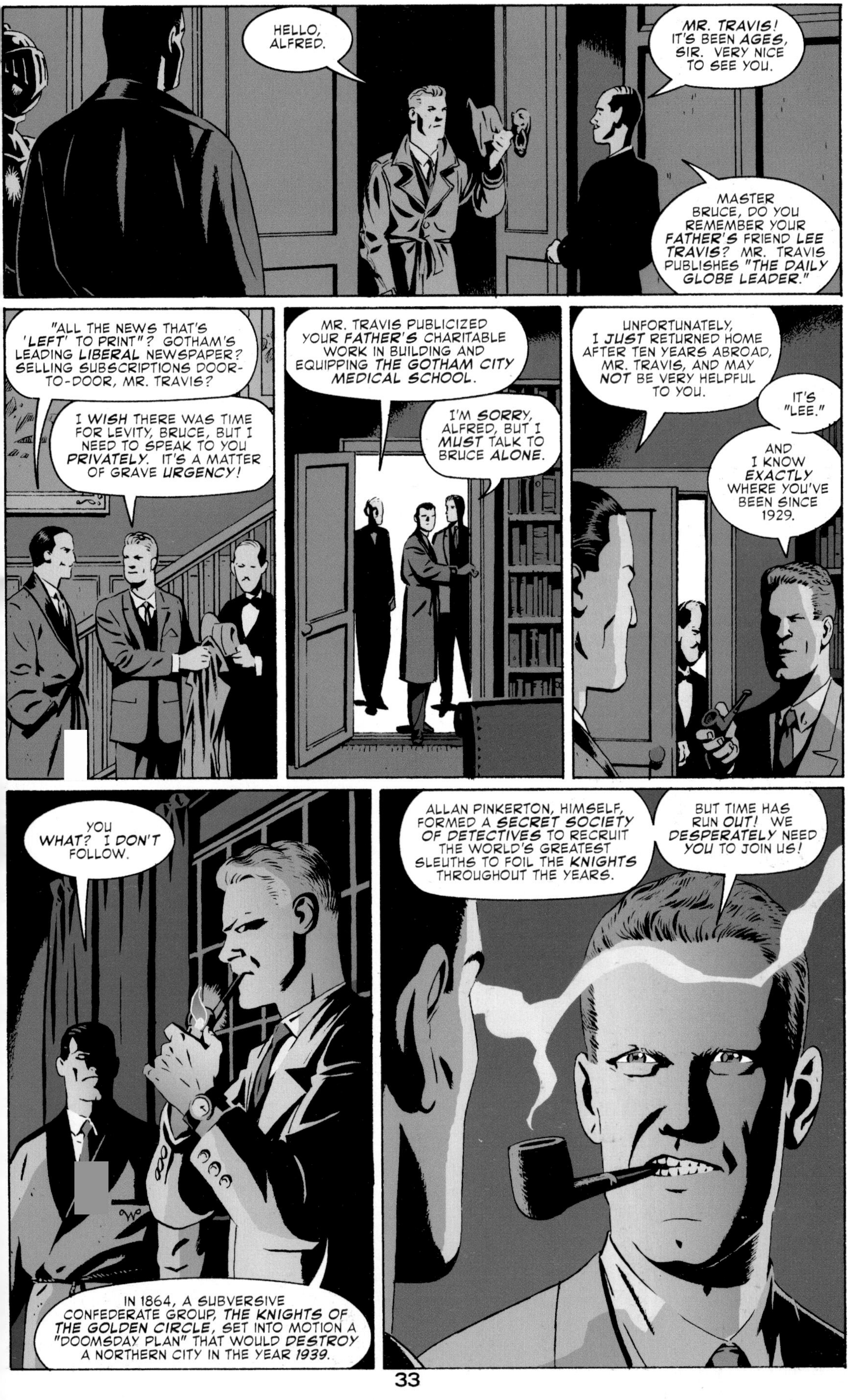
HELLO, ALFRED.
MR. TRAVIS! IT'S BEEN AGES, SIR. VERY NICE TO SEE YOU.
MASTER BRUCE, DO YOU REMEMBER YOUR FATHER'S FRIEND LEE TRAVIS? MR. TRAVIS PUBLISHES "THE DAILY GLOBE LEADER."
"ALL THE NEWS THAT'S 'LEFT' TO PRINT"? GOTHAM'S LEADING LIBERAL NEWSPAPER? SELLING SUBSCRIPTIONS DOOR-TO-DOOR, MR. TRAVIS?
I WISH THERE WAS TIME FOR LEVITY, BRUCE, BUT I NEED TO SPEAK TO YOU PRIVATELY. IT'S A MATTER OF GRAVE URGENCY!
MR. TRAVIS PUBLICIZED YOUR FATHER'S CHARITABLE WORK IN BUILDING AND EQUIPPING THE GOTHAM CITY MEDICAL SCHOOL.
I'M SORRY, ALFRED, BUT I MUST TALK TO BRUCE ALONE.
UNFORTUNATELY, I JUST RETURNED HOME AFTER TEN YEARS ABROAD, MR. TRAVIS, AND MAY NOT BE VERY HELPFUL TO YOU.
IT'S "LEE."
AND I KNOW EXACTLY WHERE YOU'VE BEEN SINCE 1929.
YOU WHAT? I DON'T FOLLOW.
IN 1864, A SUBVERSIVE CONFEDERATE GROUP, THE KNIGHTS OF THE GOLDEN CIRCLE, SET INTO MOTION A "DOOMSDAY PLAN" THAT WOULD DESTROY A NORTHERN CITY IN THE YEAR 1939.
ALLAN PINKERTON, HIMSELF, FORMED A SECRET SOCIETY OF DETECTIVES TO RECRUIT THE WORLD'S GREATEST SLEUTHS TO FOIL THE KNIGHTS THROUGHOUT THE YEARS.
BUT TIME HAS RUN OUT! WE DESPERATELY NEED YOU TO JOIN US!

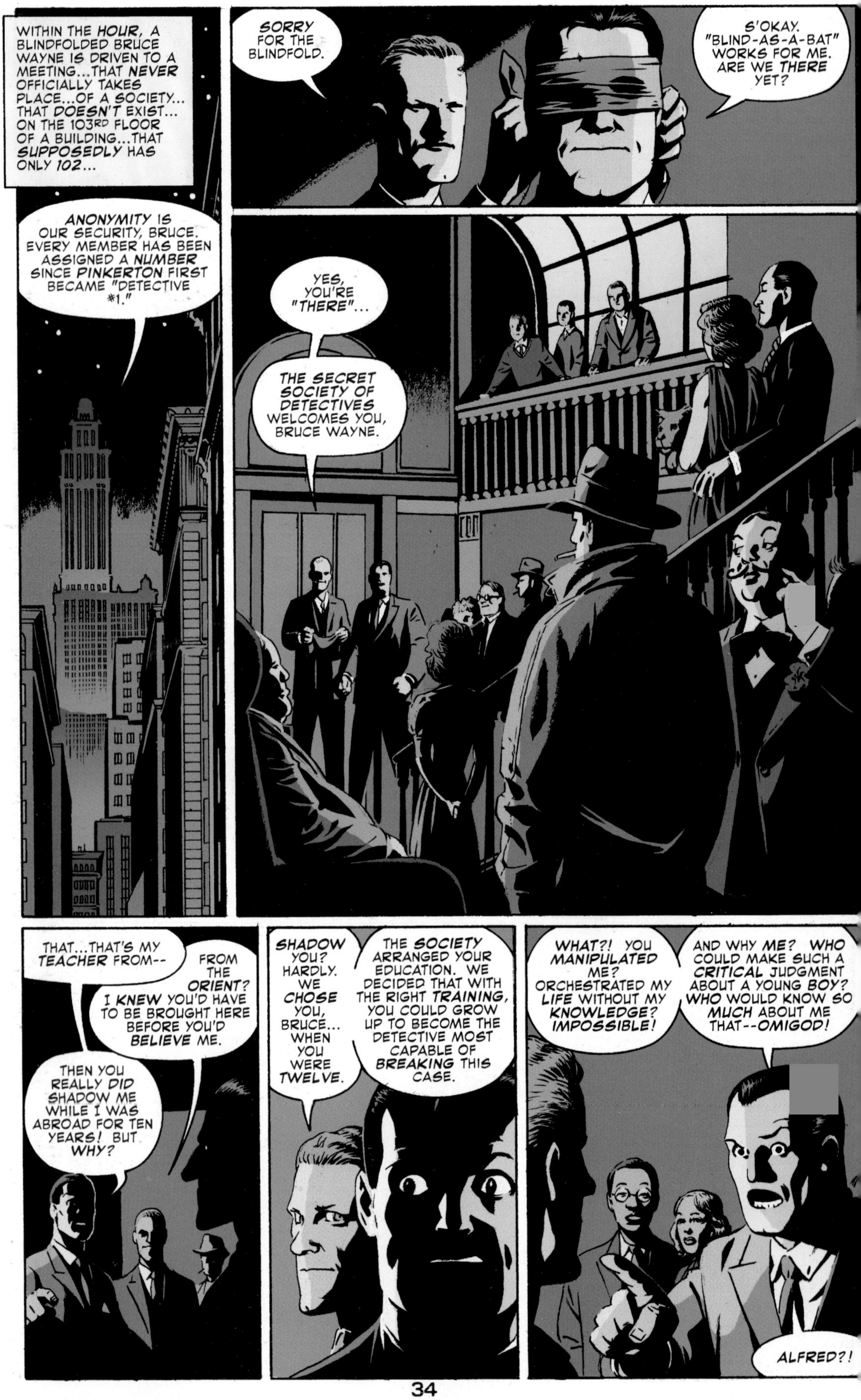

WITHIN THE HOUR, A BLINDFOLDED BRUCE WAYNE IS DRIVEN TO A MEETING...THAT NEVER OFFICIALLY TAKES PLACE...OF A SOCIETY... THAT DOESN'T EXIST... ON THE 103RD FLOOR OF A BUILDING...THAT SUPPOSEDLY HAS ONLY 102...
SORRY FOR THE BLINDFOLD.
S'OKAY. "BLIND-AS-A-BAT" WORKS FOR ME. ARE WE THERE YET?
ANONYMITY IS OUR SECURITY, BRUCE. EVERY MEMBER HAS BEEN ASSIGNED A NUMBER SINCE PINKERTON FIRST BECAME "DETECTIVE #1."
YES, YOU'RE "THERE"...
THE SECRET SOCIETY OF DETECTIVES WELCOMES YOU, BRUCE WAYNE.
THAT...THAT'S MY TEACHER FROM--
FROM THE ORIENT? I KNEW YOU'D HAVE TO BE BROUGHT HERE BEFORE YOU'D BELIEVE ME.
THEN YOU REALLY DID SHADOW ME WHILE I WAS ABROAD FOR TEN YEARS! BUT WHY?
SHADOW YOU? HARDLY. WE CHOSE YOU, BRUCE... WHEN YOU WERE TWELVE.
THE SOCIETY ARRANGED YOUR EDUCATION. WE DECIDED THAT WITH THE RIGHT TRAINING, YOU COULD GROW UP TO BECOME THE DETECTIVE MOST CAPABLE OF BREAKING THIS CASE.
WHAT?! YOU MANIPULATED ME? ORCHESTRATED MY LIFE WITHOUT MY KNOWLEDGE? IMPOSSIBLE!
AND WHY ME? WHO COULD MAKE SUCH A CRITICAL JUDGMENT ABOUT A YOUNG BOY? WHO WOULD KNOW SO MUCH ABOUT ME THAT--OMIGOD!
ALFRED?!

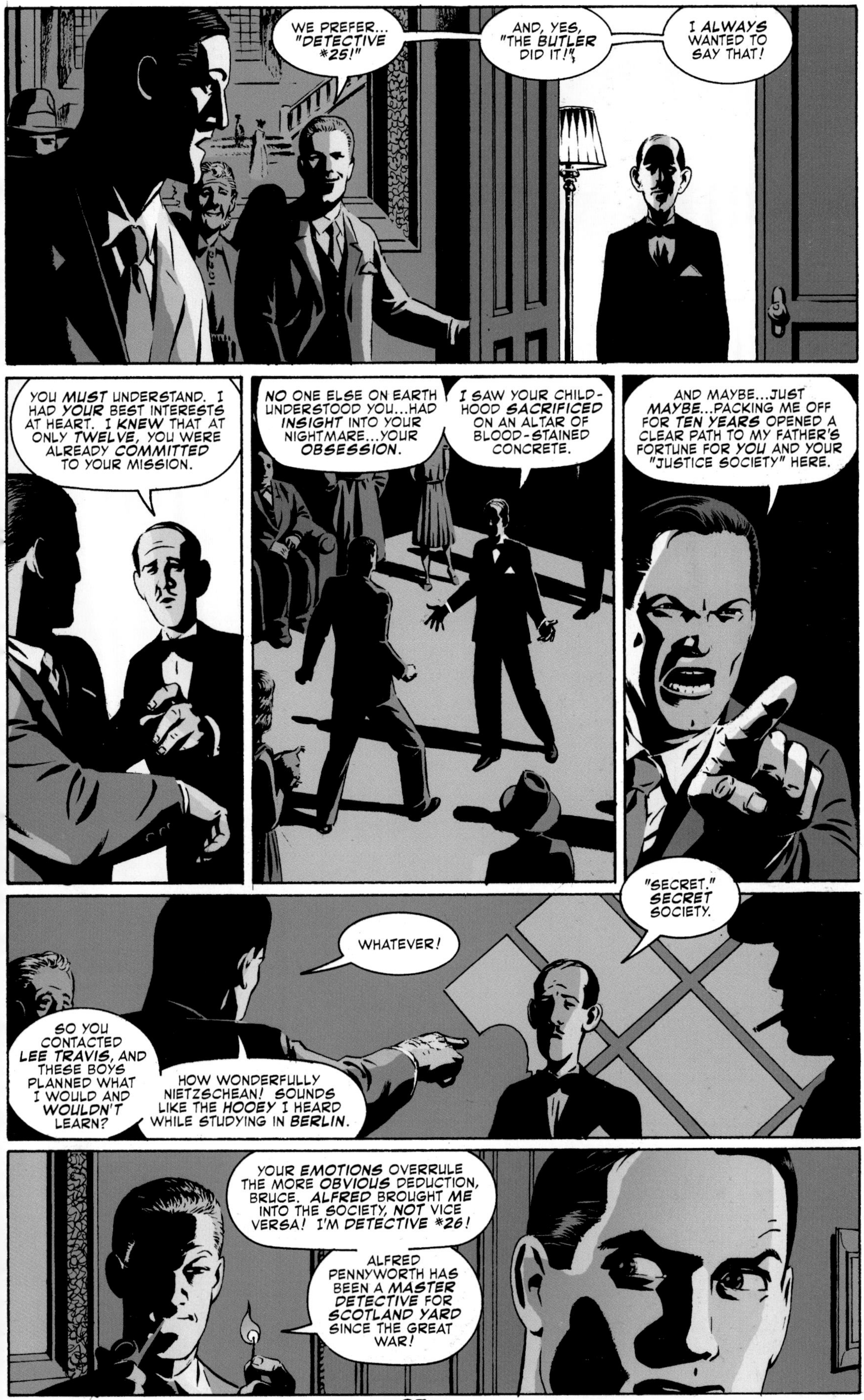
WE PREFER... "DETECTIVE #25!"
AND, YES, "THE BUTLER DID IT!"
I ALWAYS WANTED TO SAY THAT!
YOU MUST UNDERSTAND. I HAD YOUR BEST INTERESTS AT HEART. I KNEW THAT AT ONLY TWELVE, YOU WERE ALREADY COMMITTED TO YOUR MISSION.
NO ONE ELSE ON EARTH UNDERSTOOD YOU...HAD INSIGHT INTO YOUR NIGHTMARE...YOUR OBSESSION.
I SAW YOUR CHILDHOOD SACRIFICED ON AN ALTAR OF BLOOD-STAINED CONCRETE.
AND MAYBE...JUST MAYBE...PACKING ME OFF FOR TEN YEARS OPENED A CLEAR PATH TO MY FATHER'S FORTUNE FOR YOU AND YOUR "JUSTICE SOCIETY" HERE.
"SECRET." SECRET SOCIETY.
WHATEVER!
SO YOU CONTACTED LEE TRAVIS, AND THESE BOYS PLANNED WHAT I WOULD AND WOULDN'T LEARN?
HOW WONDERFULLY NIETZSCHEAN! SOUNDS LIKE THE HOOEY I HEARD WHILE STUDYING IN BERLIN.
YOUR EMOTIONS OVERRULE THE MORE OBVIOUS DEDUCTION, BRUCE. ALFRED BROUGHT ME INTO THE SOCIETY, NOT VICE VERSA! I'M DETECTIVE #26!
ALFRED PENNYWORTH HAS BEEN A MASTER DETECTIVE FOR SCOTLAND YARD SINCE THE GREAT WAR!

ALFRED... WHAT--?!

AS MR. TRAVIS EXPLAINED EN ROUTE, *THE SECRET SOCIETY* MONITORS ANY *DOCTOR*, *PROFESSOR* OR *BOTANIST* SHOWING A *SUDDEN RISE IN PERSONAL WEALTH*... A POSSIBLE SIGN OF RECRUITMENT BY *THE KNIGHTS.*

WHAT COULD THAT *POSSIBLY* HAVE TO DO WITH--?

DR. THOMAS WAYNE'S FORTUNE *AUTOMATICALLY* MADE HIM A *SUSPECT.* I WAS SENT TO GOTHAM TO DETERMINE THE *SOURCE* OF HIS MONEY.

WHO THE HELL *ARE* YOU?! I NO LONGER HAVE A *CLUE!*

YOU *INFILTRATED* MY FAMILY TO *SPY* ON MY *FATHER*... A MAN WHO CONSIDERED YOU A *FRIEND* AND PROVIDED FOR YOU IN HIS *WILL?!*

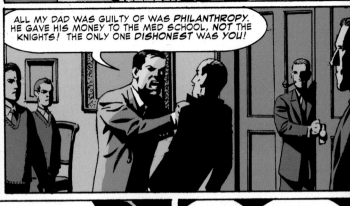

ALL MY DAD WAS GUILTY OF WAS *PHILANTHROPY.* HE GAVE HIS MONEY TO THE MED SCHOOL, *NOT* THE KNIGHTS! THE ONLY ONE *DISHONEST* WAS *YOU!*

MY FEELINGS FOR YOU AND YOUR PARENTS WERE *GENUINE.*

I UNCOVERED *NO EVIDENCE* AGAINST *DR. WAYNE* AND WAS ABOUT TO *CONFESS* MY IDENTITY TO THEM WHEN...WHEN--

NONE OF THIS MATTERS! THE *DOOMSDAY PLOT'S* A LOT MORE IMPORTANT THAN YOUR FAMILY SPAT!

SO LET'S CUT TO THE CHASE, WAYNE...WE NEED YOUR HELP. YOU *IN OR NOT?*

YOU BOYS PICKED THE *WRONG* GUY TO BE YOUR TRAINED *MONKEY!*

THAT SAID, I BID YOU ALL A *GOOD NIGHT*...AND *WARN* YOU THAT I'LL *FLATTEN* ANYONE WHO TRIES TO *STOP* ME FROM LEAVING!

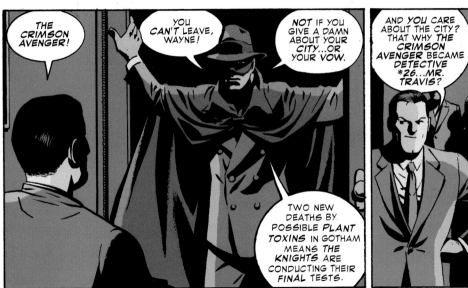

THE CRIMSON AVENGER!

YOU CAN'T LEAVE, WAYNE!

NOT IF YOU GIVE A DAMN ABOUT YOUR CITY...OR YOUR VOW.

TWO NEW DEATHS BY POSSIBLE *PLANT TOXINS* IN GOTHAM MEANS *THE KNIGHTS* ARE CONDUCTING THEIR *FINAL TESTS.*

AND *YOU* CARE ABOUT THE CITY? THAT WHY *THE CRIMSON AVENGER* BECAME DETECTIVE #26...MR. TRAVIS?

YOU *KNOW?!?* YOU'RE EVEN *BETTER* THAN YOUR TEACHERS INDICATED.

IT WAS *EASY.* THIS *SOCIETY* IS COMPOSED OF THE WORLD'S GREATEST *DETECTIVES,* NOT THE WORLD'S GREATEST NEWSPAPER PUBLISHERS.

ERGO, LEE TRAVIS IS *SECRETLY* A STELLAR DETECTIVE.

AND *LOGIC* DICTATED THE REST. BRAVO!

PLEASE, BRUCE. *JOIN* US.

I *STILL* HAVE TO WORRY ABOUT *ALFRED*...HIS ROLE HERE. COULD *THE KNIGHTS* HAVE RECRUITED HIM TO THEIR CAUSE?

I WAS HIS RESPONSIBILITY UNTIL *21.* WHATEVER HE'S BECOME...HE'S *MY* RESPONSIBILITY.

COUNT ME *IN!*

IS THERE A *SECRET HANDSHAKE* OR DE-CODER RING?

NOT EVEN A CAPE.

WELCOME TO THE SECRET SOCIETY... DETECTIVE #27!

END ACT ONE

ACT TWO

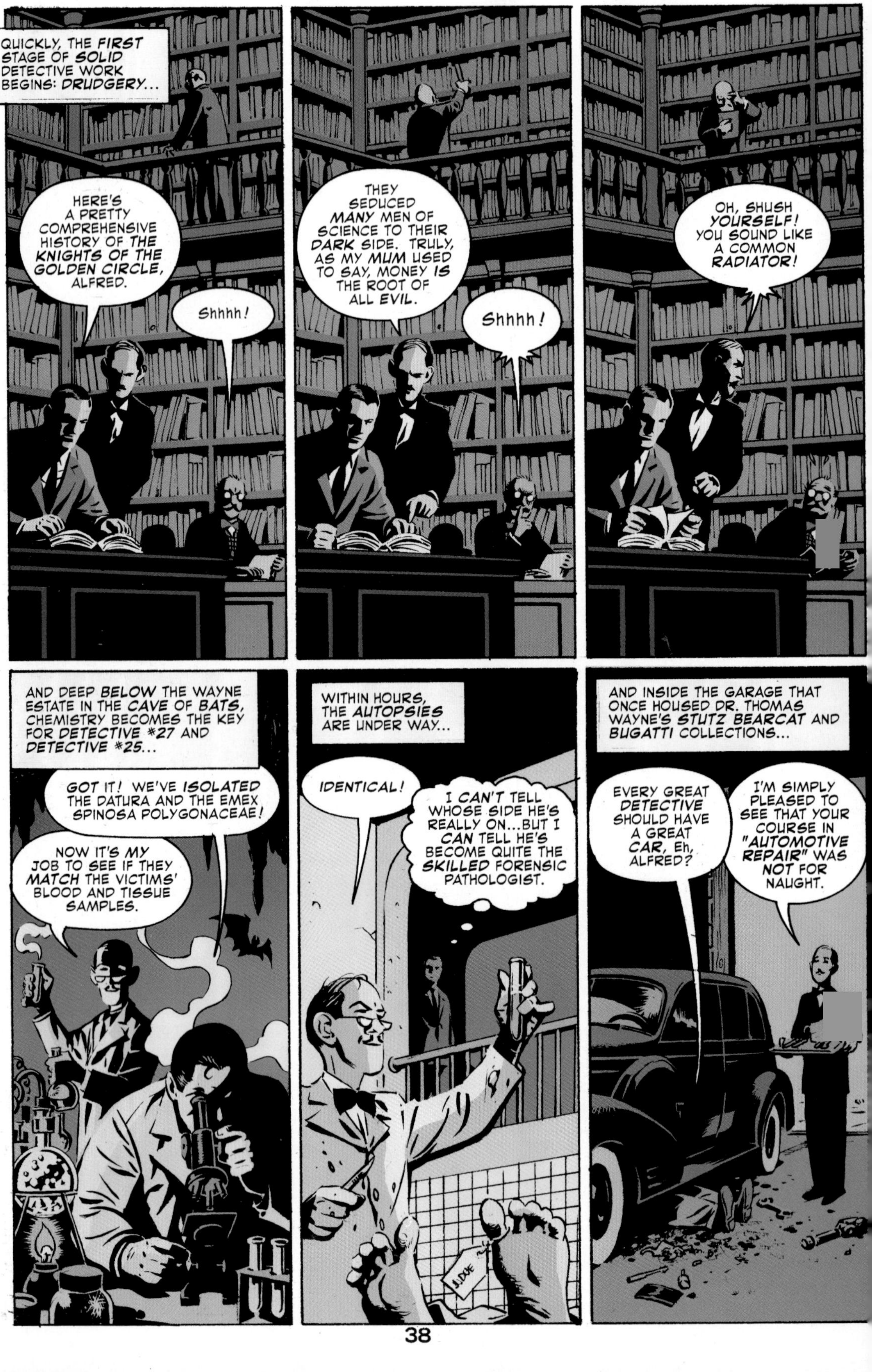

QUICKLY, THE FIRST STAGE OF SOLID DETECTIVE WORK BEGINS: DRUDGERY...
HERE'S A PRETTY COMPREHENSIVE HISTORY OF THE KNIGHTS OF THE GOLDEN CIRCLE, ALFRED.
Shhhh!
THEY SEDUCED MANY MEN OF SCIENCE TO THEIR DARK SIDE. TRULY, AS MY MUM USED TO SAY, MONEY IS THE ROOT OF ALL EVIL.
Shhhh!
OH, SHUSH YOURSELF! YOU SOUND LIKE A COMMON RADIATOR!
AND DEEP BELOW THE WAYNE ESTATE IN THE CAVE OF BATS, CHEMISTRY BECOMES THE KEY FOR DETECTIVE #27 AND DETECTIVE #25...
GOT IT! WE'VE ISOLATED THE DATURA AND THE EMEX SPINOSA POLYGONACEAE!
NOW IT'S MY JOB TO SEE IF THEY MATCH THE VICTIMS' BLOOD AND TISSUE SAMPLES.
WITHIN HOURS, THE AUTOPSIES ARE UNDER WAY...
IDENTICAL!
I CAN'T TELL WHOSE SIDE HE'S REALLY ON...BUT I CAN TELL HE'S BECOME QUITE THE SKILLED FORENSIC PATHOLOGIST.
J. DOE
AND INSIDE THE GARAGE THAT ONCE HOUSED DR. THOMAS WAYNE'S STUTZ BEARCAT AND BUGATTI COLLECTIONS...
EVERY GREAT DETECTIVE SHOULD HAVE A GREAT CAR, Eh, ALFRED?
I'M SIMPLY PLEASED TO SEE THAT YOUR COURSE IN "AUTOMOTIVE REPAIR" WAS NOT FOR NAUGHT.

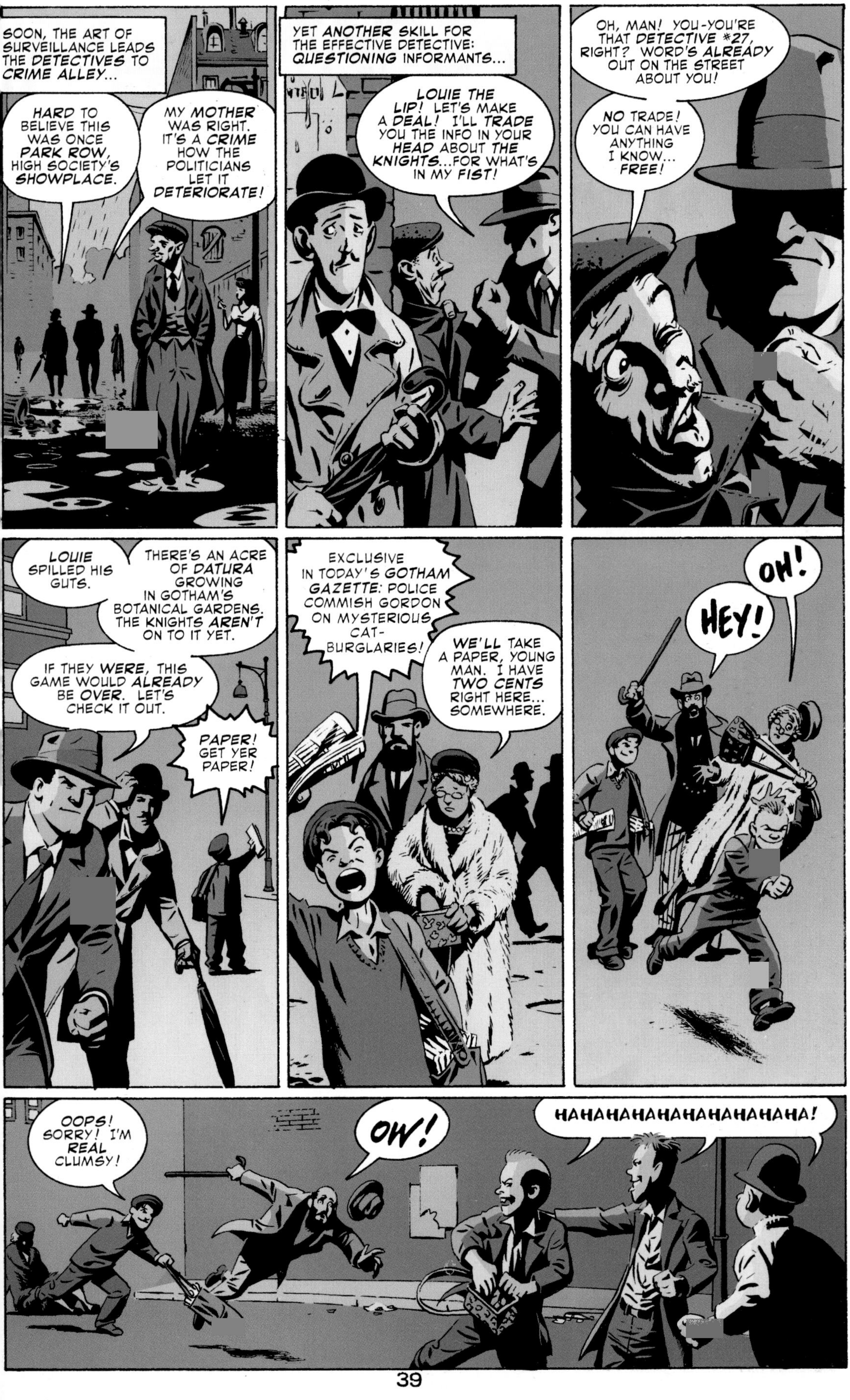
SOON, THE ART OF SURVEILLANCE LEADS THE DETECTIVES TO CRIME ALLEY...
HARD TO BELIEVE THIS WAS ONCE PARK ROW, HIGH SOCIETY'S SHOWPLACE.
MY MOTHER WAS RIGHT. IT'S A CRIME HOW THE POLITICIANS LET IT DETERIORATE!
YET ANOTHER SKILL FOR THE EFFECTIVE DETECTIVE: QUESTIONING INFORMANTS...
LOUIE THE LIP! LET'S MAKE A DEAL! I'LL TRADE YOU THE INFO IN YOUR HEAD ABOUT THE KNIGHTS...FOR WHAT'S IN MY FIST!
OH, MAN! YOU-YOU'RE THAT DETECTIVE #27, RIGHT? WORD'S ALREADY OUT ON THE STREET ABOUT YOU!
NO TRADE! YOU CAN HAVE ANYTHING I KNOW... FREE!
LOUIE SPILLED HIS GUTS.
THERE'S AN ACRE OF DATURA GROWING IN GOTHAM'S BOTANICAL GARDENS. THE KNIGHTS AREN'T ON TO IT YET.
IF THEY WERE, THIS GAME WOULD ALREADY BE OVER. LET'S CHECK IT OUT.
PAPER! GET YER PAPER!
EXCLUSIVE IN TODAY'S GOTHAM GAZETTE: POLICE COMMISH GORDON ON MYSTERIOUS CAT-BURGLARIES!
WE'LL TAKE A PAPER, YOUNG MAN. I HAVE TWO CENTS RIGHT HERE... SOMEWHERE.
OH!
HEY!
OOPS! SORRY! I'M REAL CLUMSY!
OW!
HAHAHAHAHAHAHAHAHAHAHA!

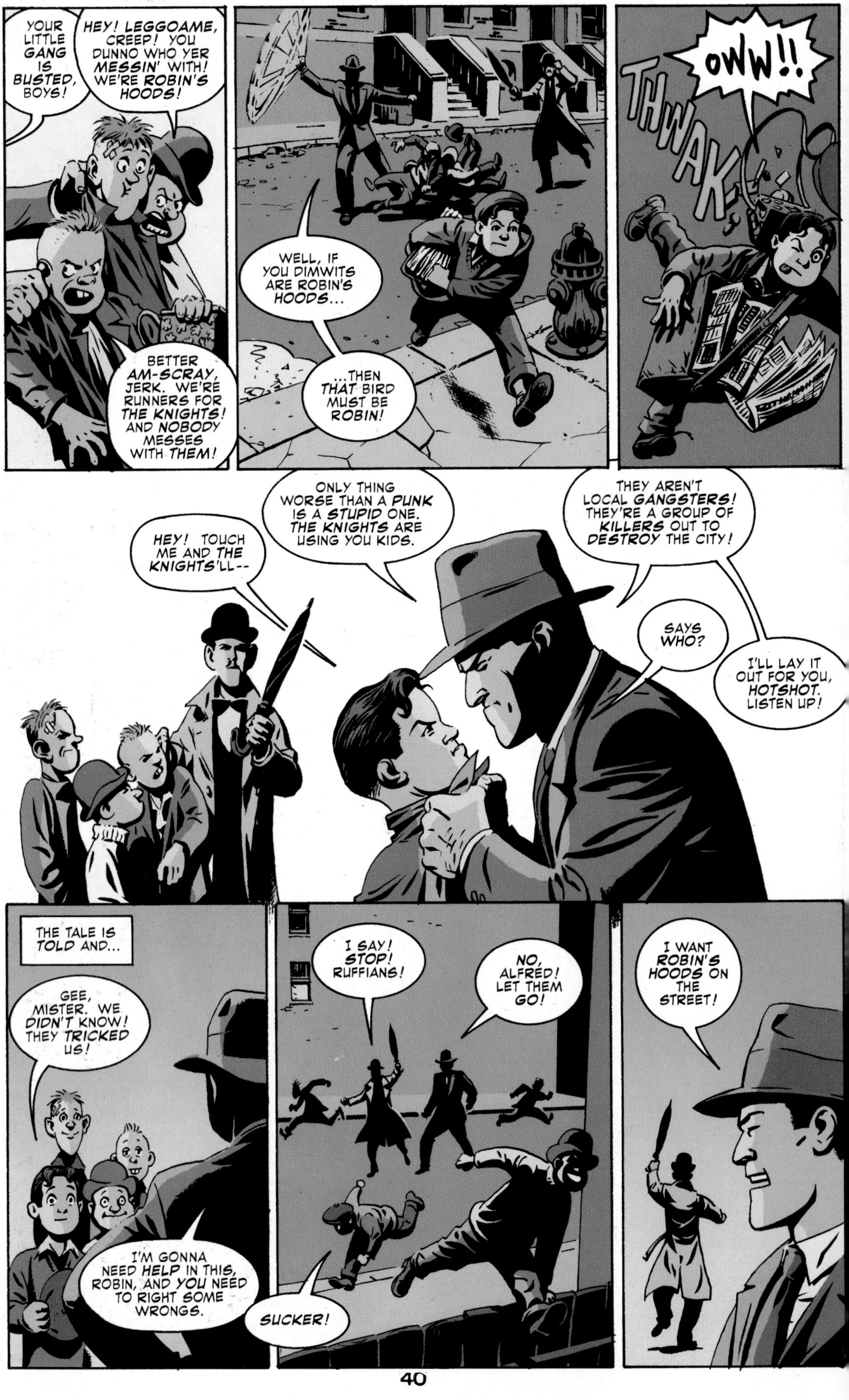

YOUR LITTLE GANG IS BUSTED, BOYS!
HEY! LEGGOAME, CREEP! YOU DUNNO WHO YER MESSIN' WITH! WE'RE ROBIN'S HOODS!
BETTER AM-SCRAY, JERK. WE'RE RUNNERS FOR THE KNIGHTS! AND NOBODY MESSES WITH THEM!
WELL, IF YOU DIMWITS ARE ROBIN'S HOODS...
...THEN THAT BIRD MUST BE ROBIN!
THWAK
OWW!!
HEY! TOUCH ME AND THE KNIGHTS'LL--
ONLY THING WORSE THAN A PUNK IS A STUPID ONE. THE KNIGHTS ARE USING YOU KIDS.
THEY AREN'T LOCAL GANGSTERS! THEY'RE A GROUP OF KILLERS OUT TO DESTROY THE CITY!
SAYS WHO?
I'LL LAY IT OUT FOR YOU, HOTSHOT. LISTEN UP!
THE TALE IS TOLD AND...
GEE, MISTER. WE DIDN'T KNOW! THEY TRICKED US!
I'M GONNA NEED HELP IN THIS, ROBIN, AND YOU NEED TO RIGHT SOME WRONGS.
I SAY! STOP! RUFFIANS!
NO, ALFRED! LET THEM GO!
SUCKER!
I WANT ROBIN'S HOODS ON THE STREET!

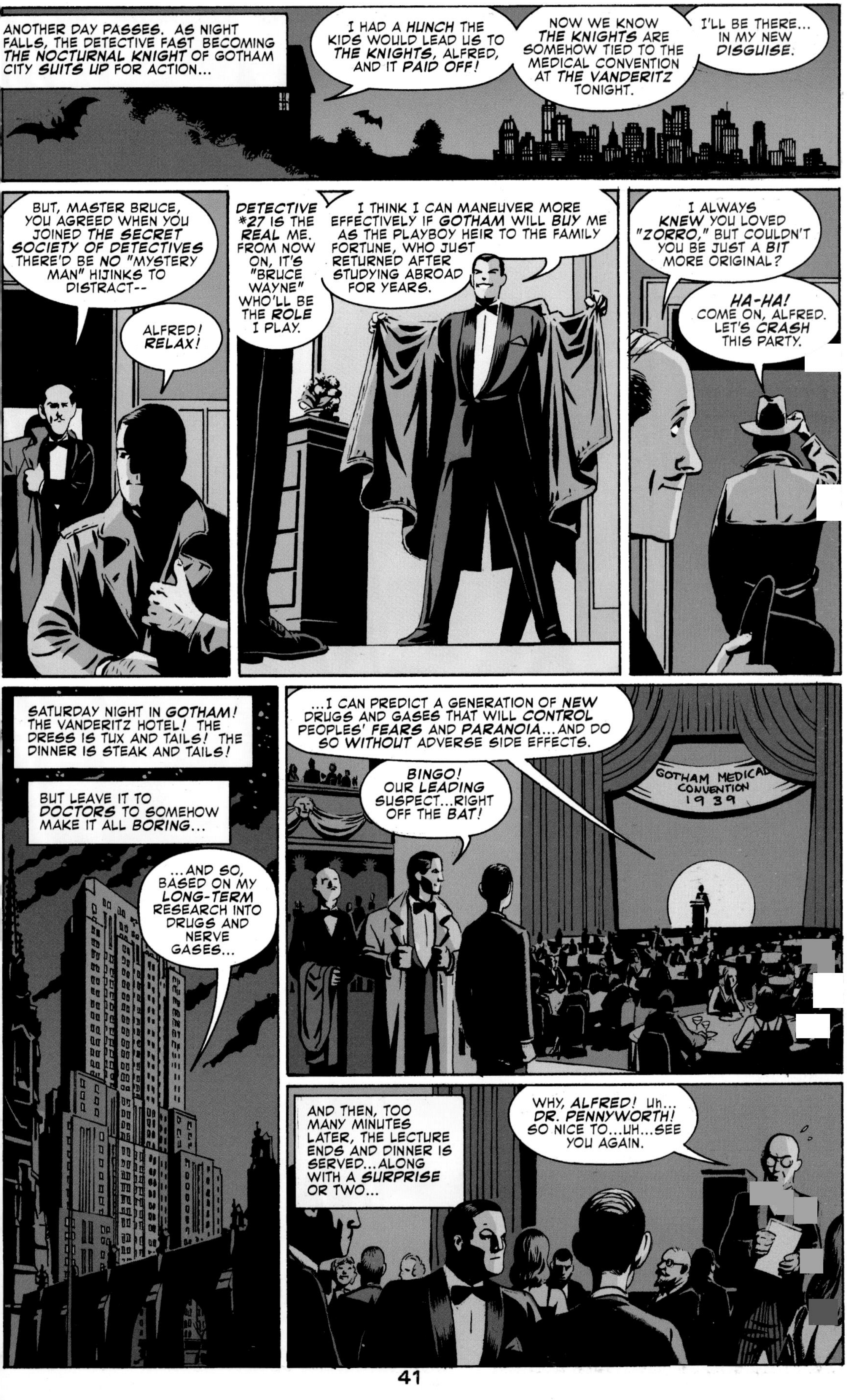
ANOTHER DAY PASSES. AS NIGHT FALLS, THE DETECTIVE FAST BECOMING THE NOCTURNAL KNIGHT OF GOTHAM CITY SUITS UP FOR ACTION...
I HAD A HUNCH THE KIDS WOULD LEAD US TO THE KNIGHTS, ALFRED, AND IT PAID OFF!
NOW WE KNOW THE KNIGHTS ARE SOMEHOW TIED TO THE MEDICAL CONVENTION AT THE VANDERITZ TONIGHT.
I'LL BE THERE... IN MY NEW DISGUISE.
BUT, MASTER BRUCE, YOU AGREED WHEN YOU JOINED THE SECRET SOCIETY OF DETECTIVES THERE'D BE NO "MYSTERY MAN" HIJINKS TO DISTRACT--
ALFRED! RELAX!
DETECTIVE #27 IS THE REAL ME. FROM NOW ON, IT'S "BRUCE WAYNE" WHO'LL BE THE ROLE I PLAY.
I THINK I CAN MANEUVER MORE EFFECTIVELY IF GOTHAM WILL BUY ME AS THE PLAYBOY HEIR TO THE FAMILY FORTUNE, WHO JUST RETURNED AFTER STUDYING ABROAD FOR YEARS.
I ALWAYS KNEW YOU LOVED "ZORRO," BUT COULDN'T YOU BE JUST A BIT MORE ORIGINAL?
HA-HA! COME ON, ALFRED. LET'S CRASH THIS PARTY.
SATURDAY NIGHT IN GOTHAM! THE VANDERITZ HOTEL! THE DRESS IS TUX AND TAILS! THE DINNER IS STEAK AND TAILS!
BUT LEAVE IT TO DOCTORS TO SOMEHOW MAKE IT ALL BORING...
...AND SO, BASED ON MY LONG-TERM RESEARCH INTO DRUGS AND NERVE GASES...
...I CAN PREDICT A GENERATION OF NEW DRUGS AND GASES THAT WILL CONTROL PEOPLES' FEARS AND PARANOIA...AND DO SO WITHOUT ADVERSE SIDE EFFECTS.
GOTHAM MEDICAL CONVENTION 1939
BINGO! OUR LEADING SUSPECT...RIGHT OFF THE BAT!
AND THEN, TOO MANY MINUTES LATER, THE LECTURE ENDS AND DINNER IS SERVED...ALONG WITH A SURPRISE OR TWO...
WHY, ALFRED! UH... DR. PENNYWORTH! SO NICE TO...UH...SEE YOU AGAIN.

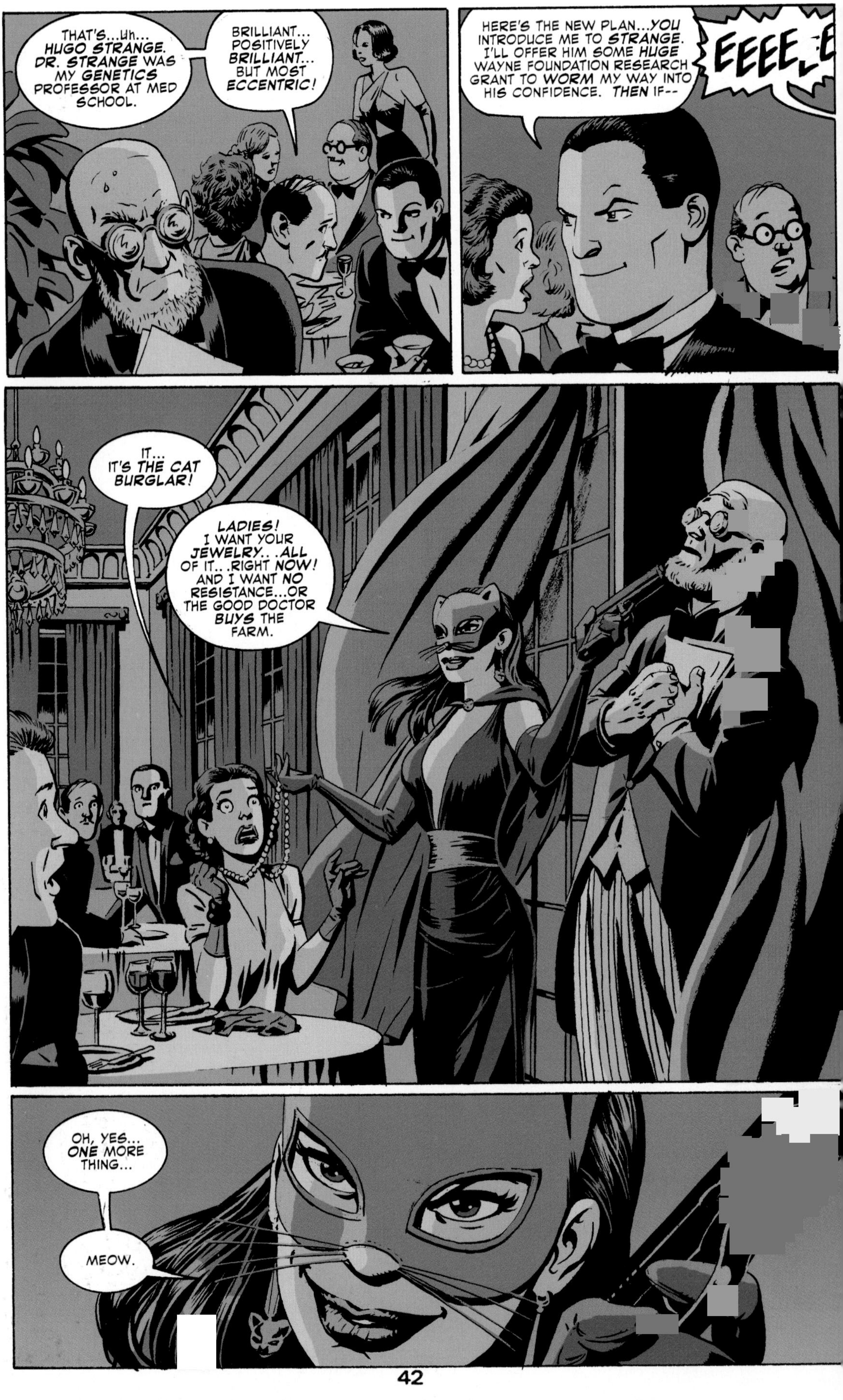

THAT'S...UH... HUGO STRANGE. DR. STRANGE WAS MY GENETICS PROFESSOR AT MED SCHOOL.
BRILLIANT... POSITIVELY BRILLIANT... BUT MOST ECCENTRIC!
HERE'S THE NEW PLAN...YOU INTRODUCE ME TO STRANGE. I'LL OFFER HIM SOME HUGE WAYNE FOUNDATION RESEARCH GRANT TO WORM MY WAY INTO HIS CONFIDENCE. THEN IF--
EEEEEE
IT... IT'S THE CAT BURGLAR!
LADIES! I WANT YOUR JEWELRY.. .ALL OF IT...RIGHT NOW! AND I WANT NO RESISTANCE...OR THE GOOD DOCTOR BUYS THE FARM.
OH, YES... ONE MORE THING...
MEOW.

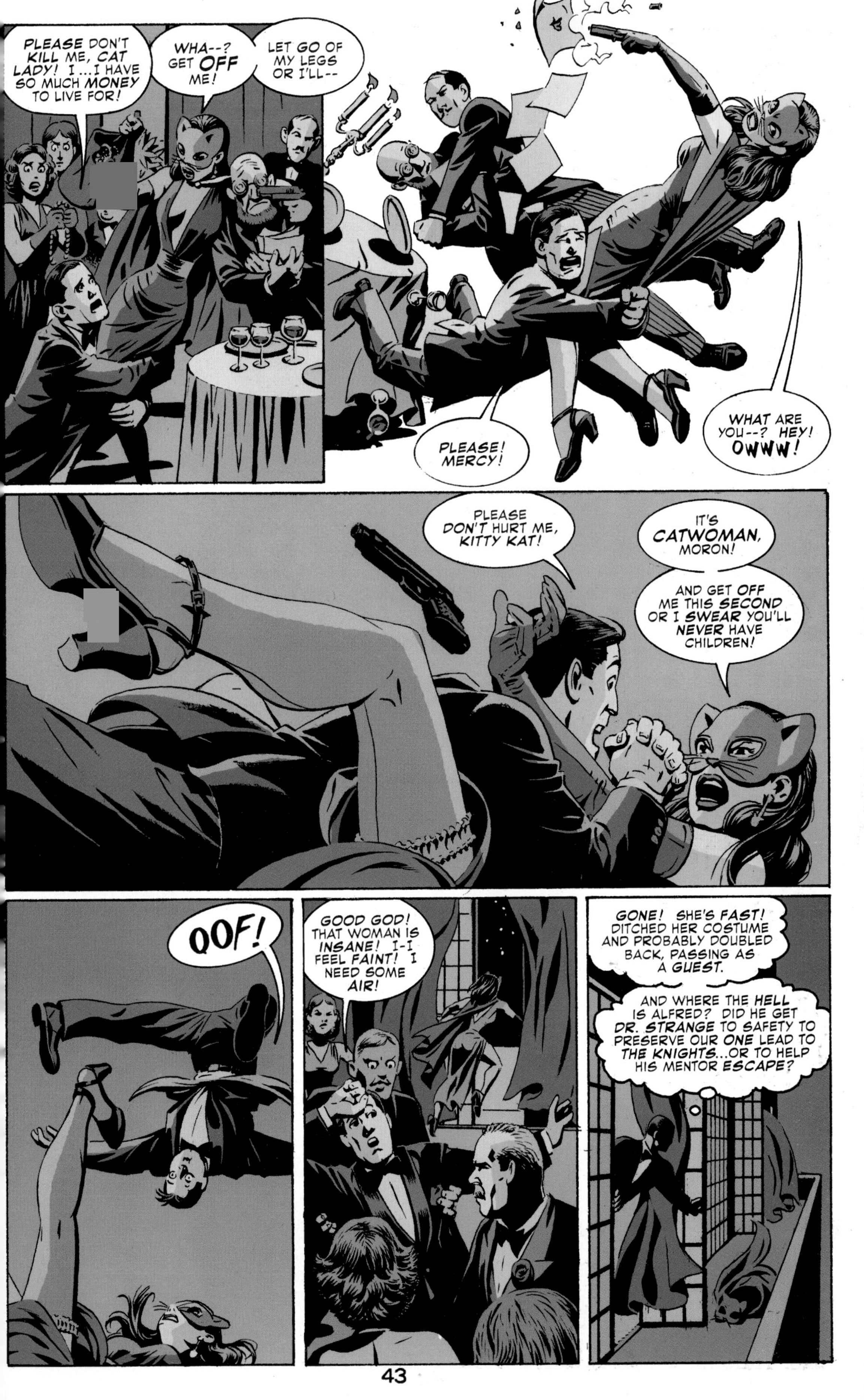
PLEASE DON'T KILL ME, CAT LADY! I...I HAVE SO MUCH MONEY TO LIVE FOR!
WHA--? GET OFF ME!
LET GO OF MY LEGS OR I'LL--
PLEASE! MERCY!
WHAT ARE YOU--? HEY! OWWW!
PLEASE DON'T HURT ME, KITTY KAT!
IT'S CATWOMAN, MORON!
AND GET OFF ME THIS SECOND OR I SWEAR YOU'LL NEVER HAVE CHILDREN!
OOF!
GOOD GOD! THAT WOMAN IS INSANE! I-I FEEL FAINT! I NEED SOME AIR!
GONE! SHE'S FAST! DITCHED HER COSTUME AND PROBABLY DOUBLED BACK, PASSING AS A GUEST.
AND WHERE THE HELL IS ALFRED? DID HE GET DR. STRANGE TO SAFETY TO PRESERVE OUR ONE LEAD TO THE KNIGHTS...OR TO HELP HIS MENTOR ESCAPE?

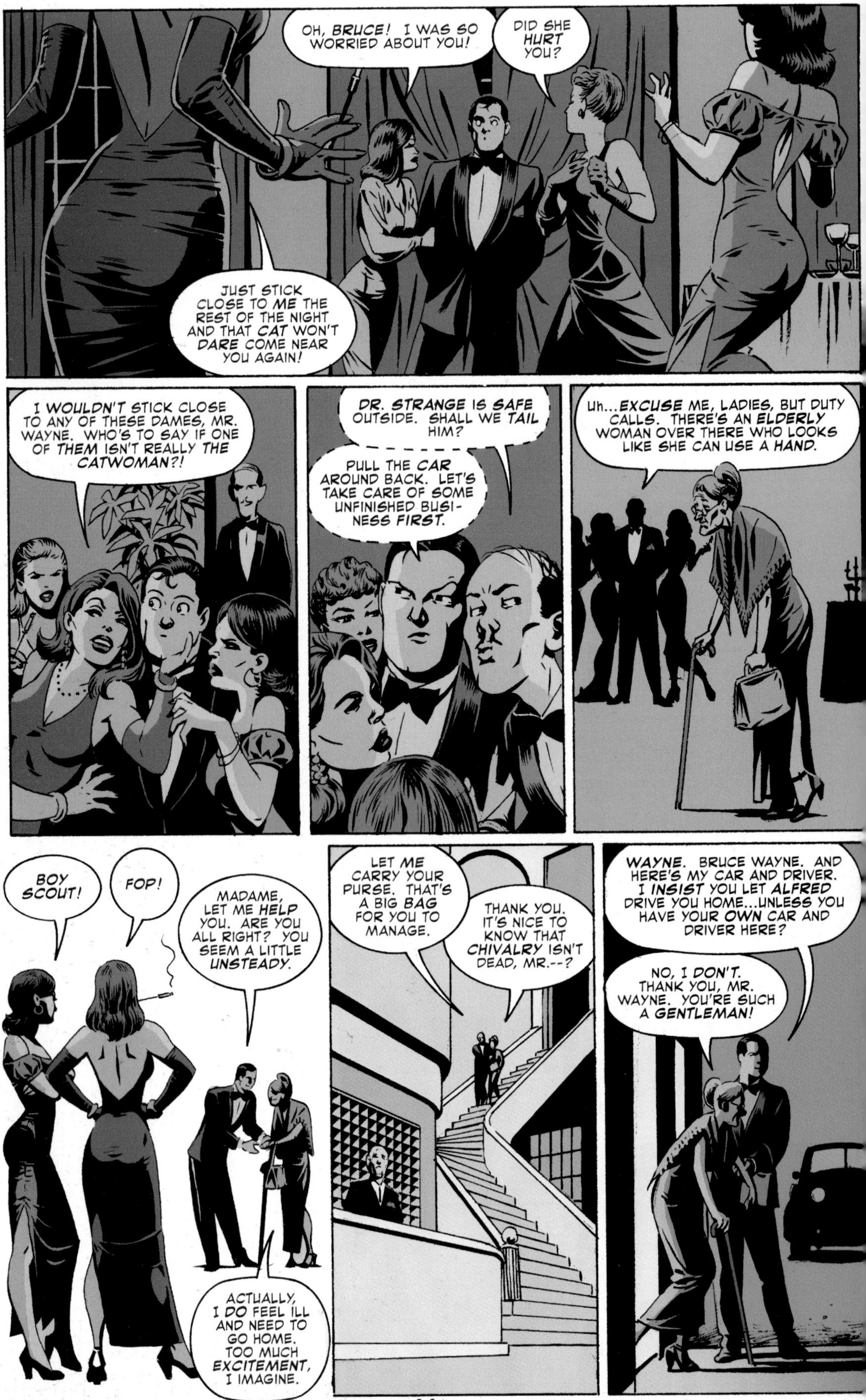
OH, BRUCE! I WAS SO WORRIED ABOUT YOU!
DID SHE HURT YOU?
JUST STICK CLOSE TO ME THE REST OF THE NIGHT AND THAT CAT WON'T DARE COME NEAR YOU AGAIN!
I WOULDN'T STICK CLOSE TO ANY OF THESE DAMES, MR. WAYNE. WHO'S TO SAY IF ONE OF THEM ISN'T REALLY THE CATWOMAN?!
DR. STRANGE IS SAFE OUTSIDE. SHALL WE TAIL HIM?
PULL THE CAR AROUND BACK. LET'S TAKE CARE OF SOME UNFINISHED BUSI-NESS FIRST.
UH...EXCUSE ME, LADIES, BUT DUTY CALLS. THERE'S AN ELDERLY WOMAN OVER THERE WHO LOOKS LIKE SHE CAN USE A HAND.
BOY SCOUT!
FOP!
MADAME, LET ME HELP YOU. ARE YOU ALL RIGHT? YOU SEEM A LITTLE UNSTEADY.
ACTUALLY, I DO FEEL ILL AND NEED TO GO HOME. TOO MUCH EXCITEMENT, I IMAGINE.
LET ME CARRY YOUR PURSE. THAT'S A BIG BAG FOR YOU TO MANAGE.
THANK YOU. IT'S NICE TO KNOW THAT CHIVALRY ISN'T DEAD, MR.--?
WAYNE. BRUCE WAYNE. AND HERE'S MY CAR AND DRIVER. I INSIST YOU LET ALFRED DRIVE YOU HOME...UNLESS YOU HAVE YOUR OWN CAR AND DRIVER HERE?
NO, I DON'T. THANK YOU, MR. WAYNE. YOU'RE SUCH A GENTLEMAN!

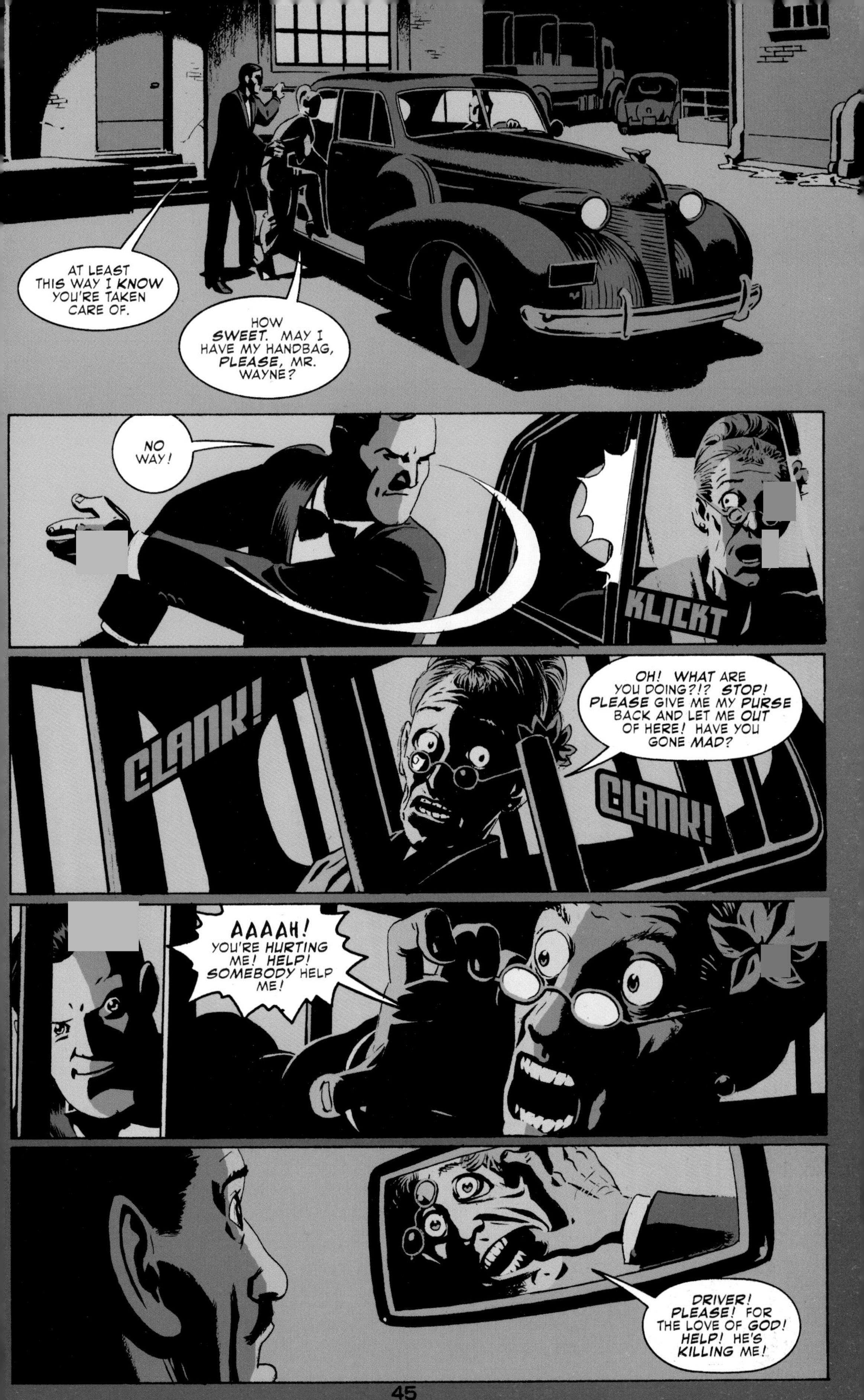

AT LEAST THIS WAY I KNOW YOU'RE TAKEN CARE OF.
HOW SWEET. MAY I HAVE MY HANDBAG, PLEASE, MR. WAYNE?
NO WAY!
KLICKT
CLANK!
OH! WHAT ARE YOU DOING?!? STOP! PLEASE GIVE ME MY PURSE BACK AND LET ME OUT OF HERE! HAVE YOU GONE MAD?
CLANK!
AAAAH! YOU'RE HURTING ME! HELP! SOMEBODY HELP ME!
DRIVER! PLEASE! FOR THE LOVE OF GOD! HELP! HE'S KILLING ME!

HELLO, *CATWOMAN...* AND *GOOD-BYE.*

ALFRED, DRIVE THIS *MOST-WANTED* WOMAN TO POLICE HEADQUARTERS... AND TAKE THIS *PURSE* WITH YOU.

JUDGING BY ITS *WEIGHT*, I'M BETTING YOU'LL FIND TONIGHT'S *STOLEN JEWELRY* INSIDE.

OWWW!

A LITTLE SOMETHING TO *REMEMBER* ME BY, MR. WAYNE...UNTIL *NEXT* TIME.

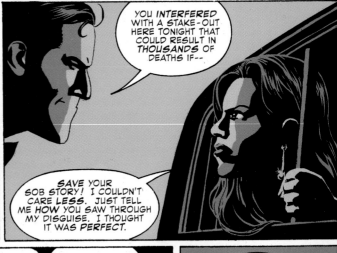

YOU *INTERFERED* WITH A STAKE-OUT HERE TONIGHT THAT COULD RESULT IN *THOUSANDS* OF DEATHS IF--

SAVE YOUR SOB STORY! I COULDN'T CARE *LESS.* JUST TELL ME *HOW* YOU SAW THROUGH MY DISGUISE. I THOUGHT IT WAS *PERFECT.*

THERE ISN'T AN OLD LADY ON *EARTH* WITH DROP-DEAD *GORGEOUS* LEGS LIKE YOURS!

...NOT MANY, *YOUNG* LADIES, EVEN, AS A MATTER OF FACT!

YOU'RE A CHARMING *LIAR...*JUST LIKE YOUR *BUTLER!*

NEXT CAT-FIGHT, MR. WAYNE, YOU'RE *DEAD!*

NOW *THAT* IS A *WOMAN!*

46

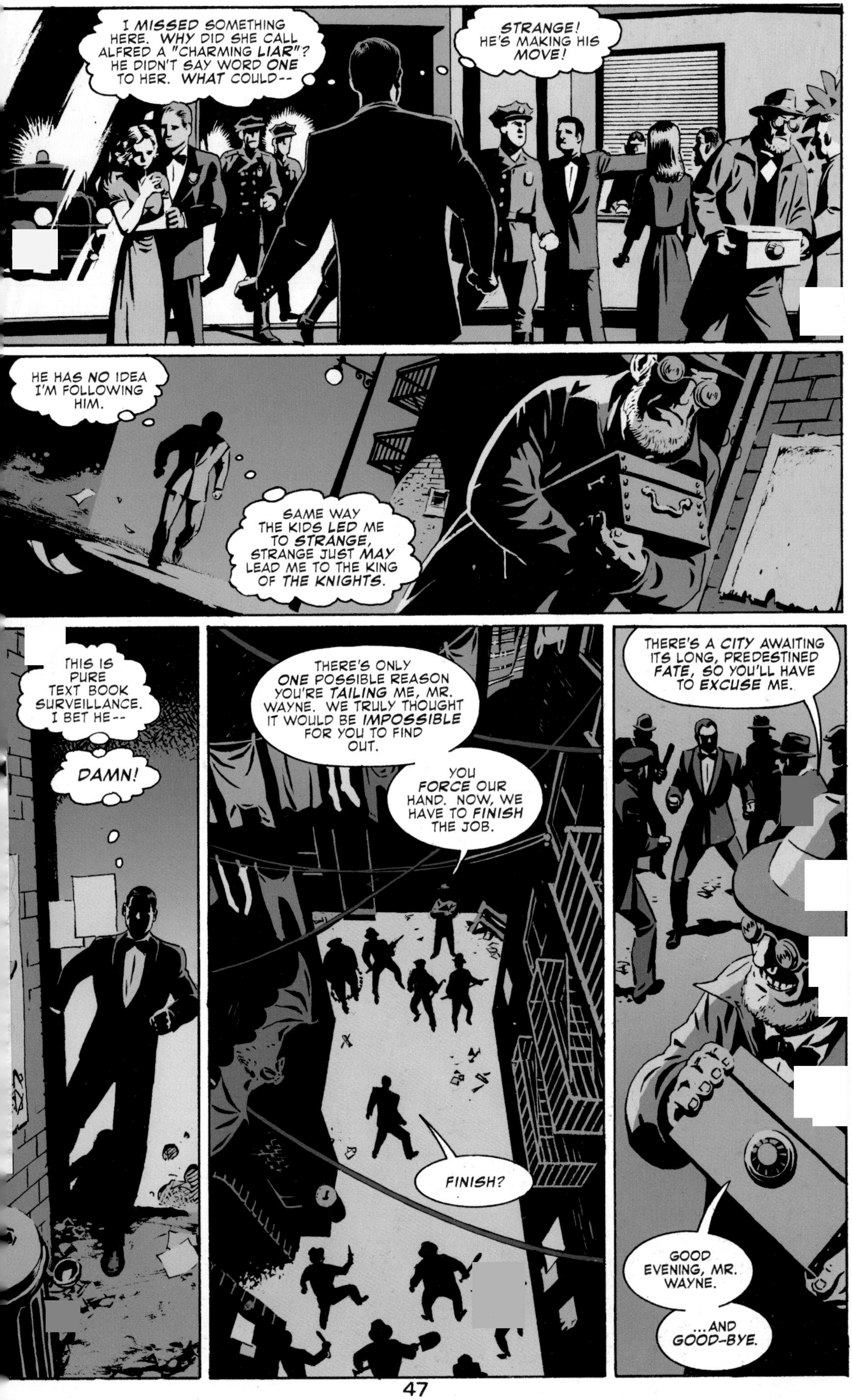
I MISSED SOMETHING HERE. WHY DID SHE CALL ALFRED A "CHARMING LIAR"? HE DIDN'T SAY WORD ONE TO HER. WHAT COULD--
STRANGE! HE'S MAKING HIS MOVE!
HE HAS NO IDEA I'M FOLLOWING HIM.
SAME WAY THE KIDS LED ME TO STRANGE, STRANGE JUST MAY LEAD ME TO THE KING OF THE KNIGHTS.
THIS IS PURE TEXT BOOK SURVEILLANCE. I BET HE--
DAMN!
THERE'S ONLY ONE POSSIBLE REASON YOU'RE TAILING ME, MR. WAYNE. WE TRULY THOUGHT IT WOULD BE IMPOSSIBLE FOR YOU TO FIND OUT.
YOU FORCE OUR HAND. NOW, WE HAVE TO FINISH THE JOB.
FINISH?
THERE'S A CITY AWAITING ITS LONG, PREDESTINED FATE, SO YOU'LL HAVE TO EXCUSE ME.
GOOD EVENING, MR. WAYNE.
...AND GOOD-BYE.

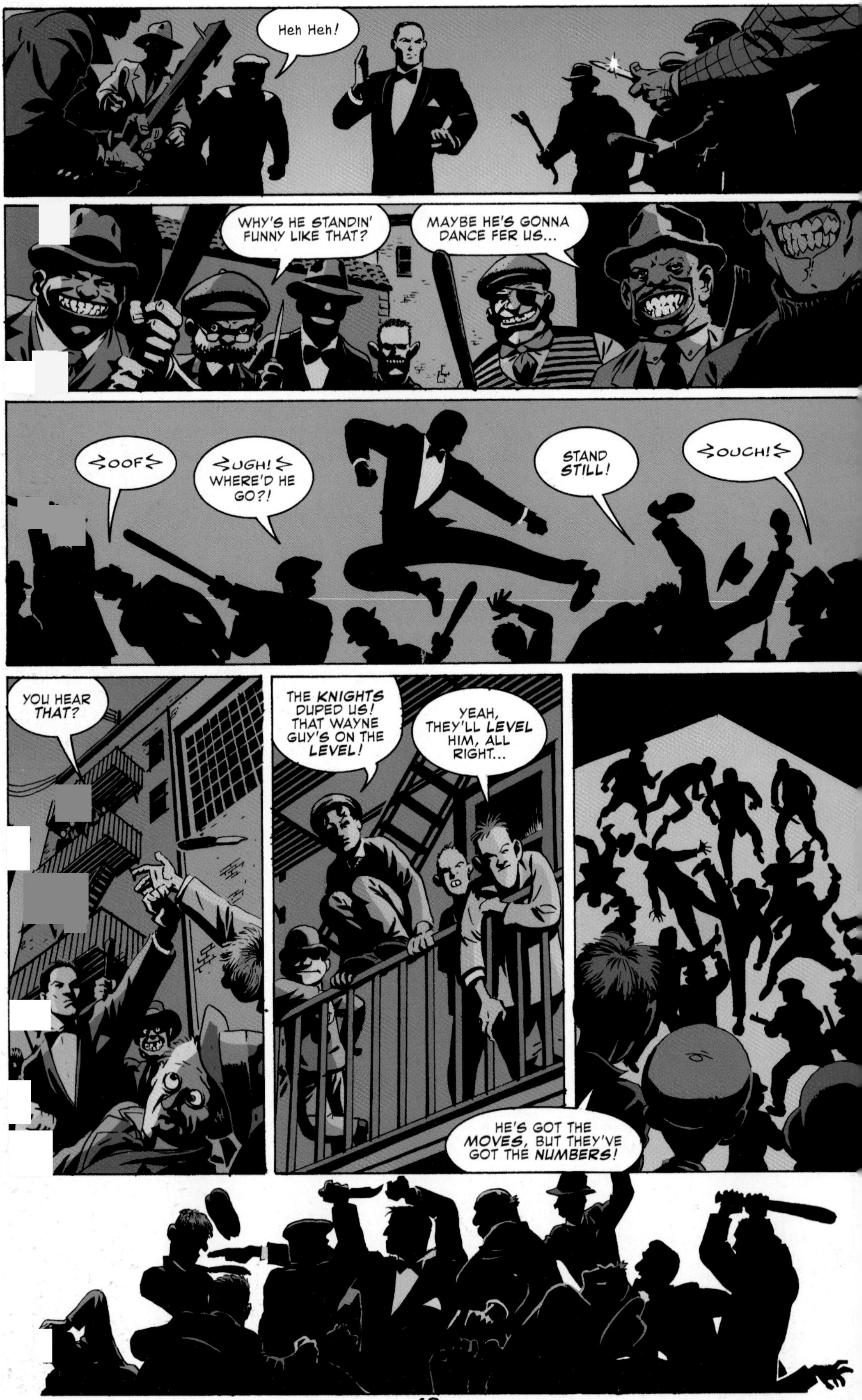
Heh Heh!
WHY'S HE STANDIN' FUNNY LIKE THAT?
MAYBE HE'S GONNA DANCE FER US...
OOF
UGH! WHERE'D HE GO?!
STAND STILL!
OUCH!
YOU HEAR THAT?
THE KNIGHTS DUPED US! THAT WAYNE GUY'S ON THE LEVEL!
YEAH, THEY'LL LEVEL HIM, ALL RIGHT...
HE'S GOT THE MOVES, BUT THEY'VE GOT THE NUMBERS!

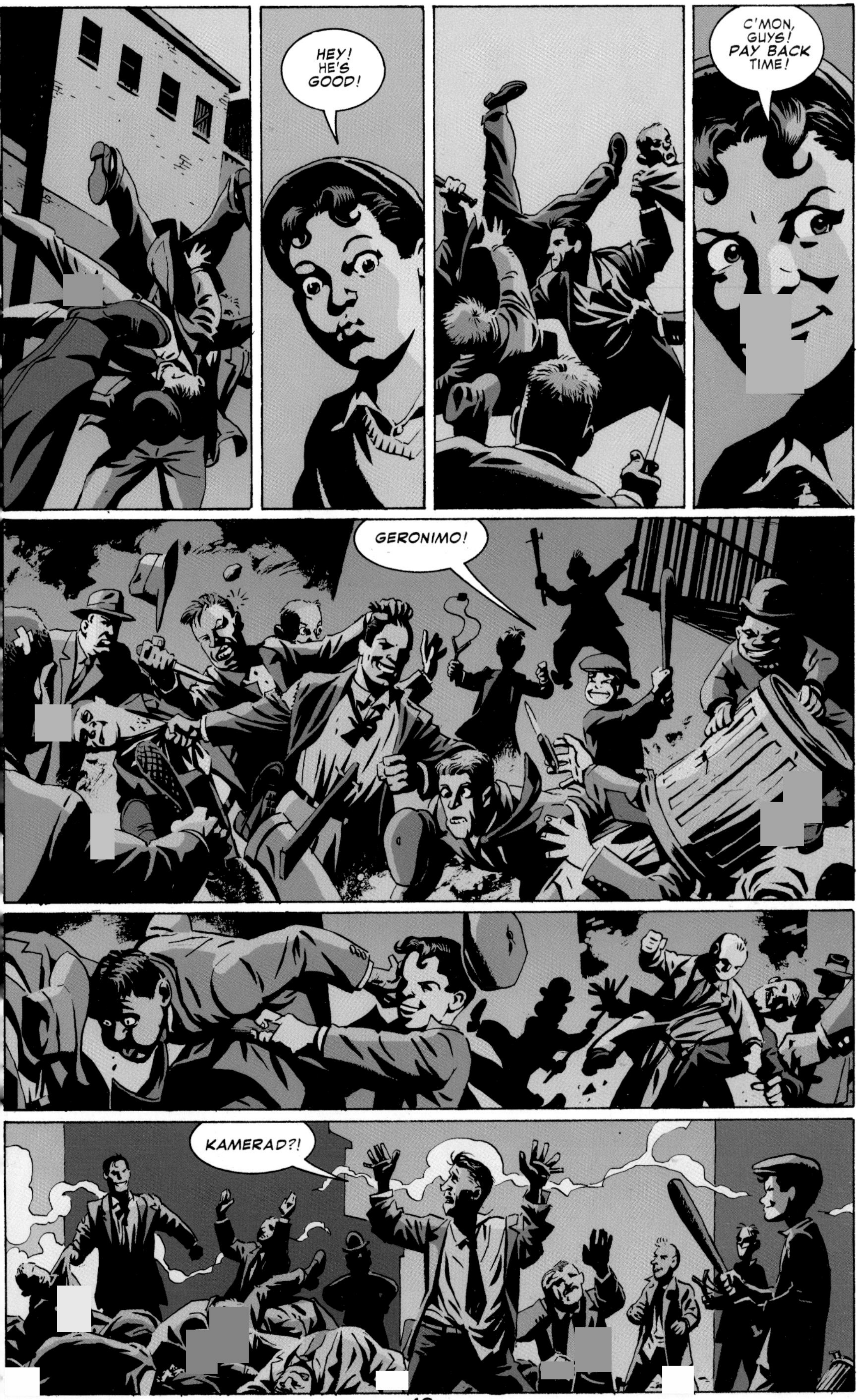
HEY! HE'S GOOD!
C'MON, GUYS! PAY BACK TIME!
GERONIMO!
KAMERAD?!

LAST CHANCE BEFORE LIGHTS OUT--IS STRANGE THE HEAD OF THE KNIGHTS OF THE GOLDEN CIRCLE?

WHERE'S THEIR NERVE CENTER? WHERE ARE THEY HIDING OUT?

WHAT'S THE BIG SECRET? SURE...STRANGE CALLS THE SHOTS! HE OPERATES OUT OF THE MED SCHOOL. GOT HIS OFFICE THERE AN' EVERYTHING.

SOME BIG-SHOT DETECTIVE YOU ARE! COULD'VE JUST LOOKED IN THE PHONE BOOK, CHUMP.

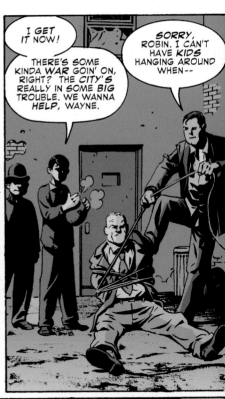

I GET IT NOW!

THERE'S SOME KINDA WAR GOIN' ON, RIGHT? THE CITY'S REALLY IN SOME BIG TROUBLE. WE WANNA HELP, WAYNE.

SORRY, ROBIN. I CAN'T HAVE KIDS HANGING AROUND WHEN--

WHEN WHAT?! YOU AIN'T EVEN GOT THE SMARTS TO STAY OUTTA A BLIND ALLEY! PAL, YOU NEED US MORE THAN WE NEED YOU!

YOU'LL NEVER HAVE BETTER EYES AND EARS ON THE STREETS THAN US.

WHADDAYA SAY, WAYNE...? IF THAT'S REALLY WHO YOU ARE...

IT'S NOT.

I'M "DETECTIVE #27".

KEEN! LIKE "OPERATOR #5" OR "SECRET AGENT X-9"? MY FAVORITE PULP AND COMIC STRIP!

WHAT ABOUT YOU BOYS? YOU'RE THE GOOD GUYS NOW! YOU CAN'T KEEP CALLING YOURSELVES "HOODS."

Nah. THIS IS A WAR AGAINST THE KNIGHTS, RIGHT? SO FROM NOW ON...WE'RE YOUR "BOY COMMANDOS!"

50

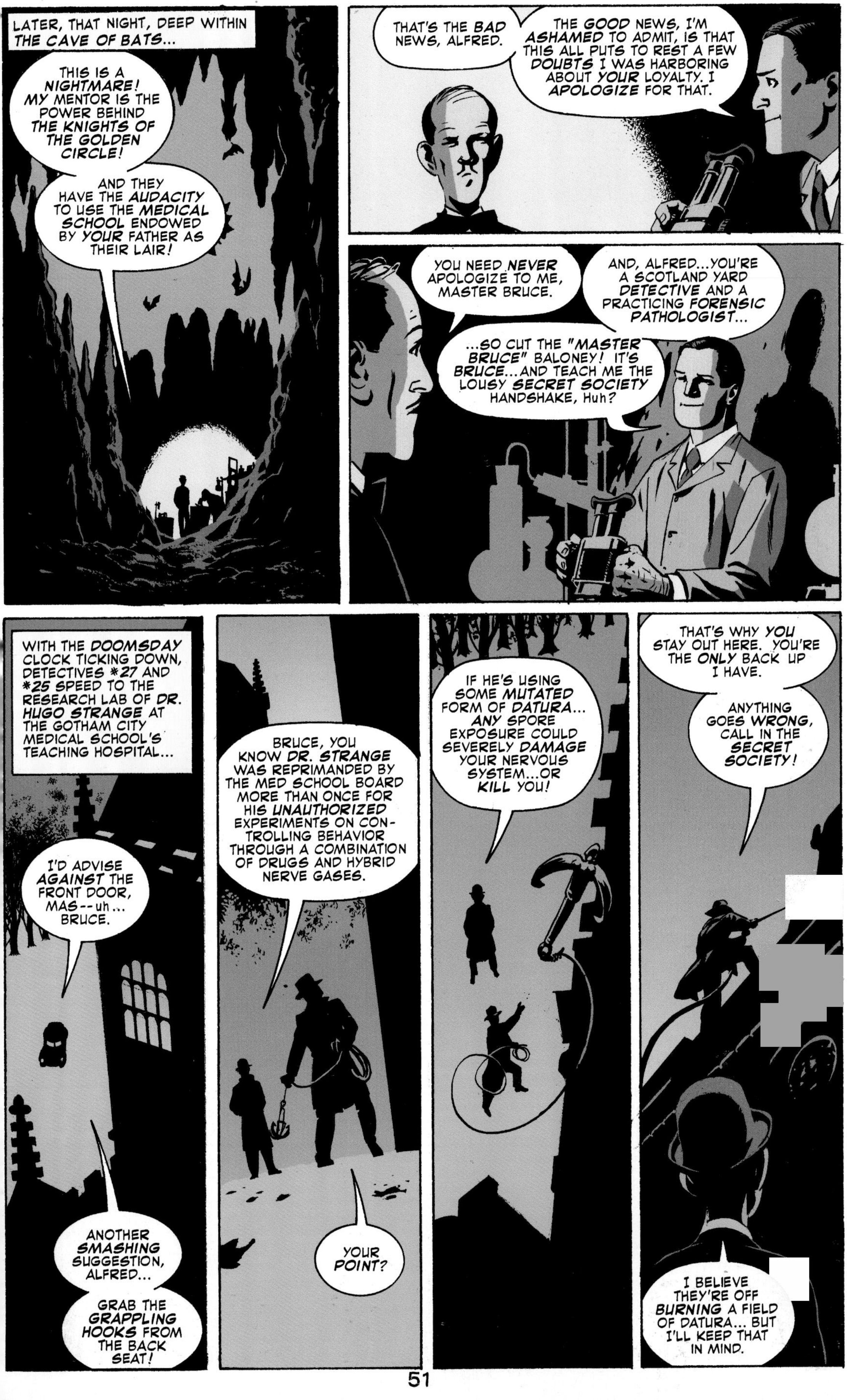
LATER, THAT NIGHT, DEEP WITHIN THE CAVE OF BATS...
THIS IS A NIGHTMARE! MY MENTOR IS THE POWER BEHIND THE KNIGHTS OF THE GOLDEN CIRCLE!
AND THEY HAVE THE AUDACITY TO USE THE MEDICAL SCHOOL ENDOWED BY YOUR FATHER AS THEIR LAIR!
THAT'S THE BAD NEWS, ALFRED.
THE GOOD NEWS, I'M ASHAMED TO ADMIT, IS THAT THIS ALL PUTS TO REST A FEW DOUBTS I WAS HARBORING ABOUT YOUR LOYALTY. I APOLOGIZE FOR THAT.
YOU NEED NEVER APOLOGIZE TO ME, MASTER BRUCE.
AND, ALFRED...YOU'RE A SCOTLAND YARD DETECTIVE AND A PRACTICING FORENSIC PATHOLOGIST...
...SO CUT THE "MASTER BRUCE" BALONEY! IT'S BRUCE...AND TEACH ME THE LOUSY SECRET SOCIETY HANDSHAKE, Huh?
WITH THE DOOMSDAY CLOCK TICKING DOWN, DETECTIVES *27 AND *25 SPEED TO THE RESEARCH LAB OF DR. HUGO STRANGE AT THE GOTHAM CITY MEDICAL SCHOOL'S TEACHING HOSPITAL...
I'D ADVISE AGAINST THE FRONT DOOR, MAS--uh... BRUCE.
ANOTHER SMASHING SUGGESTION, ALFRED...
GRAB THE GRAPPLING HOOKS FROM THE BACK SEAT!
BRUCE, YOU KNOW DR. STRANGE WAS REPRIMANDED BY THE MED SCHOOL BOARD MORE THAN ONCE FOR HIS UNAUTHORIZED EXPERIMENTS ON CONTROLLING BEHAVIOR THROUGH A COMBINATION OF DRUGS AND HYBRID NERVE GASES.
YOUR POINT?
IF HE'S USING SOME MUTATED FORM OF DATURA... ANY SPORE EXPOSURE COULD SEVERELY DAMAGE YOUR NERVOUS SYSTEM...OR KILL YOU!
THAT'S WHY YOU STAY OUT HERE. YOU'RE THE ONLY BACK UP I HAVE.
ANYTHING GOES WRONG, CALL IN THE SECRET SOCIETY!
I BELIEVE THEY'RE OFF BURNING A FIELD OF DATURA... BUT I'LL KEEP THAT IN MIND.

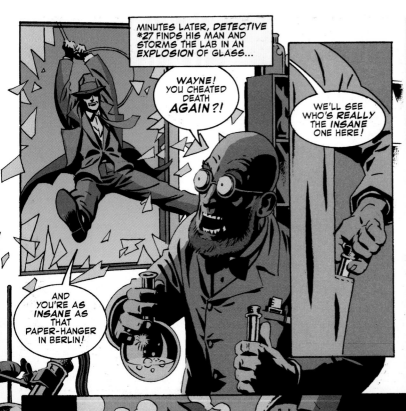

MINUTES LATER, DETECTIVE #27 FINDS HIS MAN AND STORMS THE LAB IN AN EXPLOSION OF GLASS...

WAYNE! YOU CHEATED DEATH AGAIN?!

WE'LL SEE WHO'S REALLY THE INSANE ONE HERE!

AND YOU'RE AS INSANE AS THAT PAPER-HANGER IN BERLIN!

BUNSEN BURNER! A HANDY LITTLE TOOL OF SCIENCE.

AAH!!

MUST STOP UNDERESTIMATING HIM. STUPID MISTAKE TO MAKE TWICE!

YOU! GRAB HIM! DON'T LET HIM GET AWAY!

WHA--?

PLEASE! THAT MAN'S A CRIMINAL!

JONATHAN, THIS IS THE WAYNE BOY. HE'S BEEN TRAUMATIZED FOR TEN YEARS AFTER WITNESSING HIS PARENTS' MURDERS.

TONIGHT, HE INHALED SPORES FROM THE DATURA I WAS EXPERIMENTING WITH. HE'S DELUSIONAL.

A PITY, HUGO. A TRAGEDY.

52

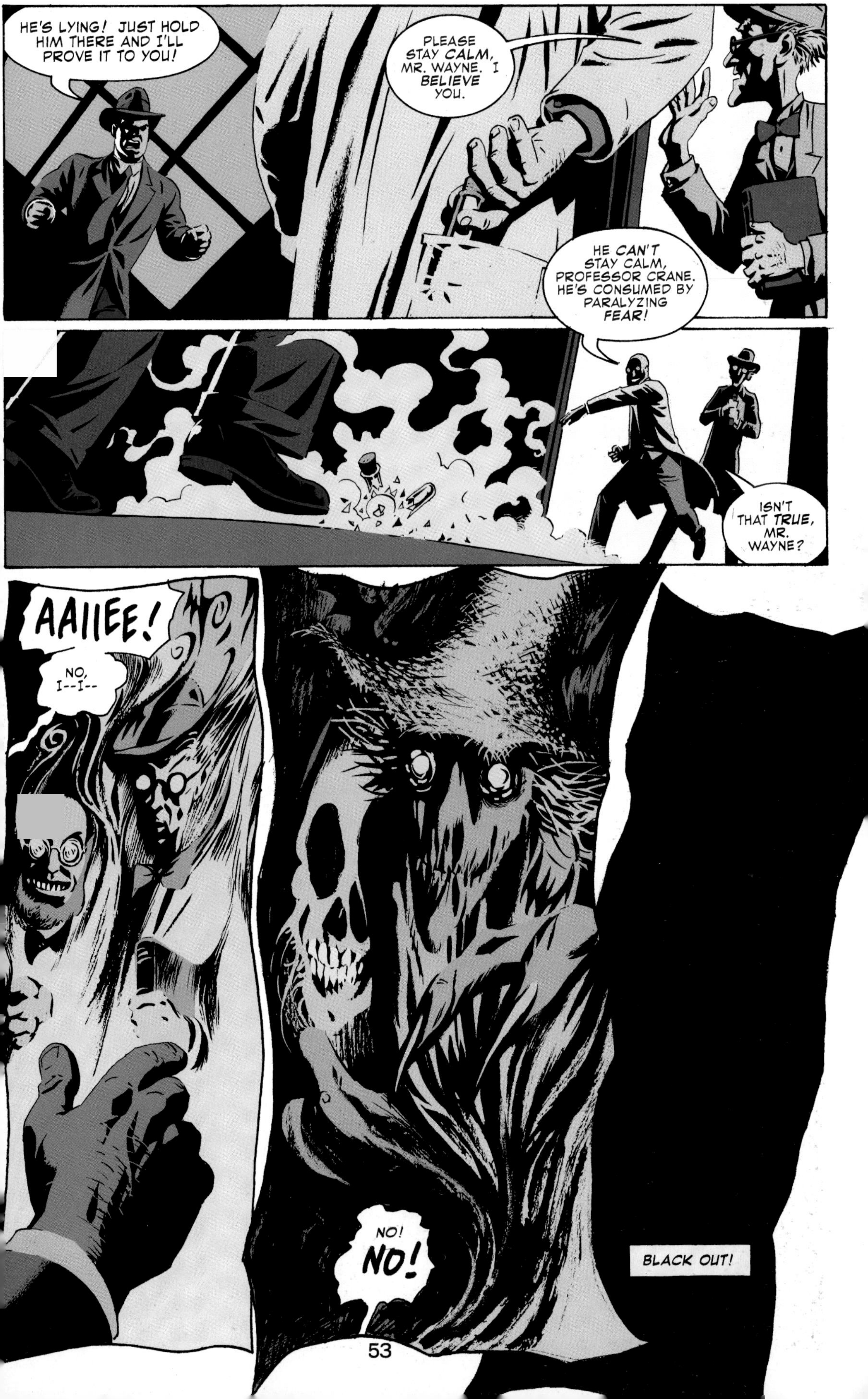
HE'S LYING! JUST HOLD HIM THERE AND I'LL PROVE IT TO YOU!
PLEASE STAY CALM, MR. WAYNE. I BELIEVE YOU.
HE CAN'T STAY CALM, PROFESSOR CRANE. HE'S CONSUMED BY PARALYZING FEAR!
ISN'T THAT TRUE, MR. WAYNE?
AAIIEE!
NO, I--I--
NO! NO!
BLACK OUT!

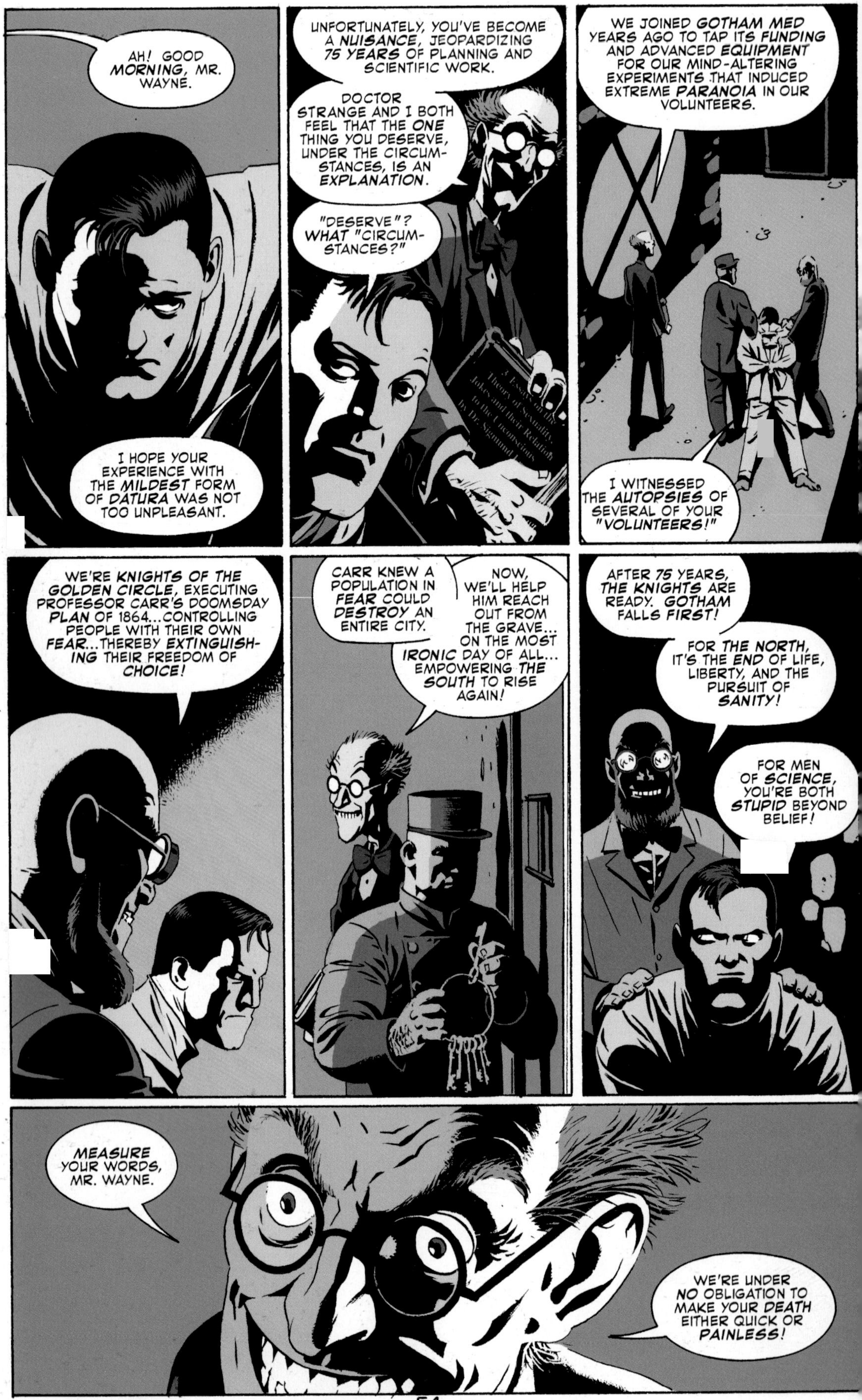

AH! GOOD MORNING, MR. WAYNE.
I HOPE YOUR EXPERIENCE WITH THE MILDEST FORM OF DATURA WAS NOT TOO UNPLEASANT.
UNFORTUNATELY, YOU'VE BECOME A NUISANCE, JEOPARDIZING 75 YEARS OF PLANNING AND SCIENTIFIC WORK.
DOCTOR STRANGE AND I BOTH FEEL THAT THE ONE THING YOU DESERVE, UNDER THE CIRCUMSTANCES, IS AN EXPLANATION.
"DESERVE"? WHAT "CIRCUMSTANCES?"
WE JOINED GOTHAM MED YEARS AGO TO TAP ITS FUNDING AND ADVANCED EQUIPMENT FOR OUR MIND-ALTERING EXPERIMENTS THAT INDUCED EXTREME PARANOIA IN OUR VOLUNTEERS.
I WITNESSED THE AUTOPSIES OF SEVERAL OF YOUR "VOLUNTEERS!"
WE'RE KNIGHTS OF THE GOLDEN CIRCLE, EXECUTING PROFESSOR CARR'S DOOMSDAY PLAN OF 1864...CONTROLLING PEOPLE WITH THEIR OWN FEAR...THEREBY EXTINGUISHING THEIR FREEDOM OF CHOICE!
CARR KNEW A POPULATION IN FEAR COULD DESTROY AN ENTIRE CITY.
NOW, WE'LL HELP HIM REACH OUT FROM THE GRAVE... ON THE MOST IRONIC DAY OF ALL... EMPOWERING THE SOUTH TO RISE AGAIN!
AFTER 75 YEARS, THE KNIGHTS ARE READY. GOTHAM FALLS FIRST!
FOR THE NORTH, IT'S THE END OF LIFE, LIBERTY, AND THE PURSUIT OF SANITY!
FOR MEN OF SCIENCE, YOU'RE BOTH STUPID BEYOND BELIEF!
MEASURE YOUR WORDS, MR. WAYNE.
WE'RE UNDER NO OBLIGATION TO MAKE YOUR DEATH EITHER QUICK OR PAINLESS!

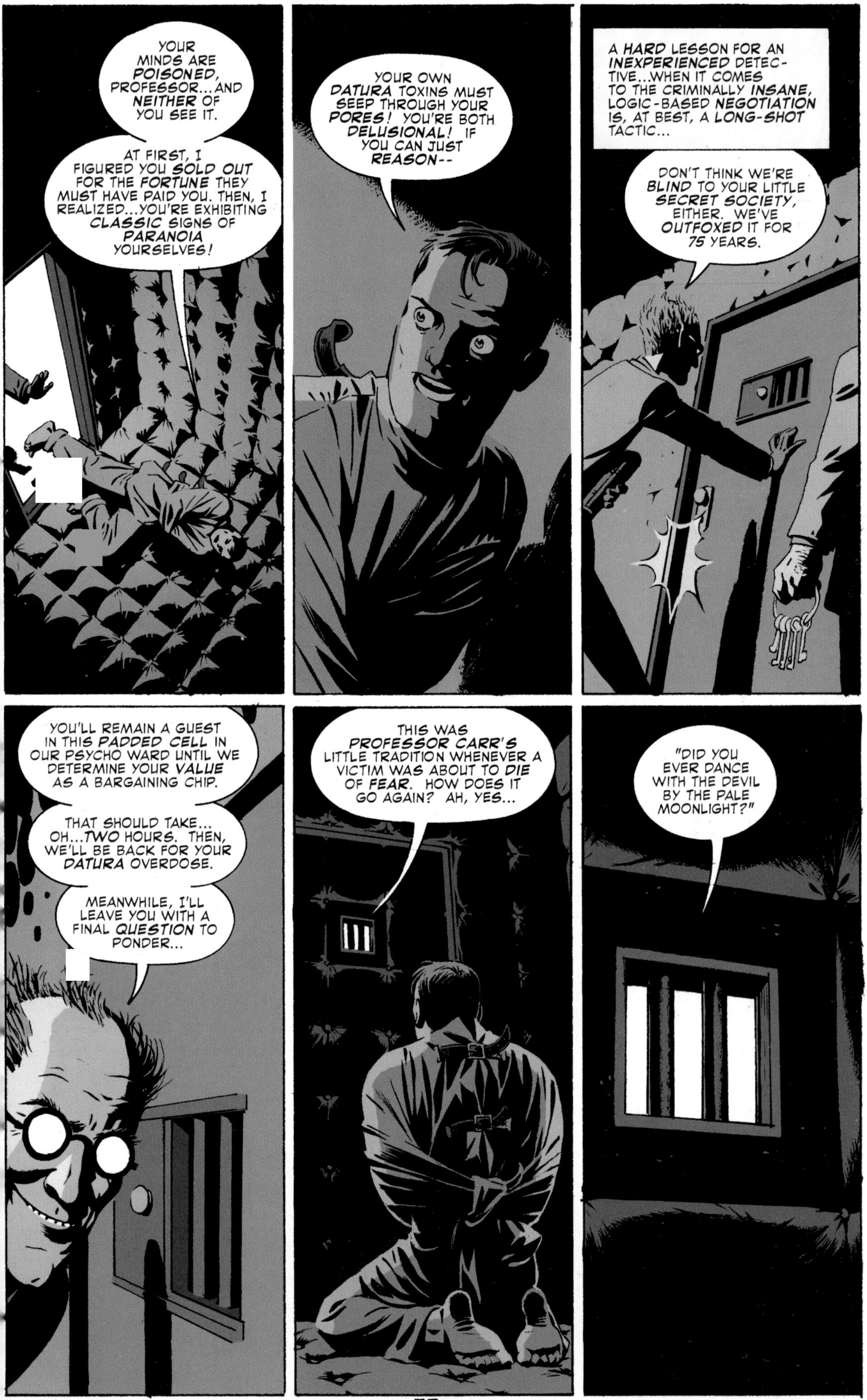
YOUR MINDS ARE POISONED, PROFESSOR...AND NEITHER OF YOU SEE IT.
AT FIRST, I FIGURED YOU SOLD OUT FOR THE FORTUNE THEY MUST HAVE PAID YOU. THEN, I REALIZED...YOU'RE EXHIBITING CLASSIC SIGNS OF PARANOIA YOURSELVES!
YOUR OWN DATURA TOXINS MUST SEEP THROUGH YOUR PORES! YOU'RE BOTH DELUSIONAL! IF YOU CAN JUST REASON--
A HARD LESSON FOR AN INEXPERIENCED DETECTIVE...WHEN IT COMES TO THE CRIMINALLY INSANE, LOGIC-BASED NEGOTIATION IS, AT BEST, A LONG-SHOT TACTIC...
DON'T THINK WE'RE BLIND TO YOUR LITTLE SECRET SOCIETY, EITHER. WE'VE OUTFOXED IT FOR 75 YEARS.
YOU'LL REMAIN A GUEST IN THIS PADDED CELL IN OUR PSYCHO WARD UNTIL WE DETERMINE YOUR VALUE AS A BARGAINING CHIP.
THAT SHOULD TAKE... OH...TWO HOURS. THEN, WE'LL BE BACK FOR YOUR DATURA OVERDOSE.
MEANWHILE, I'LL LEAVE YOU WITH A FINAL QUESTION TO PONDER...
THIS WAS PROFESSOR CARR'S LITTLE TRADITION WHENEVER A VICTIM WAS ABOUT TO DIE OF FEAR. HOW DOES IT GO AGAIN? AH, YES...
"DID YOU EVER DANCE WITH THE DEVIL BY THE PALE MOONLIGHT?"

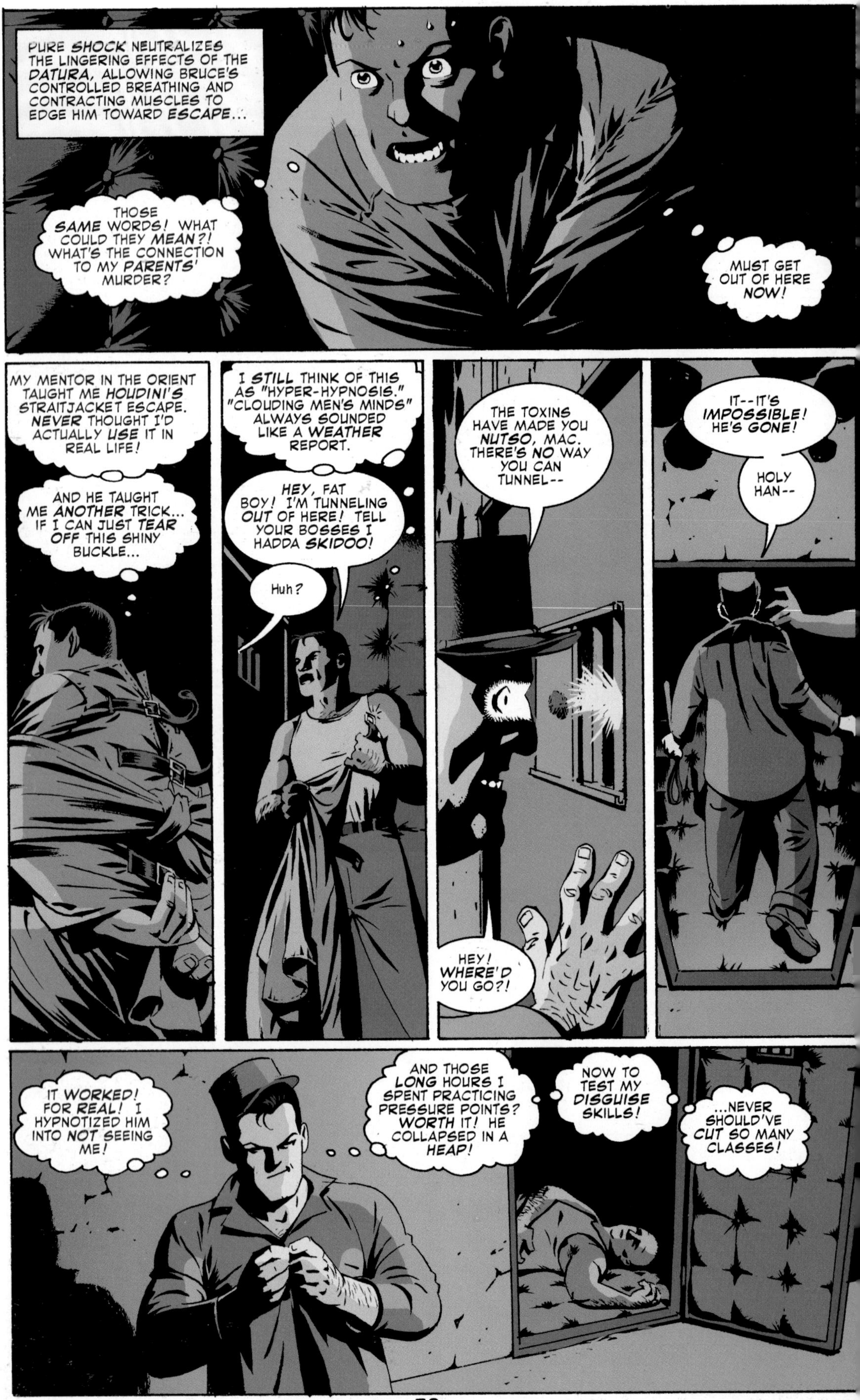

PURE SHOCK NEUTRALIZES THE LINGERING EFFECTS OF THE DATURA, ALLOWING BRUCE'S CONTROLLED BREATHING AND CONTRACTING MUSCLES TO EDGE HIM TOWARD ESCAPE...
THOSE SAME WORDS! WHAT COULD THEY MEAN?! WHAT'S THE CONNECTION TO MY PARENTS' MURDER?
MUST GET OUT OF HERE NOW!
MY MENTOR IN THE ORIENT TAUGHT ME HOUDINI'S STRAITJACKET ESCAPE. NEVER THOUGHT I'D ACTUALLY USE IT IN REAL LIFE!
AND HE TAUGHT ME ANOTHER TRICK... IF I CAN JUST TEAR OFF THIS SHINY BUCKLE...
I STILL THINK OF THIS AS "HYPER-HYPNOSIS." "CLOUDING MEN'S MINDS" ALWAYS SOUNDED LIKE A WEATHER REPORT.
HEY, FAT BOY! I'M TUNNELING OUT OF HERE! TELL YOUR BOSSES I HADDA SKIDOO!
Huh?
THE TOXINS HAVE MADE YOU NUTSO, MAC. THERE'S NO WAY YOU CAN TUNNEL--
HEY! WHERE'D YOU GO?!
IT--IT'S IMPOSSIBLE! HE'S GONE!
HOLY HAN--
IT WORKED! FOR REAL! I HYPNOTIZED HIM INTO NOT SEEING ME!
AND THOSE LONG HOURS I SPENT PRACTICING PRESSURE POINTS? WORTH IT! HE COLLAPSED IN A HEAP!
NOW TO TEST MY DISGUISE SKILLS!
...NEVER SHOULD'VE CUT SO MANY CLASSES!

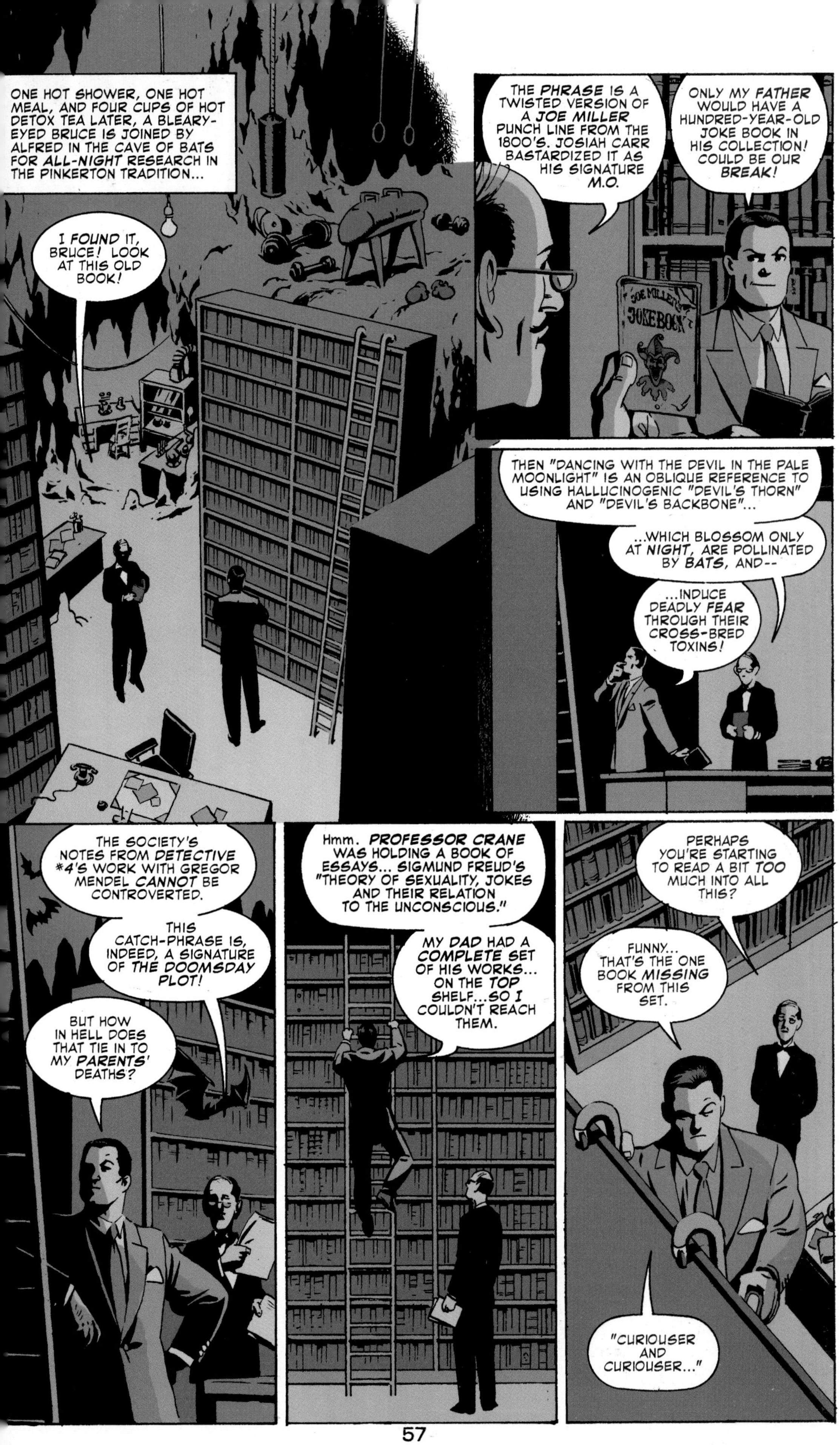
ONE HOT SHOWER, ONE HOT MEAL, AND FOUR CUPS OF HOT DETOX TEA LATER, A BLEARY-EYED BRUCE IS JOINED BY ALFRED IN THE CAVE OF BATS FOR ALL-NIGHT RESEARCH IN THE PINKERTON TRADITION...
I FOUND IT, BRUCE! LOOK AT THIS OLD BOOK!
THE PHRASE IS A TWISTED VERSION OF A JOE MILLER PUNCH LINE FROM THE 1800'S. JOSIAH CARR BASTARDIZED IT AS HIS SIGNATURE M.O.
ONLY MY FATHER WOULD HAVE A HUNDRED-YEAR-OLD JOKE BOOK IN HIS COLLECTION! COULD BE OUR BREAK!
JOE MILLER'S JOKEBOOK
THEN "DANCING WITH THE DEVIL IN THE PALE MOONLIGHT" IS AN OBLIQUE REFERENCE TO USING HALLUCINOGENIC "DEVIL'S THORN" AND "DEVIL'S BACKBONE"...
...WHICH BLOSSOM ONLY AT NIGHT, ARE POLLINATED BY BATS, AND--
...INDUCE DEADLY FEAR THROUGH THEIR CROSS-BRED TOXINS!
THE SOCIETY'S NOTES FROM DETECTIVE #4'S WORK WITH GREGOR MENDEL CANNOT BE CONTROVERTED.
THIS CATCH-PHRASE IS, INDEED, A SIGNATURE OF THE DOOMSDAY PLOT!
BUT HOW IN HELL DOES THAT TIE IN TO MY PARENTS' DEATHS?
Hmm. PROFESSOR CRANE WAS HOLDING A BOOK OF ESSAYS... SIGMUND FREUD'S "THEORY OF SEXUALITY, JOKES AND THEIR RELATION TO THE UNCONSCIOUS."
MY DAD HAD A COMPLETE SET OF HIS WORKS... ON THE TOP SHELF...SO I COULDN'T REACH THEM.
PERHAPS YOU'RE STARTING TO READ A BIT TOO MUCH INTO ALL THIS?
FUNNY... THAT'S THE ONE BOOK MISSING FROM THIS SET.
"CURIOUSER AND CURIOUSER..."

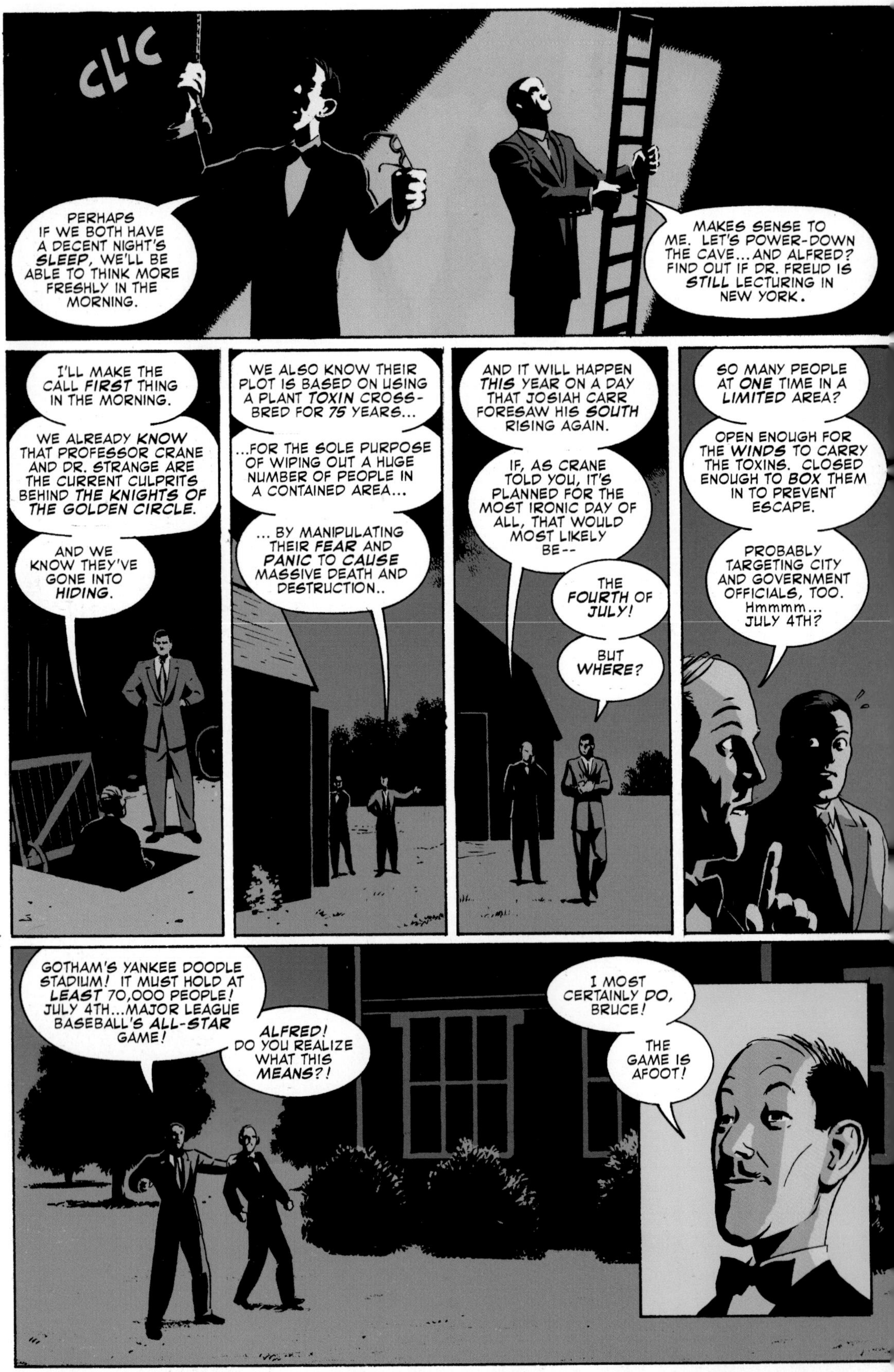
CL'C
PERHAPS IF WE BOTH HAVE A DECENT NIGHT'S SLEEP, WE'LL BE ABLE TO THINK MORE FRESHLY IN THE MORNING.
MAKES SENSE TO ME. LET'S POWER-DOWN THE CAVE...AND ALFRED? FIND OUT IF DR. FREUD IS STILL LECTURING IN NEW YORK.
I'LL MAKE THE CALL FIRST THING IN THE MORNING.
WE ALREADY KNOW THAT PROFESSOR CRANE AND DR. STRANGE ARE THE CURRENT CULPRITS BEHIND THE KNIGHTS OF THE GOLDEN CIRCLE.
AND WE KNOW THEY'VE GONE INTO HIDING.
WE ALSO KNOW THEIR PLOT IS BASED ON USING A PLANT TOXIN CROSS-BRED FOR 75 YEARS...
...FOR THE SOLE PURPOSE OF WIPING OUT A HUGE NUMBER OF PEOPLE IN A CONTAINED AREA...
... BY MANIPULATING THEIR FEAR AND PANIC TO CAUSE MASSIVE DEATH AND DESTRUCTION..
AND IT WILL HAPPEN THIS YEAR ON A DAY THAT JOSIAH CARR FORESAW HIS SOUTH RISING AGAIN.
IF, AS CRANE TOLD YOU, IT'S PLANNED FOR THE MOST IRONIC DAY OF ALL, THAT WOULD MOST LIKELY BE--
THE FOURTH OF JULY!
BUT WHERE?
SO MANY PEOPLE AT ONE TIME IN A LIMITED AREA?
OPEN ENOUGH FOR THE WINDS TO CARRY THE TOXINS. CLOSED ENOUGH TO BOX THEM IN TO PREVENT ESCAPE.
PROBABLY TARGETING CITY AND GOVERNMENT OFFICIALS, TOO. Hmmmm... JULY 4TH?
GOTHAM'S YANKEE DOODLE STADIUM! IT MUST HOLD AT LEAST 70,000 PEOPLE! JULY 4TH...MAJOR LEAGUE BASEBALL'S ALL-STAR GAME!
ALFRED! DO YOU REALIZE WHAT THIS MEANS?!
I MOST CERTAINLY DO, BRUCE!
THE GAME IS AFOOT!

END ACT TWO

ACT THREE

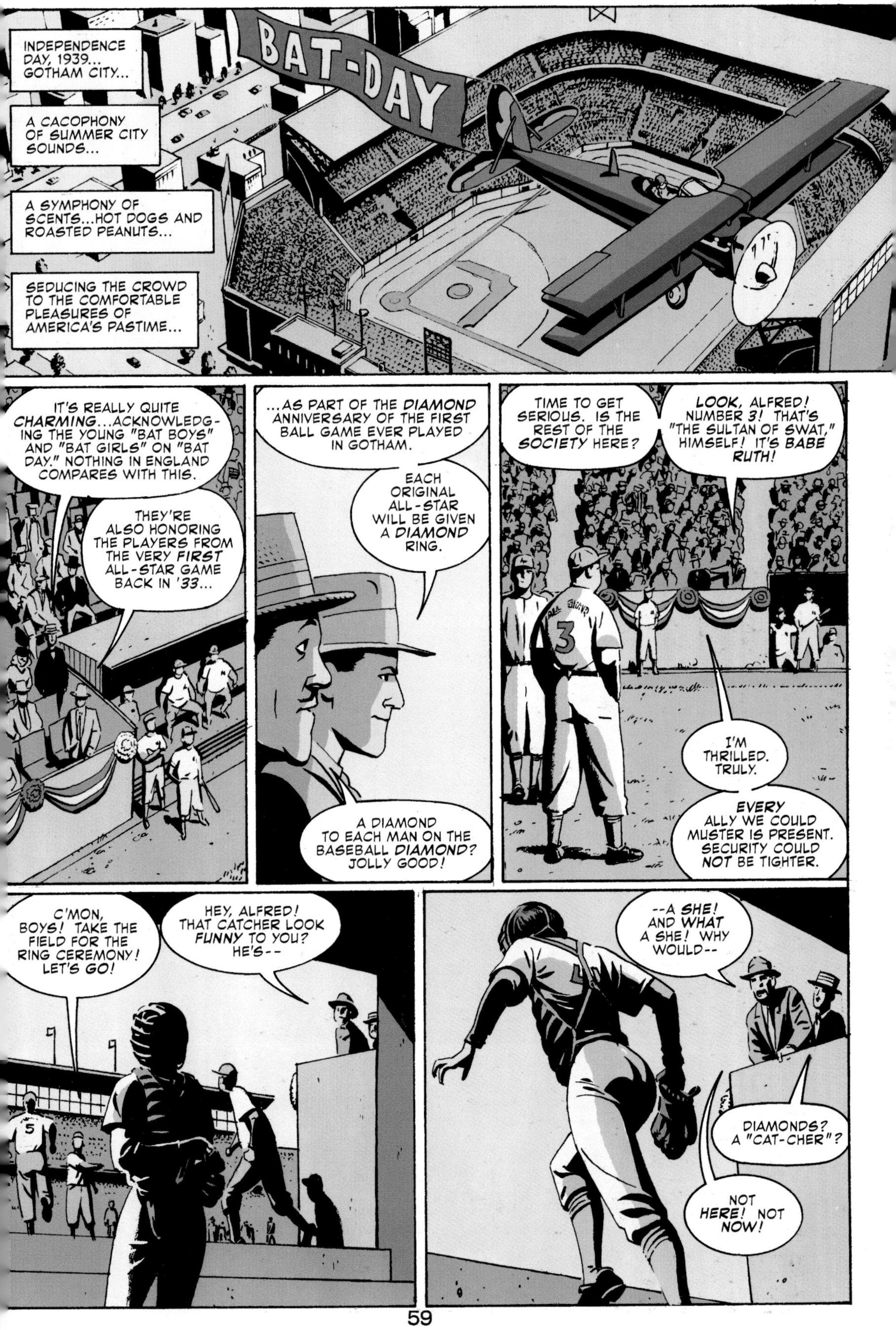

INDEPENDENCE DAY, 1939... GOTHAM CITY...
BAT-DAY
A CACOPHONY OF SUMMER CITY SOUNDS...
A SYMPHONY OF SCENTS...HOT DOGS AND ROASTED PEANUTS...
SEDUCING THE CROWD TO THE COMFORTABLE PLEASURES OF AMERICA'S PASTIME...
IT'S REALLY QUITE CHARMING...ACKNOWLEDGING THE YOUNG "BAT BOYS" AND "BAT GIRLS" ON "BAT DAY." NOTHING IN ENGLAND COMPARES WITH THIS.
THEY'RE ALSO HONORING THE PLAYERS FROM THE VERY FIRST ALL-STAR GAME BACK IN '33...
...AS PART OF THE DIAMOND ANNIVERSARY OF THE FIRST BALL GAME EVER PLAYED IN GOTHAM.
EACH ORIGINAL ALL-STAR WILL BE GIVEN A DIAMOND RING.
A DIAMOND TO EACH MAN ON THE BASEBALL DIAMOND? JOLLY GOOD!
TIME TO GET SERIOUS. IS THE REST OF THE SOCIETY HERE?
LOOK, ALFRED! NUMBER 3! THAT'S "THE SULTAN OF SWAT," HIMSELF! IT'S BABE RUTH!
I'M THRILLED. TRULY.
EVERY ALLY WE COULD MUSTER IS PRESENT. SECURITY COULD NOT BE TIGHTER.
C'MON, BOYS! TAKE THE FIELD FOR THE RING CEREMONY! LET'S GO!
HEY, ALFRED! THAT CATCHER LOOK FUNNY TO YOU? HE'S--
--A SHE! AND WHAT A SHE! WHY WOULD--
DIAMONDS? A "CAT-CHER"?
NOT HERE! NOT NOW!

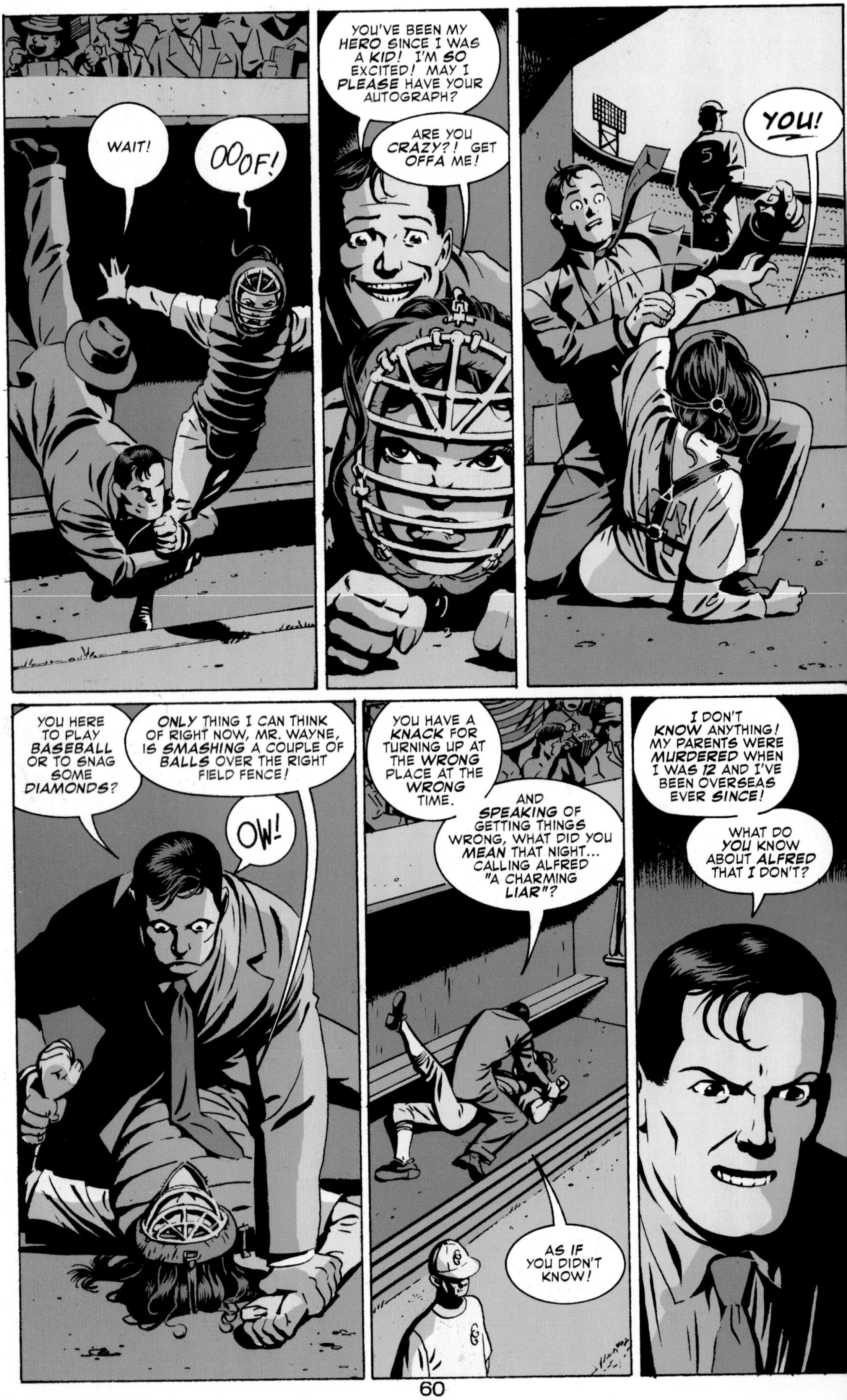
WAIT!
OOOF!
YOU'VE BEEN MY HERO SINCE I WAS A KID! I'M SO EXCITED! MAY I PLEASE HAVE YOUR AUTOGRAPH?
ARE YOU CRAZY?! GET OFFA ME!
YOU!
YOU HERE TO PLAY BASEBALL OR TO SNAG SOME DIAMONDS?
ONLY THING I CAN THINK OF RIGHT NOW, MR. WAYNE, IS SMASHING A COUPLE OF BALLS OVER THE RIGHT FIELD FENCE!
OW!
YOU HAVE A KNACK FOR TURNING UP AT THE WRONG PLACE AT THE WRONG TIME.
AND SPEAKING OF GETTING THINGS WRONG, WHAT DID YOU MEAN THAT NIGHT... CALLING ALFRED "A CHARMING LIAR"?
AS IF YOU DIDN'T KNOW!
I DON'T KNOW ANYTHING! MY PARENTS WERE MURDERED WHEN I WAS 12 AND I'VE BEEN OVERSEAS EVER SINCE!
WHAT DO YOU KNOW ABOUT ALFRED THAT I DON'T?

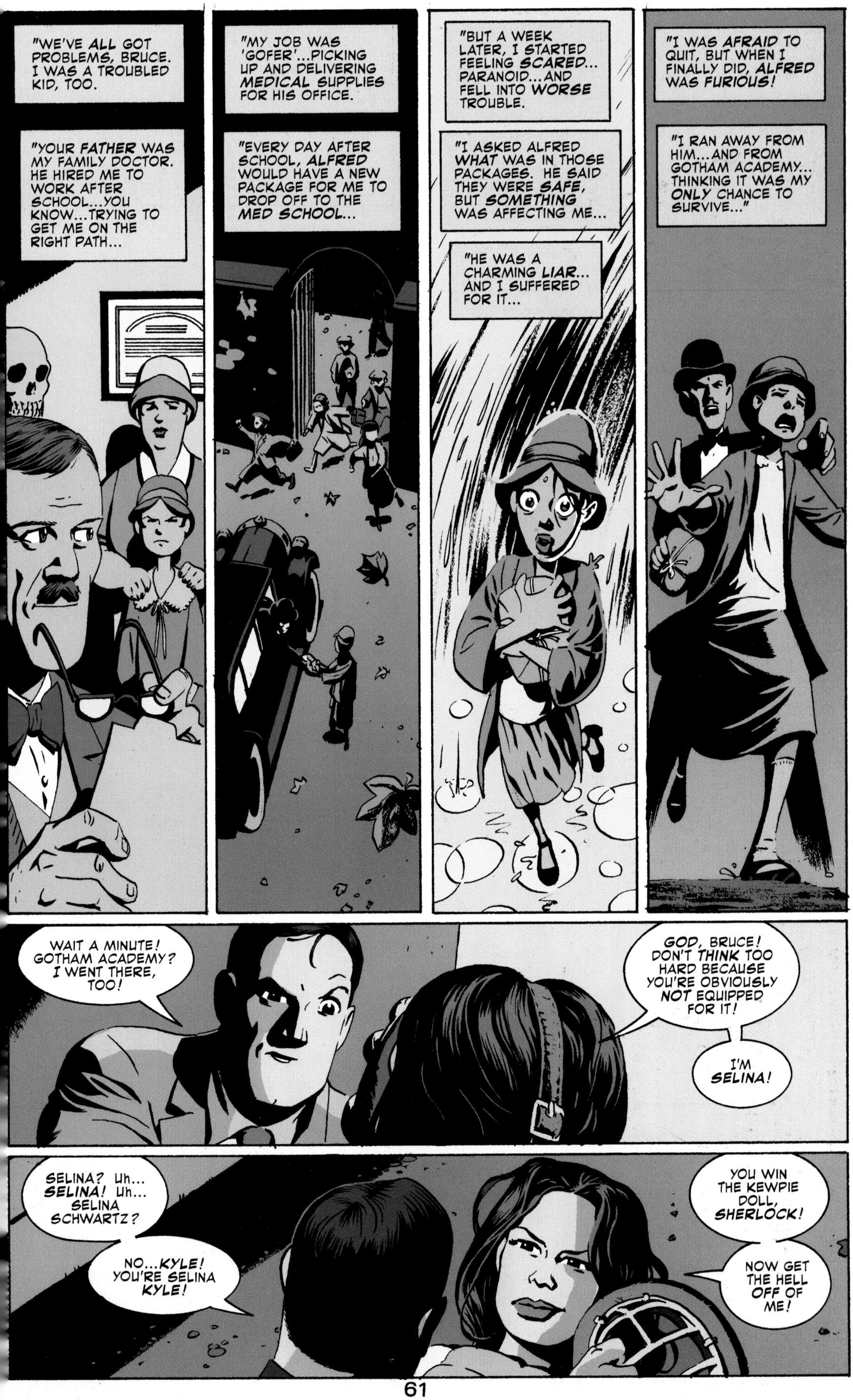

"WE'VE ALL GOT PROBLEMS, BRUCE. I WAS A TROUBLED KID, TOO.
"YOUR FATHER WAS MY FAMILY DOCTOR. HE HIRED ME TO WORK AFTER SCHOOL...YOU KNOW...TRYING TO GET ME ON THE RIGHT PATH...
"MY JOB WAS 'GOFER'...PICKING UP AND DELIVERING MEDICAL SUPPLIES FOR HIS OFFICE.
"EVERY DAY AFTER SCHOOL, ALFRED WOULD HAVE A NEW PACKAGE FOR ME TO DROP OFF TO THE MED SCHOOL...
"BUT A WEEK LATER, I STARTED FEELING SCARED...PARANOID...AND FELL INTO WORSE TROUBLE.
"I ASKED ALFRED WHAT WAS IN THOSE PACKAGES. HE SAID THEY WERE SAFE, BUT SOMETHING WAS AFFECTING ME...
"HE WAS A CHARMING LIAR...AND I SUFFERED FOR IT...
"I WAS AFRAID TO QUIT, BUT WHEN I FINALLY DID, ALFRED WAS FURIOUS!
"I RAN AWAY FROM HIM...AND FROM GOTHAM ACADEMY...THINKING IT WAS MY ONLY CHANCE TO SURVIVE..."
WAIT A MINUTE! GOTHAM ACADEMY? I WENT THERE, TOO!
GOD, BRUCE! DON'T THINK TOO HARD BECAUSE YOU'RE OBVIOUSLY NOT EQUIPPED FOR IT!
I'M SELINA!
SELINA? Uh... SELINA! Uh... SELINA SCHWARTZ?
NO...KYLE! YOU'RE SELINA KYLE!
YOU WIN THE KEWPIE DOLL, SHERLOCK!
NOW GET THE HELL OFF OF ME!

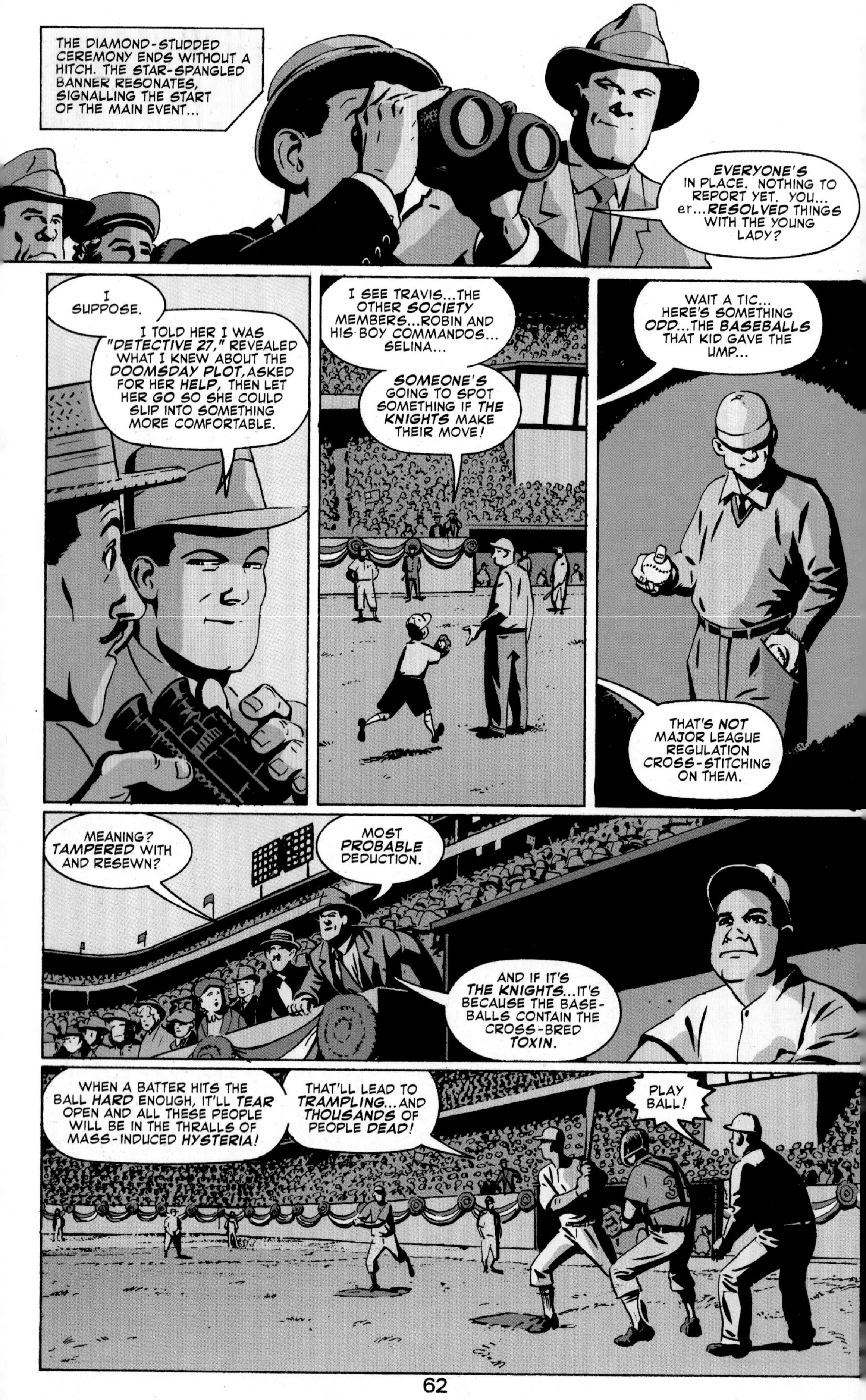
THE DIAMOND-STUDDED CEREMONY ENDS WITHOUT A HITCH. THE STAR-SPANGLED BANNER RESONATES, SIGNALLING THE START OF THE MAIN EVENT...
EVERYONE'S IN PLACE. NOTHING TO REPORT YET. YOU... er...RESOLVED THINGS WITH THE YOUNG LADY?
I SUPPOSE.
I TOLD HER I WAS "DETECTIVE 27," REVEALED WHAT I KNEW ABOUT THE DOOMSDAY PLOT, ASKED FOR HER HELP, THEN LET HER GO SO SHE COULD SLIP INTO SOMETHING MORE COMFORTABLE.
I SEE TRAVIS...THE OTHER SOCIETY MEMBERS...ROBIN AND HIS BOY COMMANDOS... SELINA...
SOMEONE'S GOING TO SPOT SOMETHING IF THE KNIGHTS MAKE THEIR MOVE!
WAIT A TIC... HERE'S SOMETHING ODD...THE BASEBALLS THAT KID GAVE THE UMP...
THAT'S NOT MAJOR LEAGUE REGULATION CROSS-STITCHING ON THEM.
MEANING? TAMPERED WITH AND RESEWN?
MOST PROBABLE DEDUCTION.
AND IF IT'S THE KNIGHTS...IT'S BECAUSE THE BASE-BALLS CONTAIN THE CROSS-BRED TOXIN.
WHEN A BATTER HITS THE BALL HARD ENOUGH, IT'LL TEAR OPEN AND ALL THESE PEOPLE WILL BE IN THE THRALLS OF MASS-INDUCED HYSTERIA!
THAT'LL LEAD TO TRAMPLING...AND THOUSANDS OF PEOPLE DEAD!
PLAY BALL!

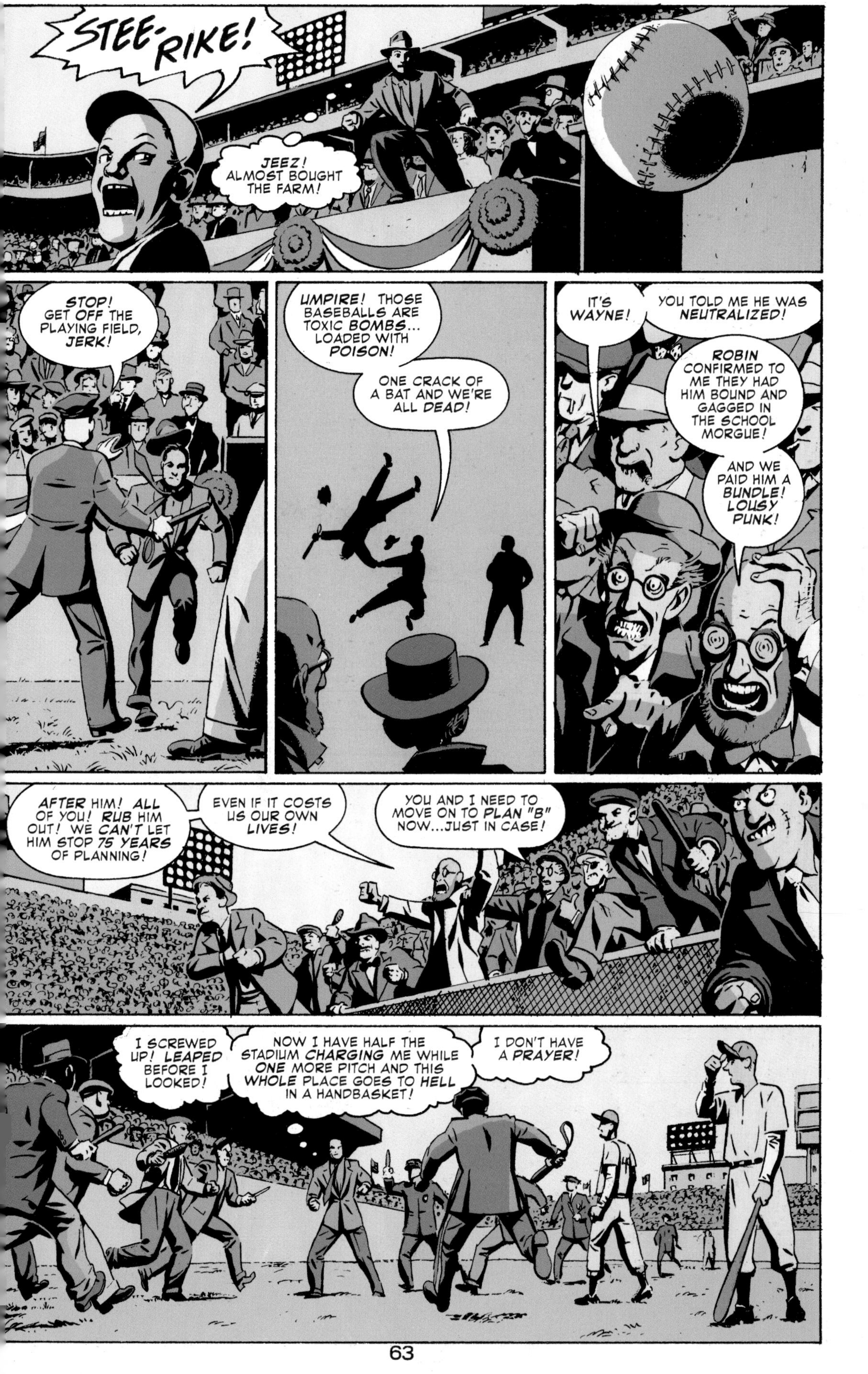
STEE-RIKE!
JEEZ! ALMOST BOUGHT THE FARM!
STOP! GET OFF THE PLAYING FIELD, JERK!
UMPIRE! THOSE BASEBALLS ARE TOXIC BOMBS... LOADED WITH POISON!
ONE CRACK OF A BAT AND WE'RE ALL DEAD!
IT'S WAYNE!
YOU TOLD ME HE WAS NEUTRALIZED!
ROBIN CONFIRMED TO ME THEY HAD HIM BOUND AND GAGGED IN THE SCHOOL MORGUE!
AND WE PAID HIM A BUNDLE! LOUSY PUNK!
AFTER HIM! ALL OF YOU! RUB HIM OUT! WE CAN'T LET HIM STOP 75 YEARS OF PLANNING!
EVEN IF IT COSTS US OUR OWN LIVES!
YOU AND I NEED TO MOVE ON TO PLAN "B" NOW...JUST IN CASE!
I SCREWED UP! LEAPED BEFORE I LOOKED!
NOW I HAVE HALF THE STADIUM CHARGING ME WHILE ONE MORE PITCH AND THIS WHOLE PLACE GOES TO HELL IN A HANDBASKET!
I DON'T HAVE A PRAYER!

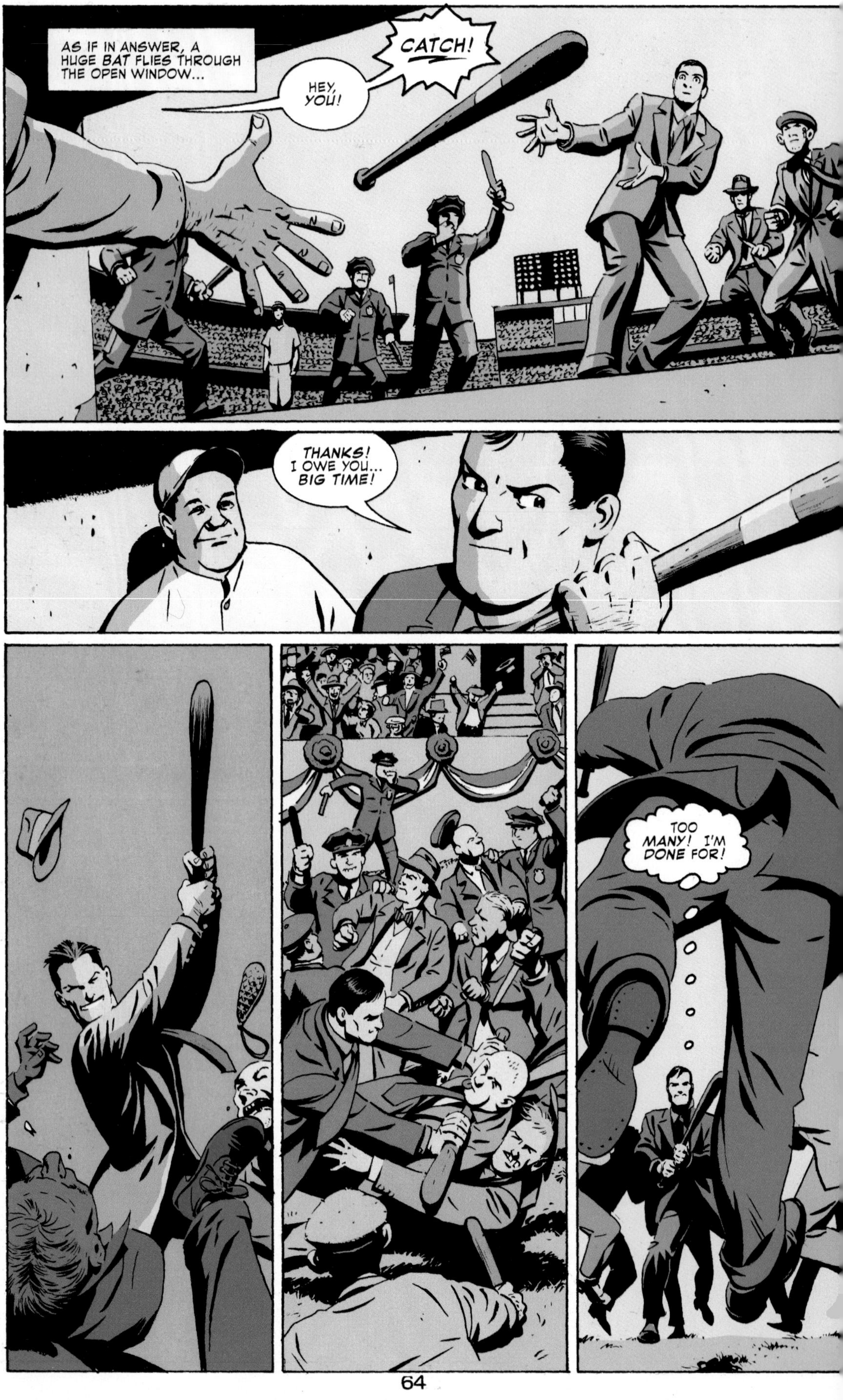
AS IF IN ANSWER, A HUGE BAT FLIES THROUGH THE OPEN WINDOW...
HEY, YOU!
CATCH!
THANKS! I OWE YOU... BIG TIME!
TOO MANY! I'M DONE FOR!

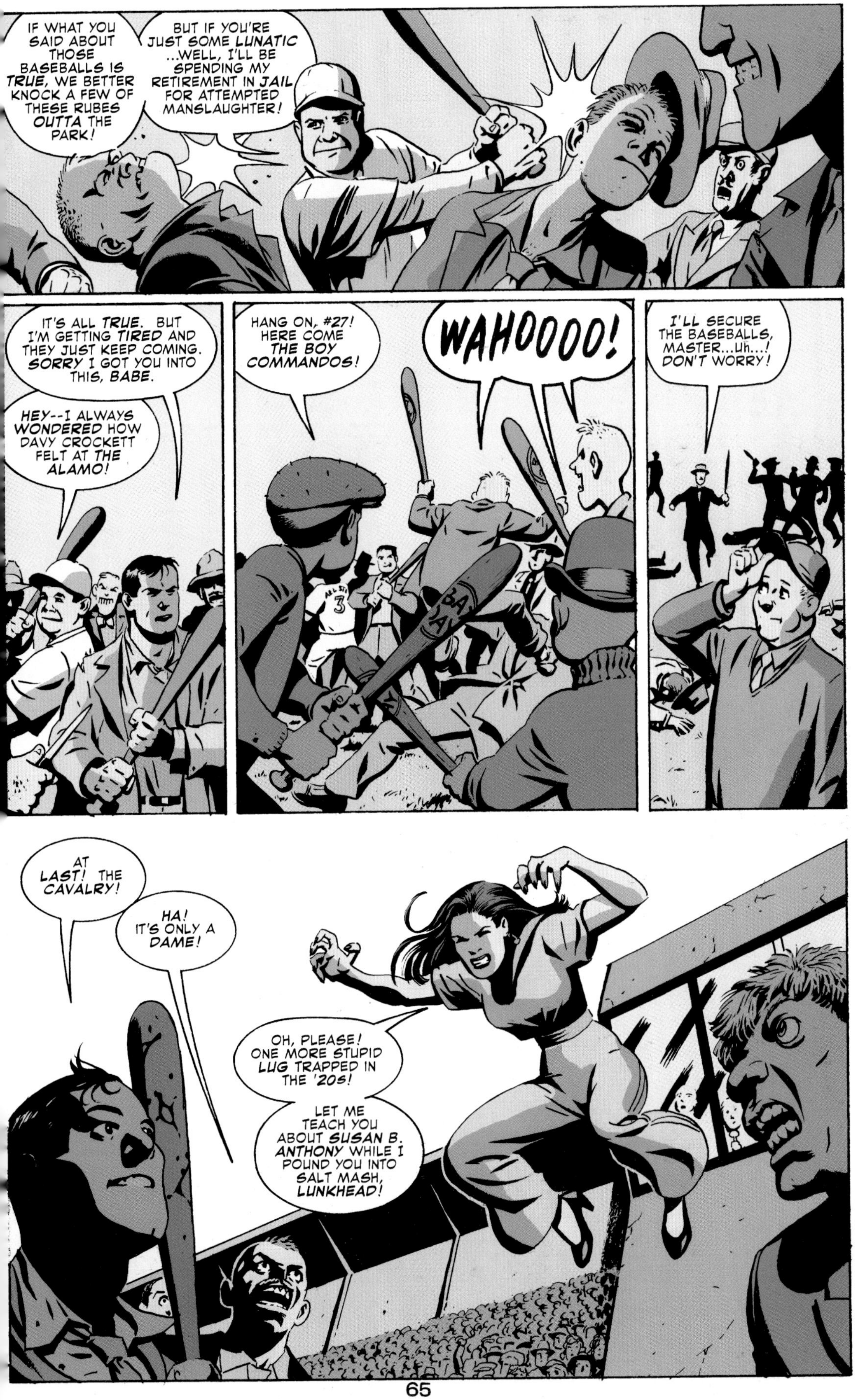

IF WHAT YOU SAID ABOUT THOSE BASEBALLS IS TRUE, WE BETTER KNOCK A FEW OF THESE RUBES OUTTA THE PARK!
BUT IF YOU'RE JUST SOME LUNATIC ...WELL, I'LL BE SPENDING MY RETIREMENT IN JAIL FOR ATTEMPTED MANSLAUGHTER!
IT'S ALL TRUE. BUT I'M GETTING TIRED AND THEY JUST KEEP COMING. SORRY I GOT YOU INTO THIS, BABE.
HEY--I ALWAYS WONDERED HOW DAVY CROCKETT FELT AT THE ALAMO!
HANG ON, #27! HERE COME THE BOY COMMANDOS!
WAHOOOO!
I'LL SECURE THE BASEBALLS, MASTER...uh...! DON'T WORRY!
AT LAST! THE CAVALRY!
HA! IT'S ONLY A DAME!
OH, PLEASE! ONE MORE STUPID LUG TRAPPED IN THE '20s!
LET ME TEACH YOU ABOUT SUSAN B. ANTHONY WHILE I POUND YOU INTO SALT MASH, LUNKHEAD!

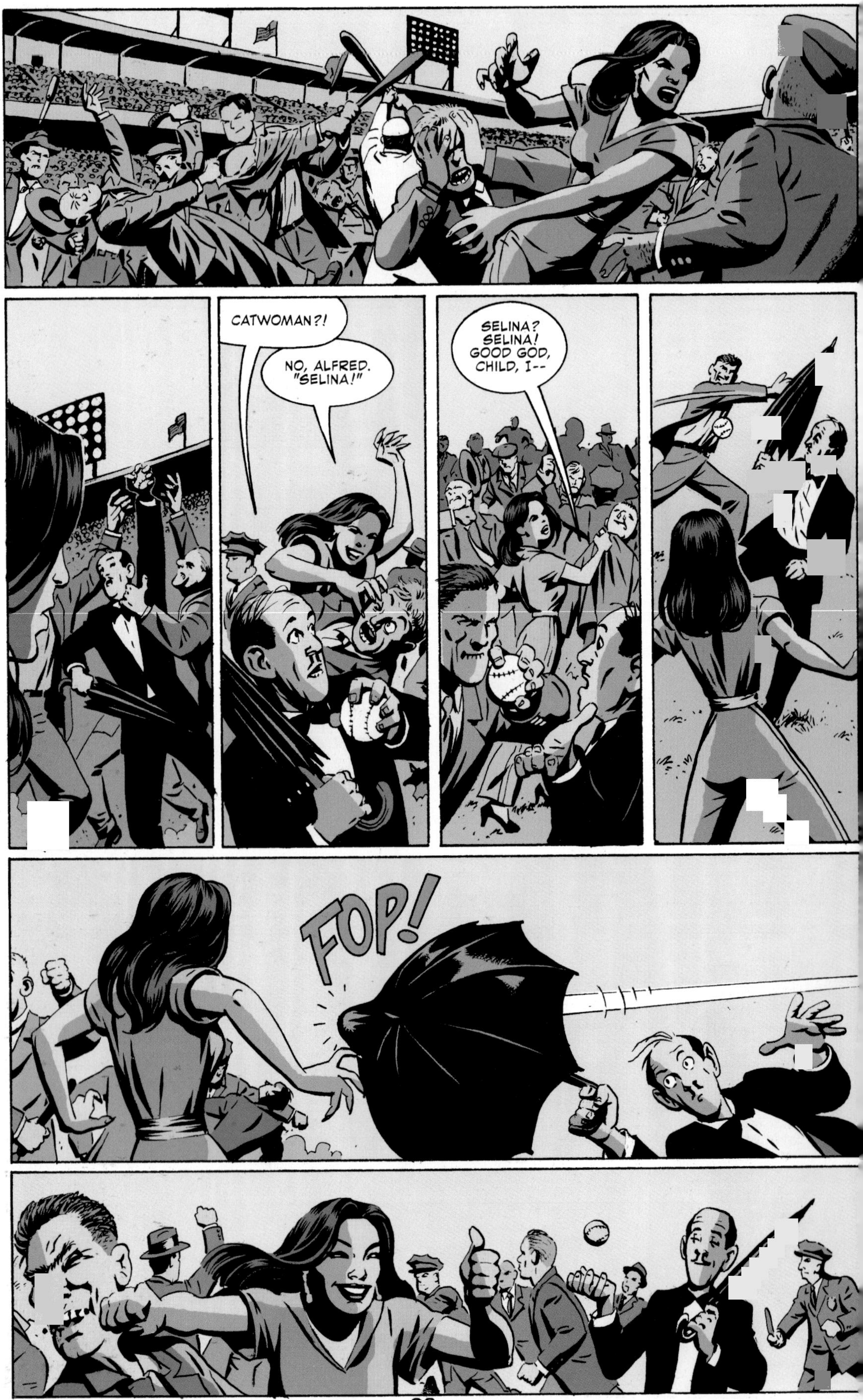
CATWOMAN?!
NO, ALFRED. "SELINA!"
SELINA? SELINA! GOOD GOD, CHILD, I--
FOP!

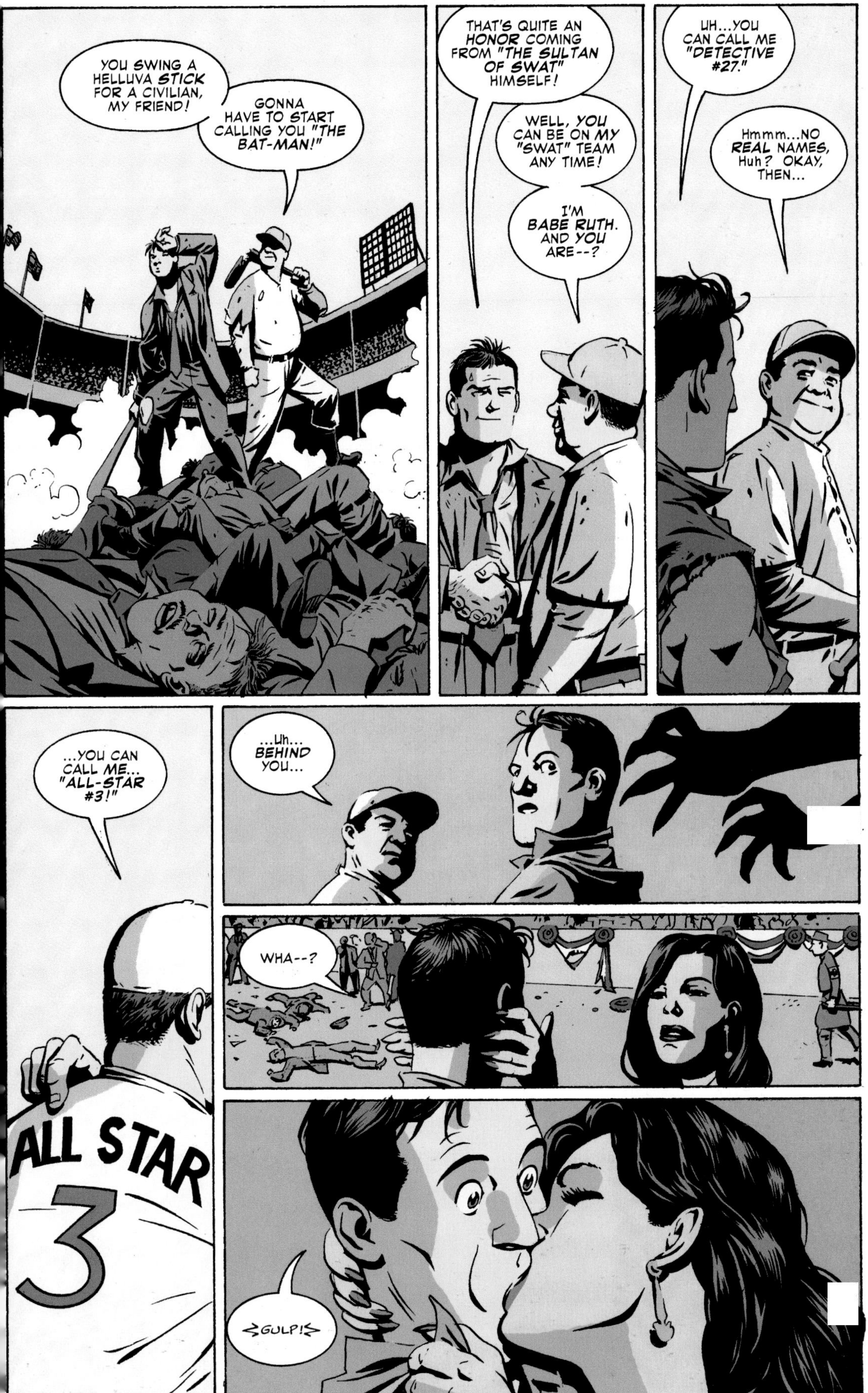
YOU SWING A HELLUVA STICK FOR A CIVILIAN, MY FRIEND!
GONNA HAVE TO START CALLING YOU "THE BAT-MAN!"
THAT'S QUITE AN HONOR COMING FROM "THE SULTAN OF SWAT" HIMSELF!
WELL, YOU CAN BE ON MY "SWAT" TEAM ANY TIME!
I'M BABE RUTH. AND YOU ARE--?
UH...YOU CAN CALL ME "DETECTIVE #27."
Hmmm...NO REAL NAMES, Huh? OKAY, THEN...
...YOU CAN CALL ME... "ALL-STAR #3!"
ALL STAR
3
...Uh... BEHIND YOU...
WHA--?
GULP!

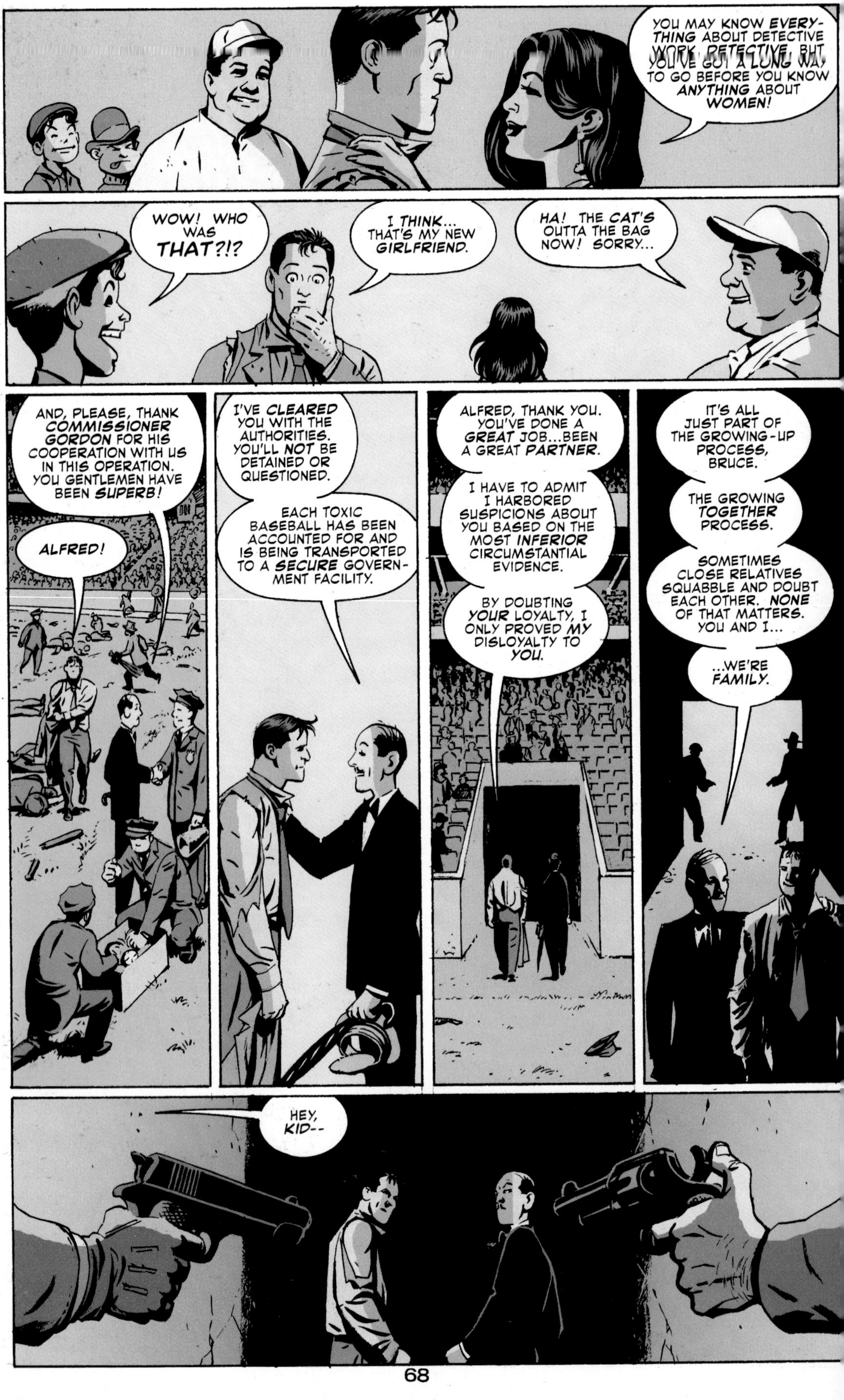

YOU MAY KNOW EVERYTHING ABOUT DETECTIVE WORK, DETECTIVE, BUT YOU'VE GOT A LONG WAY TO GO BEFORE YOU KNOW ANYTHING ABOUT WOMEN!
WOW! WHO WAS THAT?!?
I THINK... THAT'S MY NEW GIRLFRIEND.
HA! THE CAT'S OUTTA THE BAG NOW! SORRY...
AND, PLEASE, THANK COMMISSIONER GORDON FOR HIS COOPERATION WITH US IN THIS OPERATION. YOU GENTLEMEN HAVE BEEN SUPERB!
ALFRED!
I'VE CLEARED YOU WITH THE AUTHORITIES. YOU'LL NOT BE DETAINED OR QUESTIONED.
EACH TOXIC BASEBALL HAS BEEN ACCOUNTED FOR AND IS BEING TRANSPORTED TO A SECURE GOVERNMENT FACILITY.
ALFRED, THANK YOU. YOU'VE DONE A GREAT JOB...BEEN A GREAT PARTNER.
I HAVE TO ADMIT I HARBORED SUSPICIONS ABOUT YOU BASED ON THE MOST INFERIOR CIRCUMSTANTIAL EVIDENCE.
BY DOUBTING YOUR LOYALTY, I ONLY PROVED MY DISLOYALTY TO YOU.
IT'S ALL JUST PART OF THE GROWING-UP PROCESS, BRUCE.
THE GROWING TOGETHER PROCESS.
SOMETIMES CLOSE RELATIVES SQUABBLE AND DOUBT EACH OTHER. NONE OF THAT MATTERS. YOU AND I...
...WE'RE FAMILY.
HEY, KID--

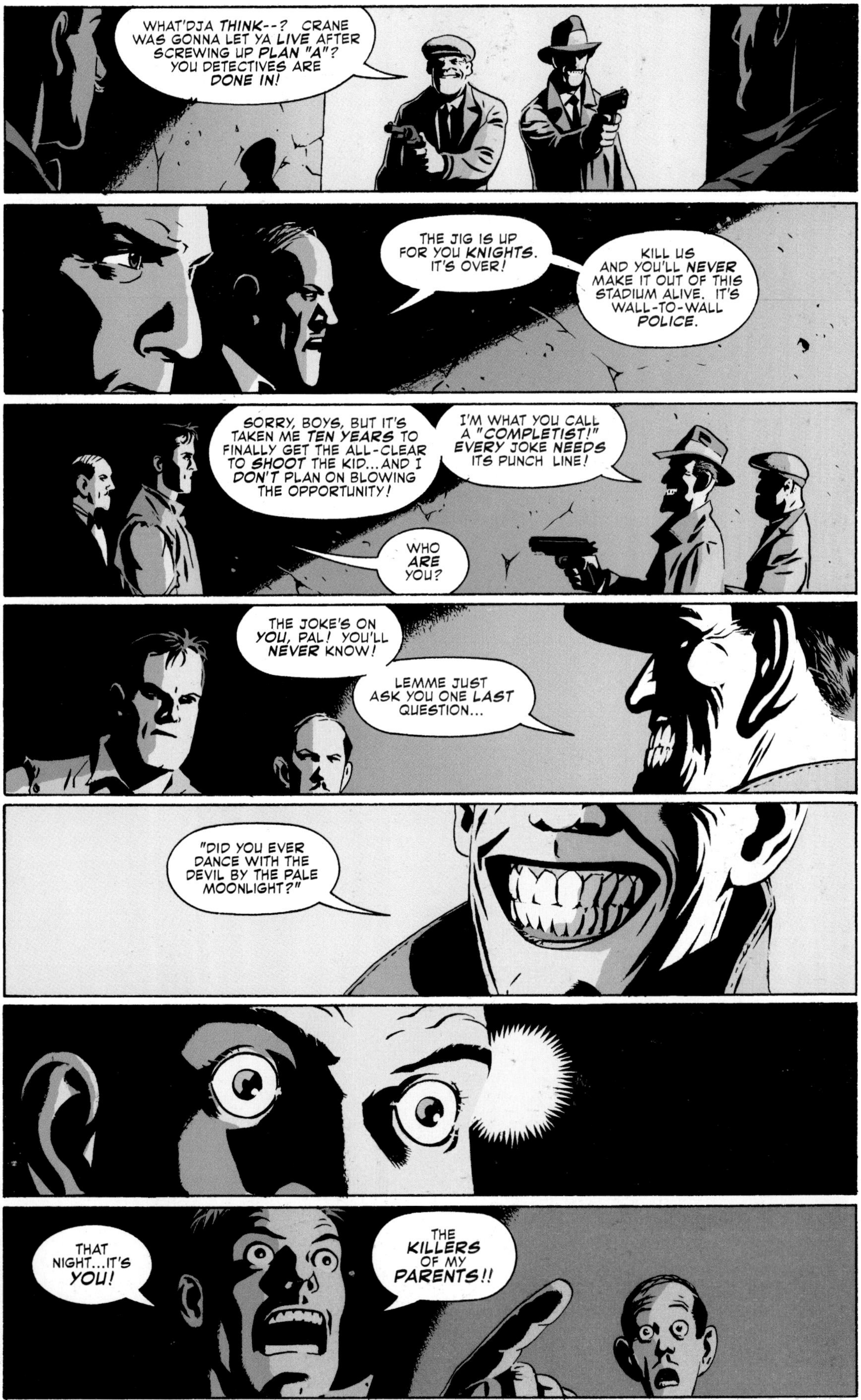
WHAT'DJA THINK--? CRANE WAS GONNA LET YA LIVE AFTER SCREWING UP PLAN "A"? YOU DETECTIVES ARE DONE IN!
THE JIG IS UP FOR YOU KNIGHTS. IT'S OVER!
KILL US AND YOU'LL NEVER MAKE IT OUT OF THIS STADIUM ALIVE. IT'S WALL-TO-WALL POLICE.
SORRY, BOYS, BUT IT'S TAKEN ME TEN YEARS TO FINALLY GET THE ALL-CLEAR TO SHOOT THE KID... AND I DON'T PLAN ON BLOWING THE OPPORTUNITY!
I'M WHAT YOU CALL A "COMPLETIST!" EVERY JOKE NEEDS ITS PUNCH LINE!
WHO ARE YOU?
THE JOKE'S ON YOU, PAL! YOU'LL NEVER KNOW!
LEMME JUST ASK YOU ONE LAST QUESTION...
"DID YOU EVER DANCE WITH THE DEVIL BY THE PALE MOONLIGHT?"
THAT NIGHT... IT'S YOU!
THE KILLERS OF MY PARENTS!!

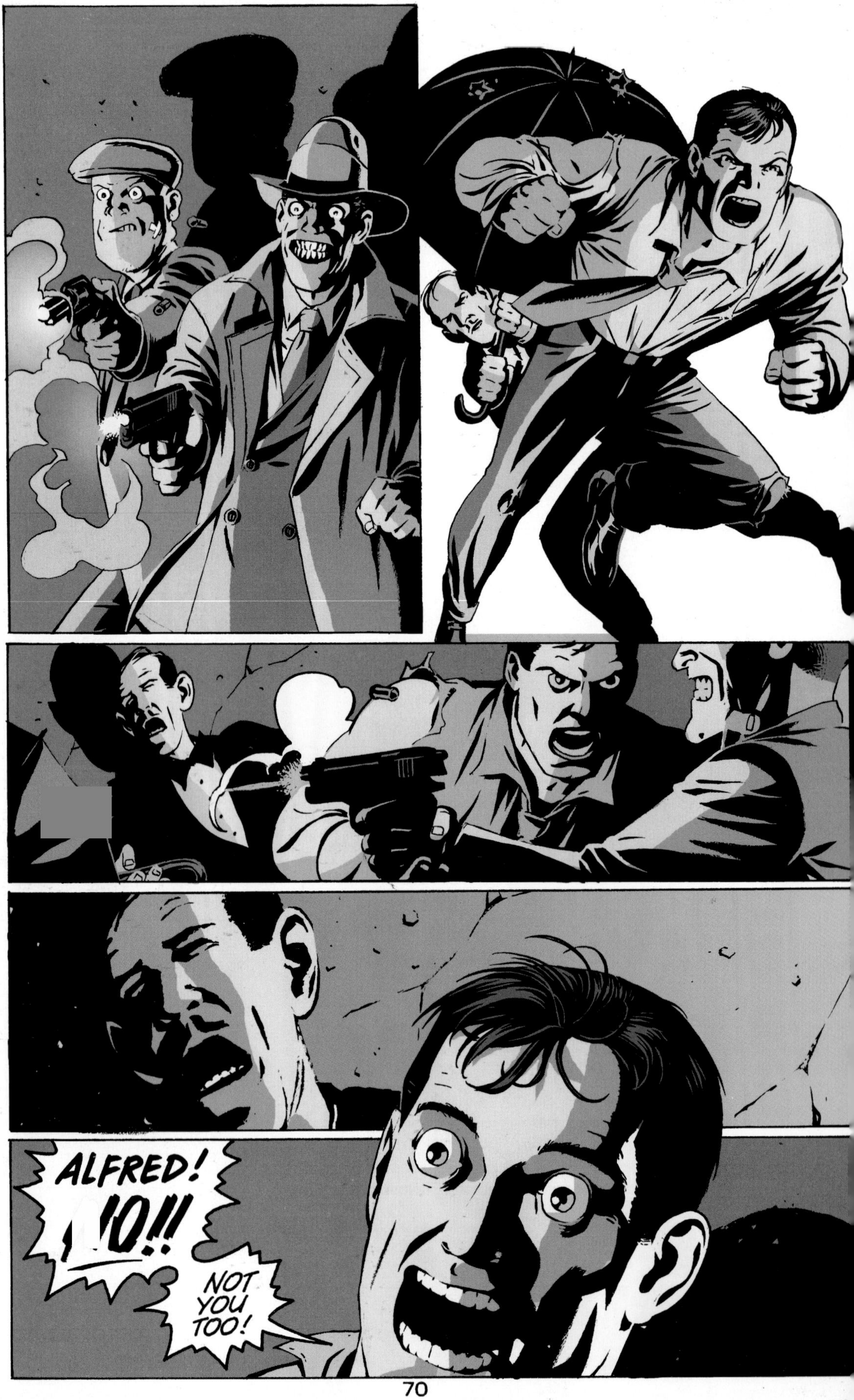
ALFRED!
NOT YOU TOO!

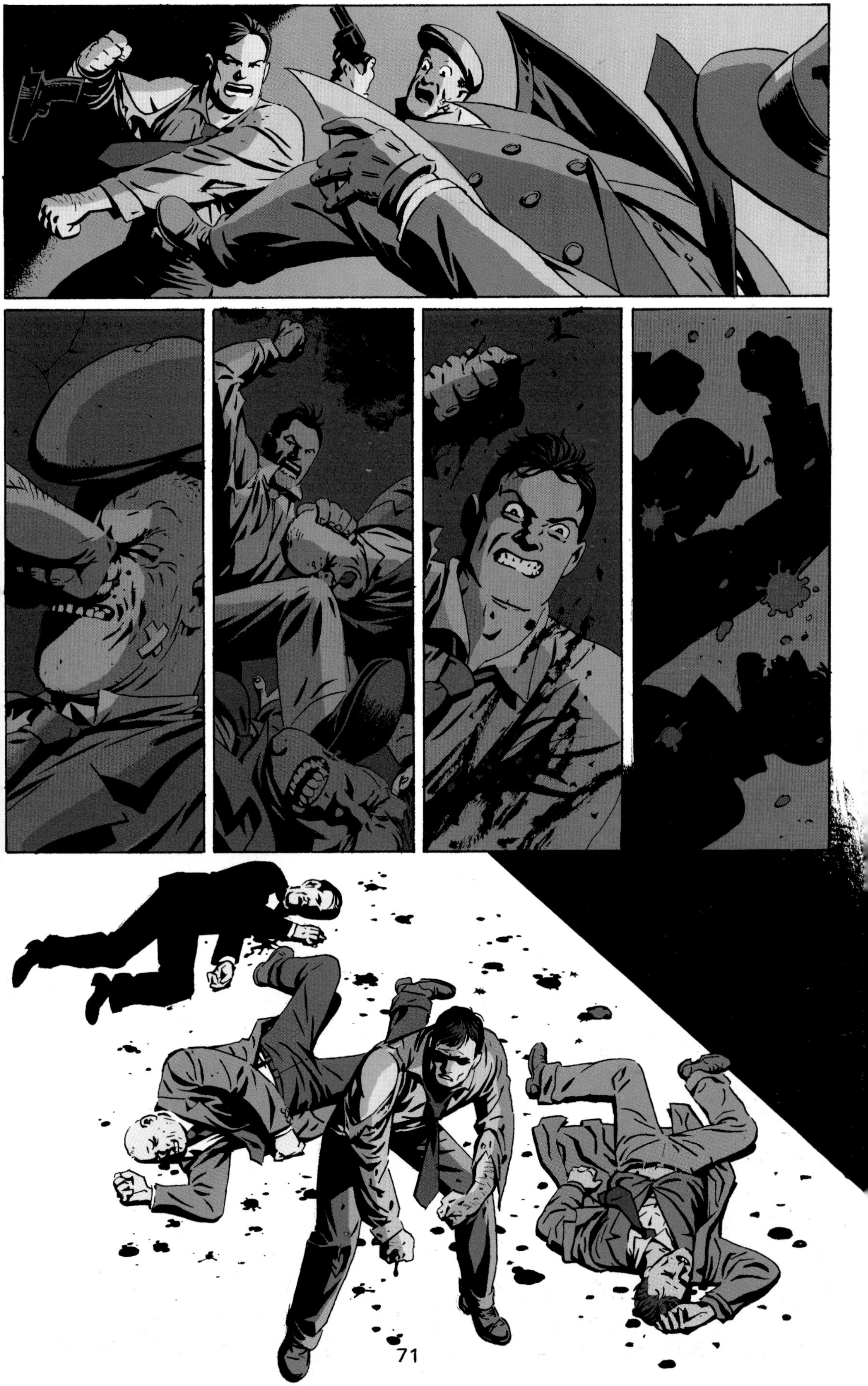

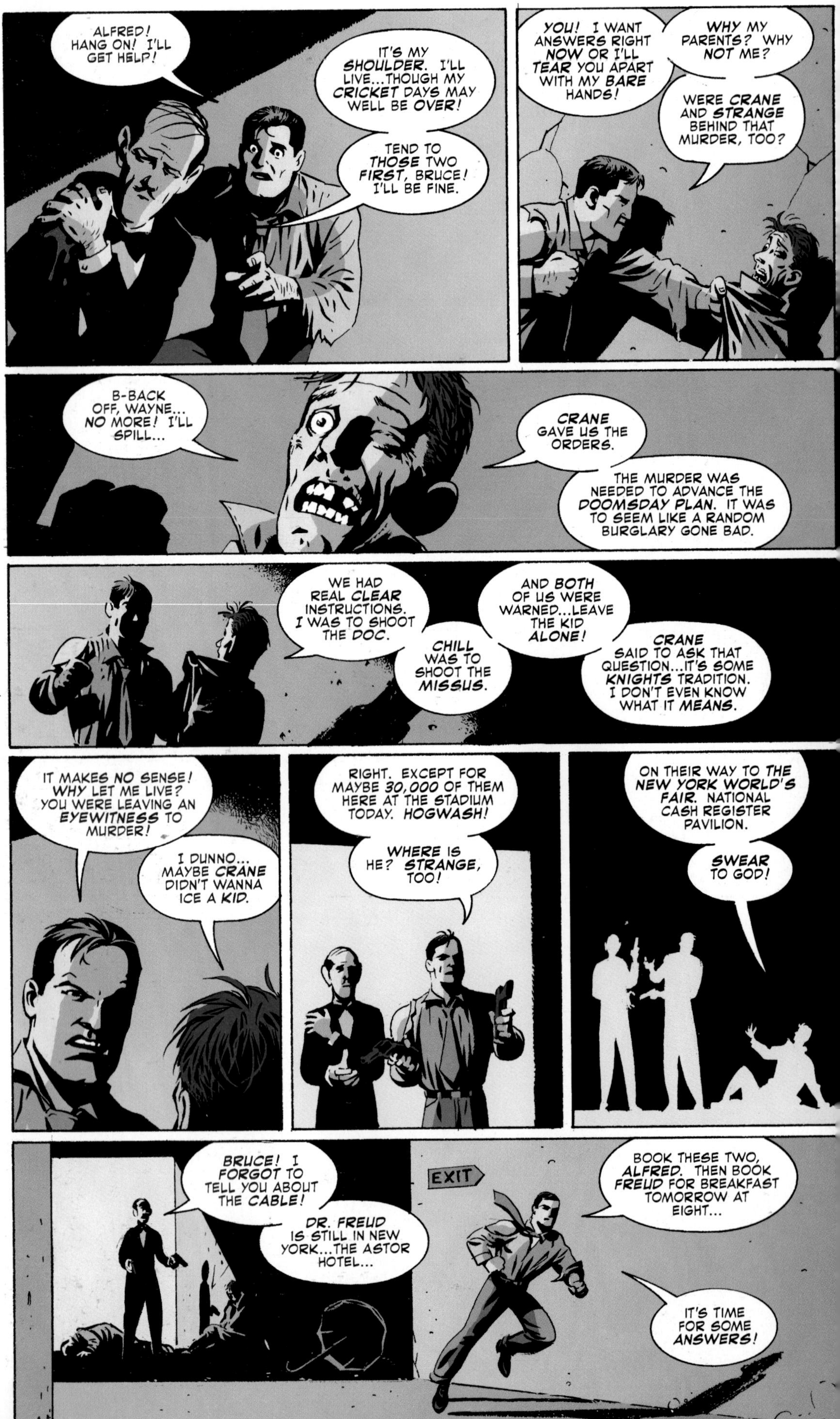
ALFRED! HANG ON! I'LL GET HELP!
IT'S MY SHOULDER. I'LL LIVE...THOUGH MY CRICKET DAYS MAY WELL BE OVER!
TEND TO THOSE TWO FIRST, BRUCE! I'LL BE FINE.
YOU! I WANT ANSWERS RIGHT NOW OR I'LL TEAR YOU APART WITH MY BARE HANDS!
WHY MY PARENTS? WHY NOT ME?
WERE CRANE AND STRANGE BEHIND THAT MURDER, TOO?
B-BACK OFF, WAYNE... NO MORE! I'LL SPILL...
CRANE GAVE US THE ORDERS.
THE MURDER WAS NEEDED TO ADVANCE THE DOOMSDAY PLAN. IT WAS TO SEEM LIKE A RANDOM BURGLARY GONE BAD.
WE HAD REAL CLEAR INSTRUCTIONS. I WAS TO SHOOT THE DOC.
CHILL WAS TO SHOOT THE MISSUS.
AND BOTH OF US WERE WARNED...LEAVE THE KID ALONE!
CRANE SAID TO ASK THAT QUESTION...IT'S SOME KNIGHTS TRADITION. I DON'T EVEN KNOW WHAT IT MEANS.
IT MAKES NO SENSE! WHY LET ME LIVE? YOU WERE LEAVING AN EYEWITNESS TO MURDER!
I DUNNO... MAYBE CRANE DIDN'T WANNA ICE A KID.
RIGHT. EXCEPT FOR MAYBE 30,000 OF THEM HERE AT THE STADIUM TODAY. HOGWASH!
WHERE IS HE? STRANGE, TOO!
ON THEIR WAY TO THE NEW YORK WORLD'S FAIR. NATIONAL CASH REGISTER PAVILION.
SWEAR TO GOD!
BRUCE! I FORGOT TO TELL YOU ABOUT THE CABLE!
DR. FREUD IS STILL IN NEW YORK...THE ASTOR HOTEL...
EXIT
BOOK THESE TWO, ALFRED. THEN BOOK FREUD FOR BREAKFAST TOMORROW AT EIGHT...
IT'S TIME FOR SOME ANSWERS!

A NEW DAWN AND A NEW HOPE...
YOUR DEDUCTIONS BASED UPON THE FACTS AS WELL AS MY THEORY OF JOKES AND THE UNCONSCIOUS ARE QUITE SOUND, DETECTIVE.
MEANING WHAT, DR. FREUD?
ASTOR
IF WHAT YOU SAY IS TRUE, I CAN CONCLUDE JOSIAH CARR WAS OBSESSED WITH HIS PREDILECTION FOR JOKES AND THE SHEER IRONY OF TYING EVENTS OF DEATH AND SADNESS TO HIS TWISTED PUNCH LINES.
AND NOW, JONATHAN CRANE AND HUGO STRANGE ARE TWO COPYCATS, EQUALLY WARPED, WITH SOME COMPELLING NEED TO EMULATE CARR'S MINDSET IN ORDER TO EXECUTE HIS PLAN OF ATTACK?
YES, EXCEPT... CARR'S "JOKE" WAS TO BE ON THE NORTH...
...HOWEVER, IT'S OBVIOUS TO ME THAT CRANE AND STRANGE HAVE MADE IT PERSONAL. THEIR FINAL JOKE MAY YET BE ON YOU, DETECTIVE. BE ALERT.
I CAN HANDLE THE JOKES, DOCTOR, JUST NOT THE DATURA AND THE FEAR IT SPARKS.
"FEAR" IS A RESPONSE, SIR...WHETHER REAL OR FALSELY PERCEIVED.
A STRONG MIND, SHARPLY FOCUSED ON THE REALITY OF THE SITUATION, WILL CONQUER ANY IRRATIONAL FEAR, DESPITE THE EFFECTS OF A DRUG OR TOXIN IMPACTING THE NERVOUS SYSTEM.
THANKS FOR YOUR HELP. YOU KNEW YOU MIGHT BE PLACING YOUR LIFE IN JEOPARDY BY MEETING WITH ME--
...AND I PLAN TO REMAIN ALIVE LONG ENOUGH TO ANALYZE THE TRAUMA YOU SUFFERED BY WITNESSING YOUR PARENTS' MURDER AS A CHILD. FASCINATING!
I'M CONFOUNDED IT HASN'T RESULTED IN SERIOUS SCHIZOPHRENIC TENDENCIES!
YOU MOST CERTAINLY PUZZLE ME, DETECTIVE. INDEED...

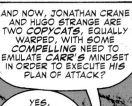

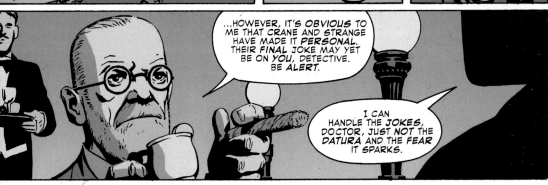

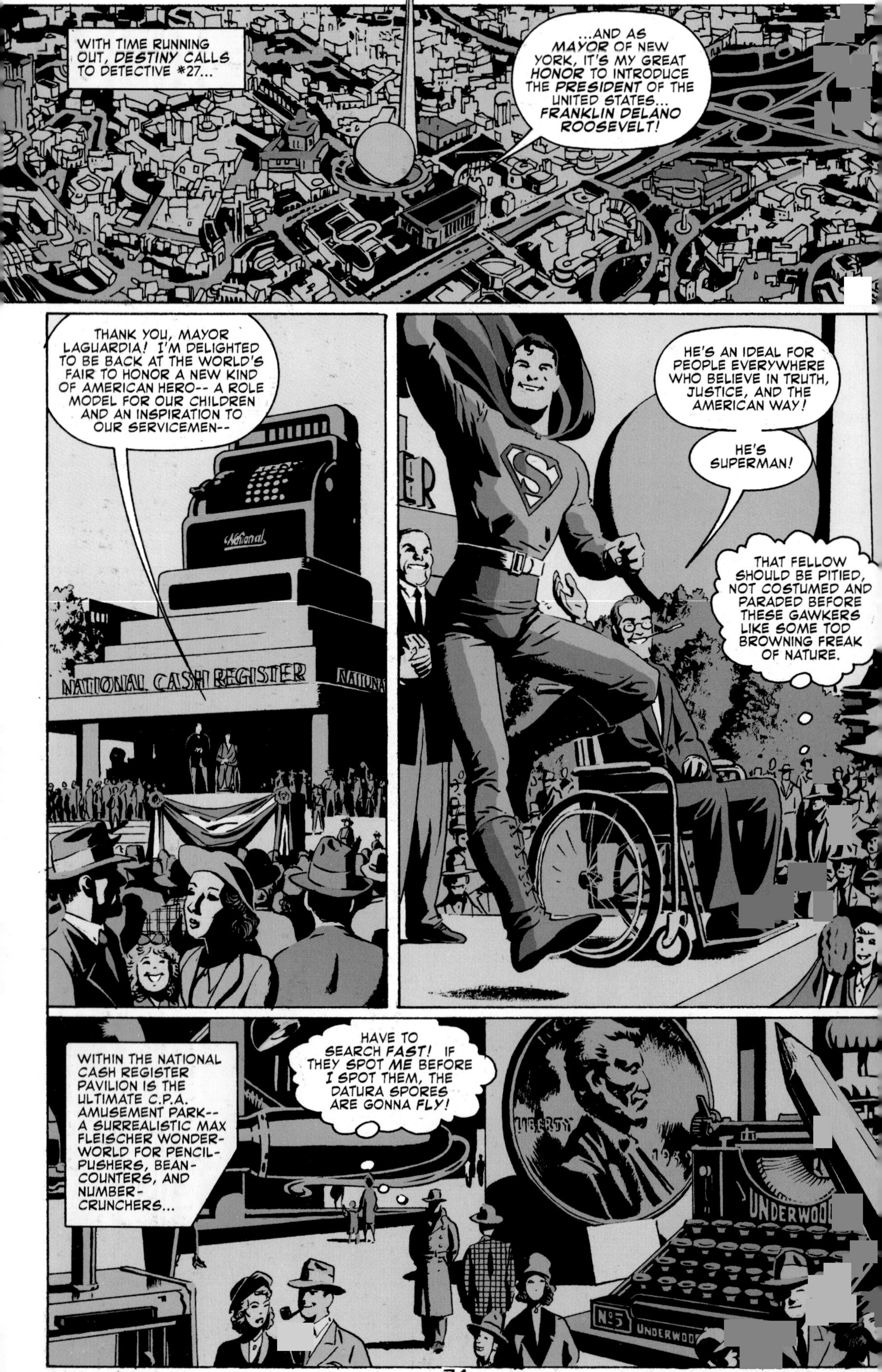
WITH TIME RUNNING OUT, DESTINY CALLS TO DETECTIVE #27...
...AND AS MAYOR OF NEW YORK, IT'S MY GREAT HONOR TO INTRODUCE THE PRESIDENT OF THE UNITED STATES... FRANKLIN DELANO ROOSEVELT!
THANK YOU, MAYOR LAGUARDIA! I'M DELIGHTED TO BE BACK AT THE WORLD'S FAIR TO HONOR A NEW KIND OF AMERICAN HERO-- A ROLE MODEL FOR OUR CHILDREN AND AN INSPIRATION TO OUR SERVICEMEN--
National
NATIONAL CASH REGISTER
HE'S AN IDEAL FOR PEOPLE EVERYWHERE WHO BELIEVE IN TRUTH, JUSTICE, AND THE AMERICAN WAY!
HE'S SUPERMAN!
THAT FELLOW SHOULD BE PITIED, NOT COSTUMED AND PARADED BEFORE THESE GAWKERS LIKE SOME TOD BROWNING FREAK OF NATURE.
WITHIN THE NATIONAL CASH REGISTER PAVILION IS THE ULTIMATE C.P.A. AMUSEMENT PARK-- A SURREALISTIC MAX FLEISCHER WONDER-WORLD FOR PENCIL-PUSHERS, BEAN-COUNTERS, AND NUMBER-CRUNCHERS...
HAVE TO SEARCH FAST! IF THEY SPOT ME BEFORE I SPOT THEM, THE DATURA SPORES ARE GONNA FLY!
LIBERTY
No 5

A VAULT! THE MOST OBVIOUS PLACE TO STORE 75 GENERATIONS OF CROSSBRED TOXINS!

Franz Jäger Berlin

IF I CAN JUST—

OH NO!

NO!!!

YOU'RE LIKE AN ATTACK DOG, REFUSING TO UNCLENCH HIS TEETH FROM HIS QUARRY'S LEG, DETECTIVE 27!

HOW NICE FOR US THAT AIRBORNE SPORES ARE HEAVY ENOUGH TO DRIFT DOWNWARD.

BUT HOW EQUALLY SAD FOR YOU!

MUST DO WHAT FREUD SAID... FIGHT FROM WITHIN... CONFRONT THE FEAR... OPPRESS IT...DON'T REPRESS IT!

IF I WANT TO LEARN THE TRUTH BEHIND MY PARENTS' MURDER, I HAVE TO! AND RIGHT NOW!

TAKING THE HIGH GROUND SHOULD HELP ME BEAT THIS FEAR!

BINGO! HERE IT IS! THE KNIGHTS' STORAGE FACILITY FOR EVERY GENERATION OF TOXIN!

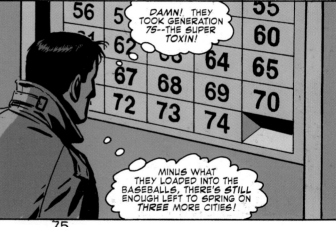

DAMN! THEY TOOK GENERATION 75—THE SUPER TOXIN!

MINUS WHAT THEY LOADED INTO THE BASEBALLS, THERE'S STILL ENOUGH LEFT TO SPRING ON THREE MORE CITIES!

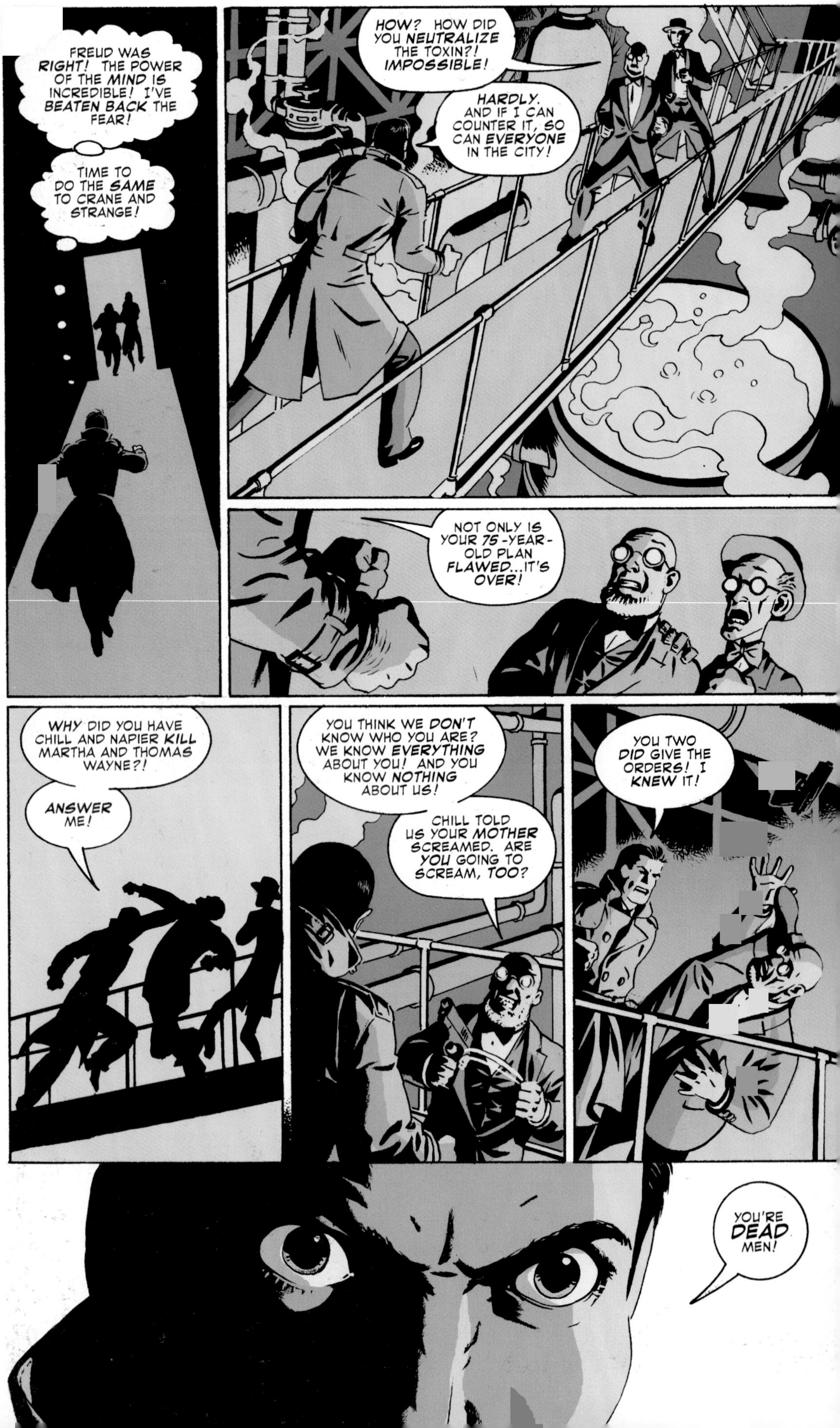
FREUD WAS RIGHT! THE POWER OF THE MIND IS INCREDIBLE! I'VE BEATEN BACK THE FEAR!
TIME TO DO THE SAME TO CRANE AND STRANGE!
HOW? HOW DID YOU NEUTRALIZE THE TOXIN?! IMPOSSIBLE!
HARDLY. AND IF I CAN COUNTER IT, SO CAN EVERYONE IN THE CITY!
NOT ONLY IS YOUR 75-YEAR-OLD PLAN FLAWED...IT'S OVER!
WHY DID YOU HAVE CHILL AND NAPIER KILL MARTHA AND THOMAS WAYNE?!
ANSWER ME!
YOU THINK WE DON'T KNOW WHO YOU ARE? WE KNOW EVERYTHING ABOUT YOU! AND YOU KNOW NOTHING ABOUT US!
CHILL TOLD US YOUR MOTHER SCREAMED. ARE YOU GOING TO SCREAM, TOO?
YOU TWO DID GIVE THE ORDERS! I KNEW IT!
YOU'RE DEAD MEN!

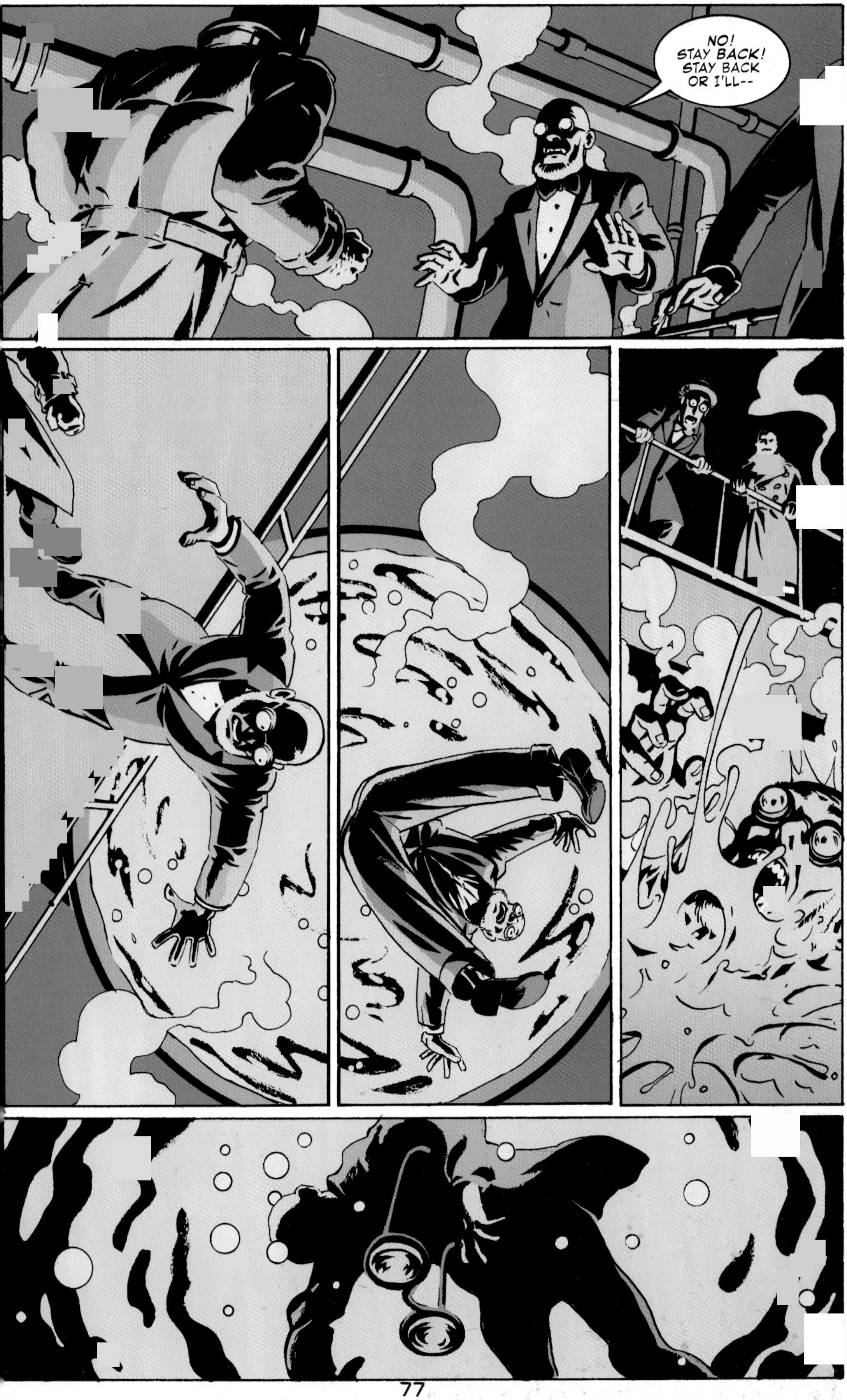
NO! STAY BACK! STAY BACK OR I'LL--

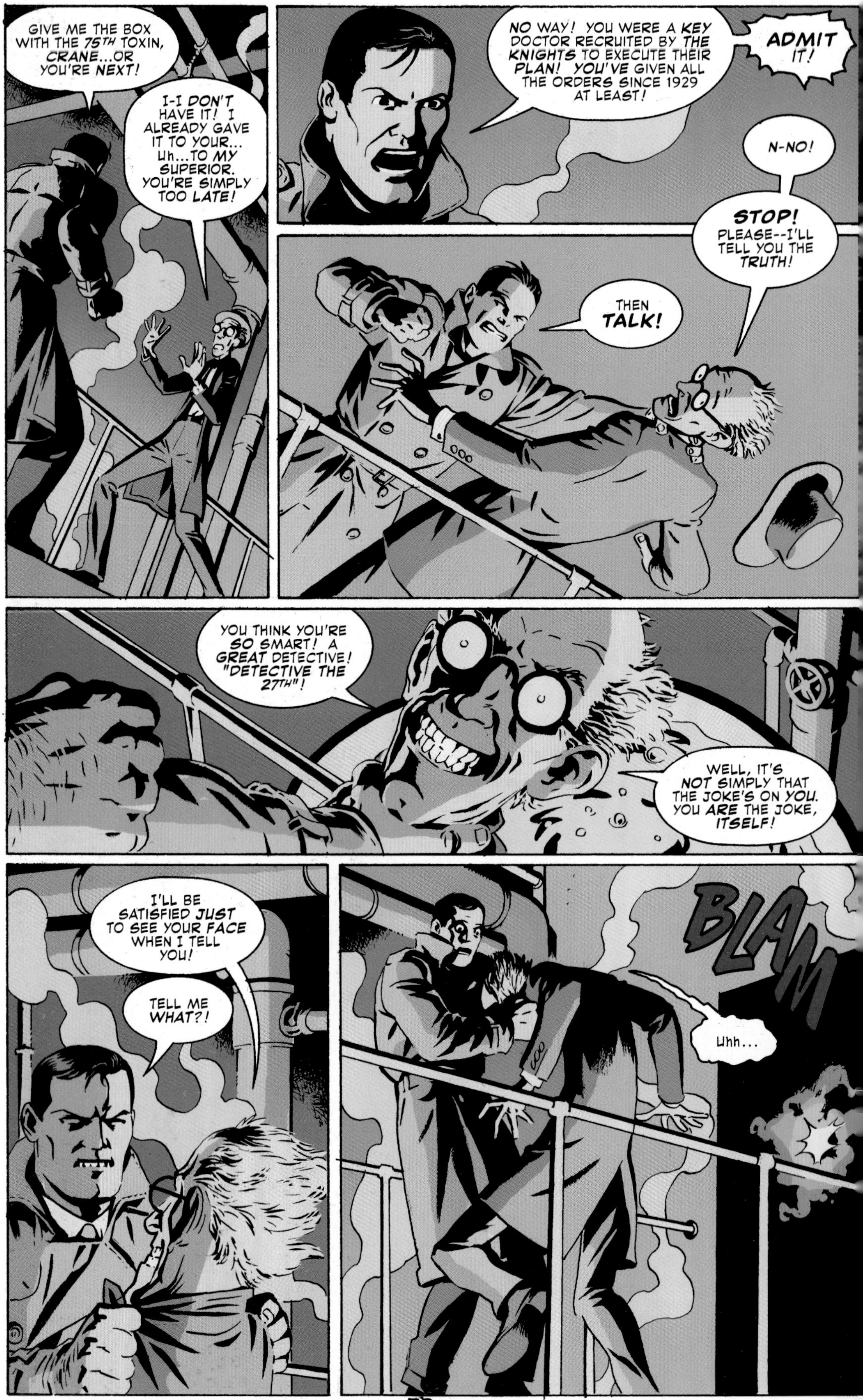
GIVE ME THE BOX WITH THE 75TH TOXIN, CRANE...OR YOU'RE NEXT!
I-I DON'T HAVE IT! I ALREADY GAVE IT TO YOUR... Uh...TO MY SUPERIOR. YOU'RE SIMPLY TOO LATE!
NO WAY! YOU WERE A KEY DOCTOR RECRUITED BY THE KNIGHTS TO EXECUTE THEIR PLAN! YOU'VE GIVEN ALL THE ORDERS SINCE 1929 AT LEAST!
ADMIT IT!
N-NO!
STOP! PLEASE--I'LL TELL YOU THE TRUTH!
THEN TALK!
YOU THINK YOU'RE SO SMART! A GREAT DETECTIVE! "DETECTIVE THE 27TH"!
WELL, IT'S NOT SIMPLY THAT THE JOKE'S ON YOU. YOU ARE THE JOKE, ITSELF!
I'LL BE SATISFIED JUST TO SEE YOUR FACE WHEN I TELL YOU!
TELL ME WHAT?!
BLAM
Uhh...

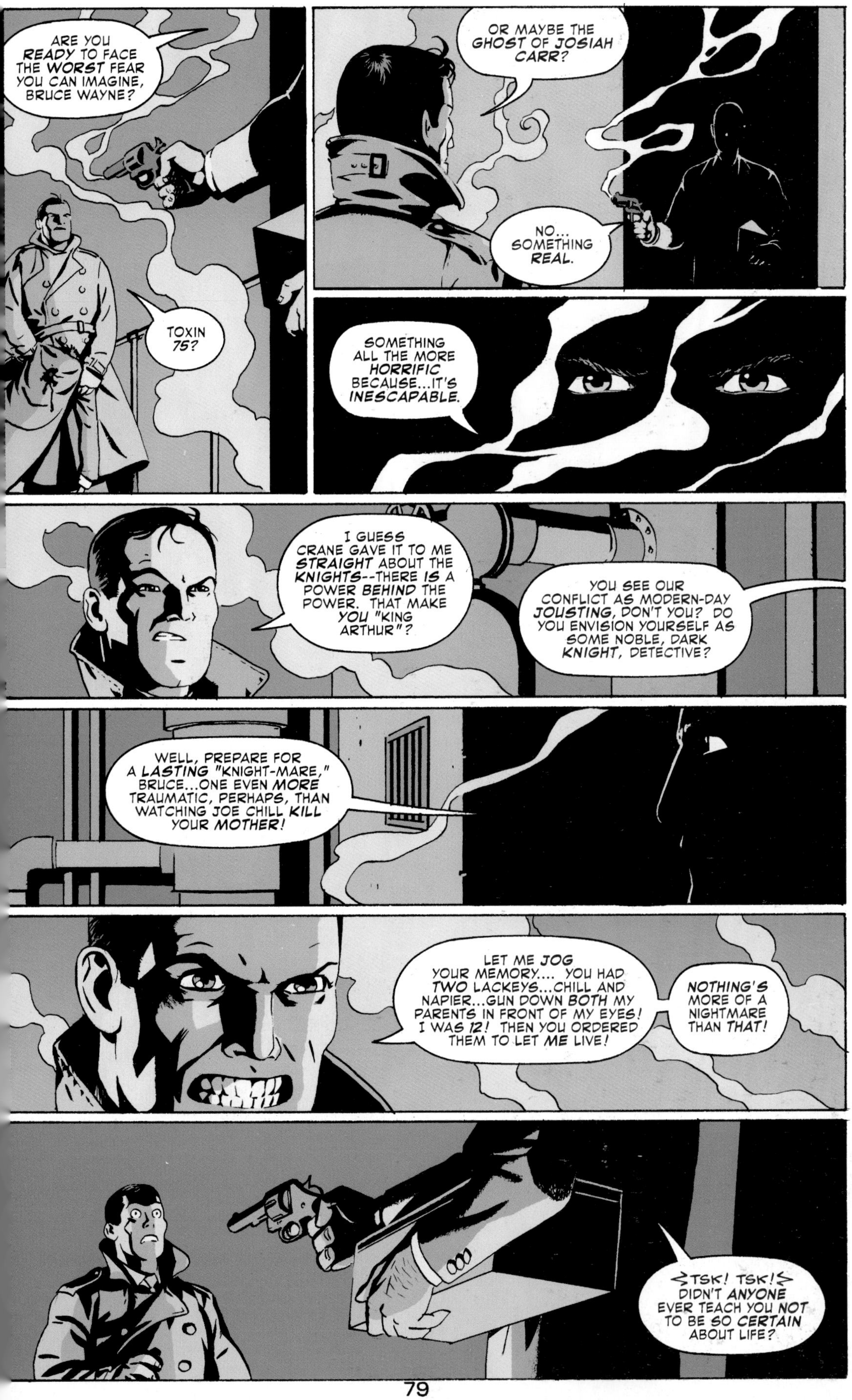

ARE YOU READY TO FACE THE WORST FEAR YOU CAN IMAGINE, BRUCE WAYNE?
TOXIN 75?
OR MAYBE THE GHOST OF JOSIAH CARR?
NO... SOMETHING REAL.
SOMETHING ALL THE MORE HORRIFIC BECAUSE...IT'S INESCAPABLE.
I GUESS CRANE GAVE IT TO ME STRAIGHT ABOUT THE KNIGHTS--THERE IS A POWER BEHIND THE POWER. THAT MAKE YOU "KING ARTHUR"?
YOU SEE OUR CONFLICT AS MODERN-DAY JOUSTING, DON'T YOU? DO YOU ENVISION YOURSELF AS SOME NOBLE, DARK KNIGHT, DETECTIVE?
WELL, PREPARE FOR A LASTING "KNIGHT-MARE," BRUCE...ONE EVEN MORE TRAUMATIC, PERHAPS, THAN WATCHING JOE CHILL KILL YOUR MOTHER!
LET ME JOG YOUR MEMORY.... YOU HAD TWO LACKEYS...CHILL AND NAPIER...GUN DOWN BOTH MY PARENTS IN FRONT OF MY EYES! I WAS 12! THEN YOU ORDERED THEM TO LET ME LIVE!
NOTHING'S MORE OF A NIGHTMARE THAN THAT!
<TSK! TSK!> DIDN'T ANYONE EVER TEACH YOU NOT TO BE SO CERTAIN ABOUT LIFE?

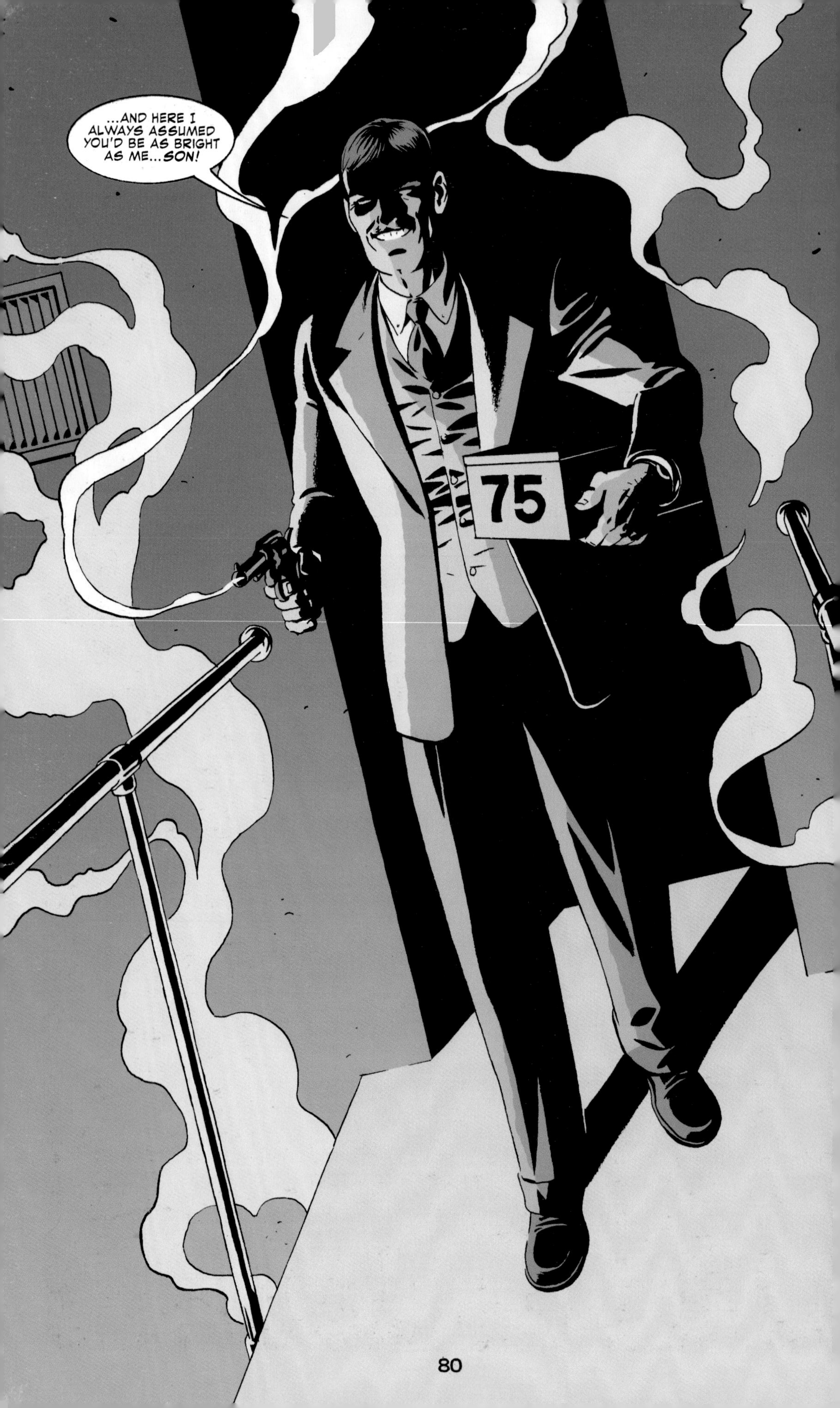
...AND HERE I ALWAYS ASSUMED YOU'D BE AS BRIGHT AS ME...*SON!*
75

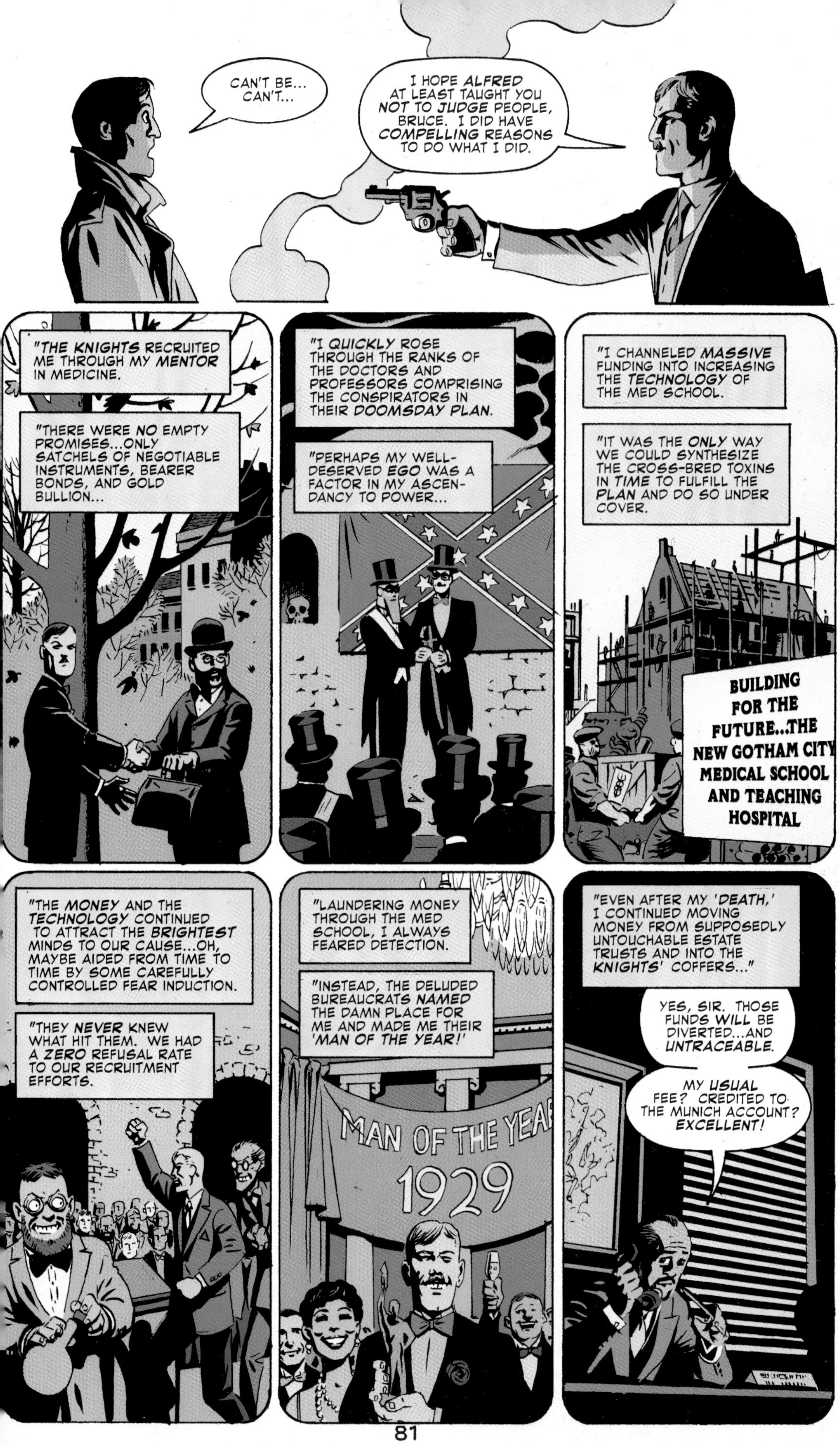
CAN'T BE... CAN'T...
I HOPE ALFRED AT LEAST TAUGHT YOU NOT TO JUDGE PEOPLE, BRUCE. I DID HAVE COMPELLING REASONS TO DO WHAT I DID.
"THE KNIGHTS RECRUITED ME THROUGH MY MENTOR IN MEDICINE.
"THERE WERE NO EMPTY PROMISES...ONLY SATCHELS OF NEGOTIABLE INSTRUMENTS, BEARER BONDS, AND GOLD BULLION...
"I QUICKLY ROSE THROUGH THE RANKS OF THE DOCTORS AND PROFESSORS COMPRISING THE CONSPIRATORS IN THEIR DOOMSDAY PLAN.
"PERHAPS MY WELL-DESERVED EGO WAS A FACTOR IN MY ASCENDANCY TO POWER...
"I CHANNELED MASSIVE FUNDING INTO INCREASING THE TECHNOLOGY OF THE MED SCHOOL.
"IT WAS THE ONLY WAY WE COULD SYNTHESIZE THE CROSS-BRED TOXINS IN TIME TO FULFILL THE PLAN AND DO SO UNDER COVER.
BUILDING FOR THE FUTURE...THE NEW GOTHAM CITY MEDICAL SCHOOL AND TEACHING HOSPITAL
"THE MONEY AND THE TECHNOLOGY CONTINUED TO ATTRACT THE BRIGHTEST MINDS TO OUR CAUSE...OH, MAYBE AIDED FROM TIME TO TIME BY SOME CAREFULLY CONTROLLED FEAR INDUCTION.
"THEY NEVER KNEW WHAT HIT THEM. WE HAD A ZERO REFUSAL RATE TO OUR RECRUITMENT EFFORTS.
"LAUNDERING MONEY THROUGH THE MED SCHOOL, I ALWAYS FEARED DETECTION.
"INSTEAD, THE DELUDED BUREAUCRATS NAMED THE DAMN PLACE FOR ME AND MADE ME THEIR 'MAN OF THE YEAR!'
MAN OF THE YEA
1929
"EVEN AFTER MY 'DEATH,' I CONTINUED MOVING MONEY FROM SUPPOSEDLY UNTOUCHABLE ESTATE TRUSTS AND INTO THE KNIGHTS' COFFERS..."
YES, SIR. THOSE FUNDS WILL BE DIVERTED...AND UNTRACEABLE.
MY USUAL FEE? CREDITED TO THE MUNICH ACCOUNT? EXCELLENT!

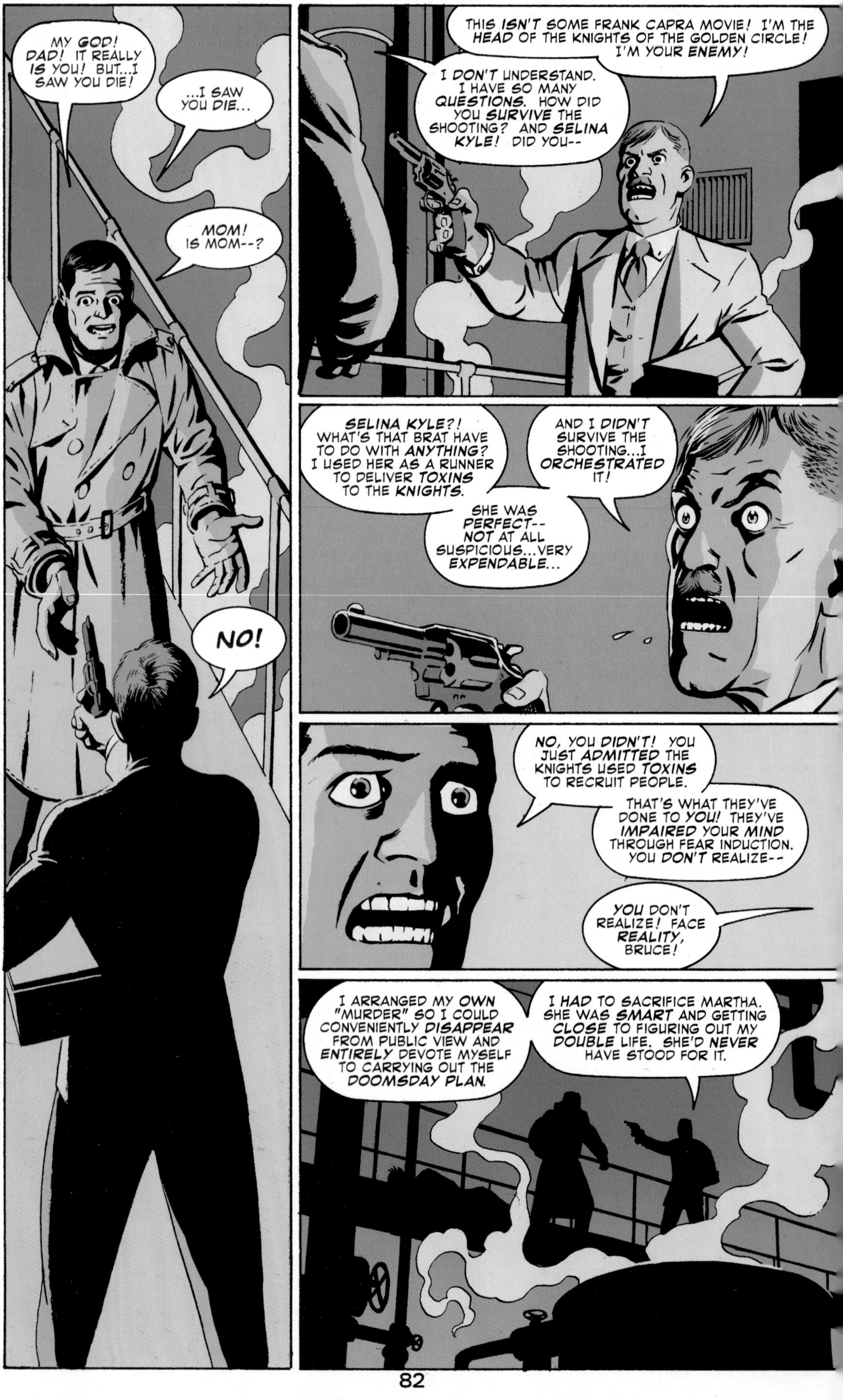
MY GOD! DAD! IT REALLY IS YOU! BUT...I SAW YOU DIE!
...I SAW YOU DIE...
MOM! IS MOM--?
NO!
THIS ISN'T SOME FRANK CAPRA MOVIE! I'M THE HEAD OF THE KNIGHTS OF THE GOLDEN CIRCLE! I'M YOUR ENEMY!
I DON'T UNDERSTAND. I HAVE SO MANY QUESTIONS. HOW DID YOU SURVIVE THE SHOOTING? AND SELINA KYLE! DID YOU--
SELINA KYLE?! WHAT'S THAT BRAT HAVE TO DO WITH ANYTHING? I USED HER AS A RUNNER TO DELIVER TOXINS TO THE KNIGHTS.
SHE WAS PERFECT--NOT AT ALL SUSPICIOUS...VERY EXPENDABLE...
AND I DIDN'T SURVIVE THE SHOOTING...I ORCHESTRATED IT!
NO, YOU DIDN'T! YOU JUST ADMITTED THE KNIGHTS USED TOXINS TO RECRUIT PEOPLE.
THAT'S WHAT THEY'VE DONE TO YOU! THEY'VE IMPAIRED YOUR MIND THROUGH FEAR INDUCTION. YOU DON'T REALIZE--
YOU DON'T REALIZE! FACE REALITY, BRUCE!
I ARRANGED MY OWN "MURDER" SO I COULD CONVENIENTLY DISAPPEAR FROM PUBLIC VIEW AND ENTIRELY DEVOTE MYSELF TO CARRYING OUT THE DOOMSDAY PLAN.
I HAD TO SACRIFICE MARTHA. SHE WAS SMART AND GETTING CLOSE TO FIGURING OUT MY DOUBLE LIFE. SHE'D NEVER HAVE STOOD FOR IT.

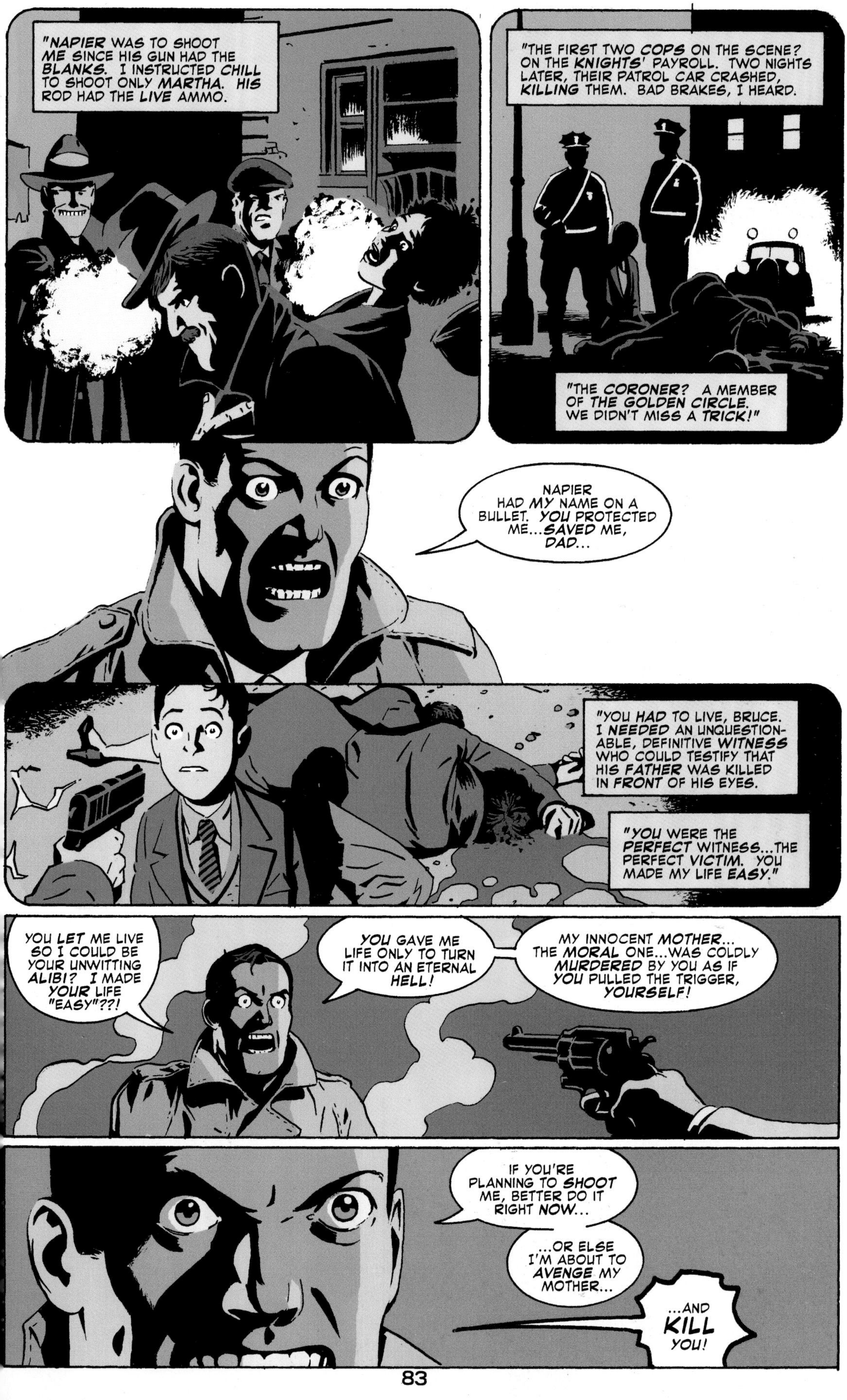
"NAPIER WAS TO SHOOT ME SINCE HIS GUN HAD THE BLANKS. I INSTRUCTED CHILL TO SHOOT ONLY MARTHA. HIS ROD HAD THE LIVE AMMO.
"THE FIRST TWO COPS ON THE SCENE? ON THE KNIGHTS' PAYROLL. TWO NIGHTS LATER, THEIR PATROL CAR CRASHED, KILLING THEM. BAD BRAKES, I HEARD.
"THE CORONER? A MEMBER OF THE GOLDEN CIRCLE. WE DIDN'T MISS A TRICK!"
NAPIER HAD MY NAME ON A BULLET. YOU PROTECTED ME...SAVED ME, DAD...
"YOU HAD TO LIVE, BRUCE. I NEEDED AN UNQUESTION-ABLE, DEFINITIVE WITNESS WHO COULD TESTIFY THAT HIS FATHER WAS KILLED IN FRONT OF HIS EYES.
"YOU WERE THE PERFECT WITNESS...THE PERFECT VICTIM. YOU MADE MY LIFE EASY."
YOU LET ME LIVE SO I COULD BE YOUR UNWITTING ALIBI? I MADE YOUR LIFE "EASY"??!
YOU GAVE ME LIFE ONLY TO TURN IT INTO AN ETERNAL HELL!
MY INNOCENT MOTHER... THE MORAL ONE...WAS COLDLY MURDERED BY YOU AS IF YOU PULLED THE TRIGGER, YOURSELF!
IF YOU'RE PLANNING TO SHOOT ME, BETTER DO IT RIGHT NOW...
...OR ELSE I'M ABOUT TO AVENGE MY MOTHER...
...AND KILL YOU!

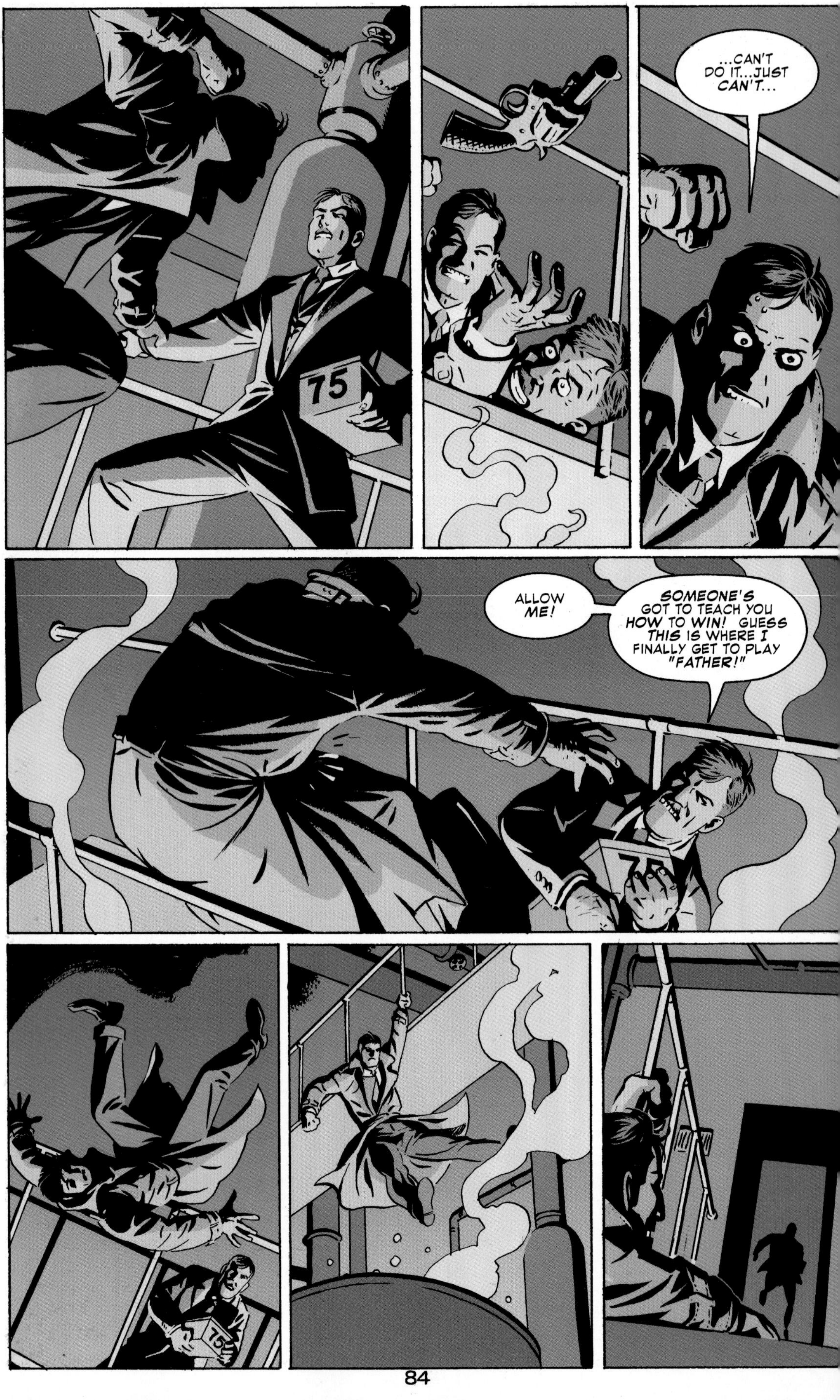

...CAN'T DO IT...JUST *CAN'T*...
ALLOW *ME!*
SOMEONE'S GOT TO TEACH YOU ***HOW*** TO ***WIN!*** GUESS ***THIS*** IS WHERE I FINALLY GET TO PLAY ***"FATHER!"***

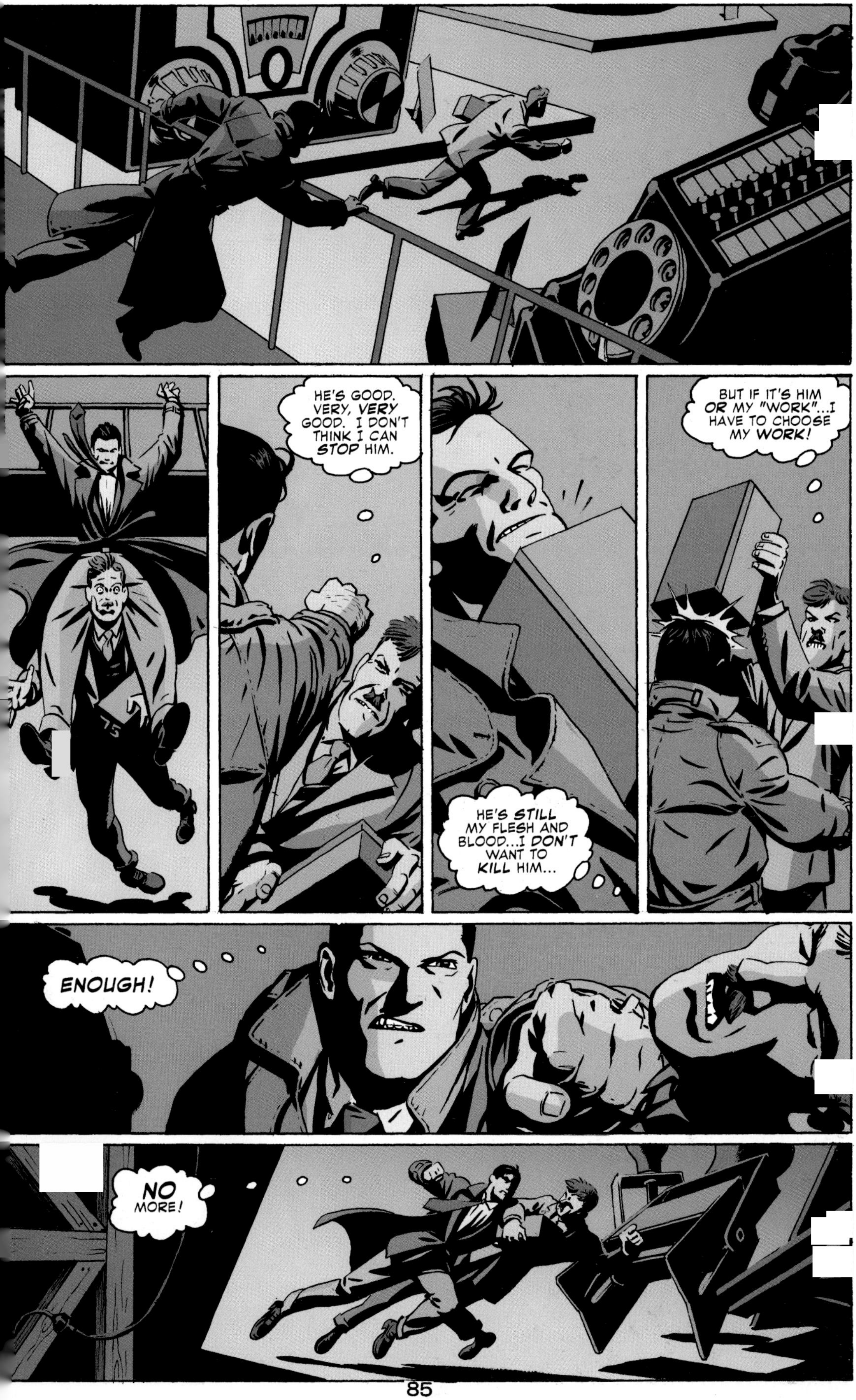
HE'S GOOD. VERY, VERY GOOD. I DON'T THINK I CAN STOP HIM.
HE'S STILL MY FLESH AND BLOOD...I DON'T WANT TO KILL HIM...
BUT IF IT'S HIM OR MY "WORK"...I HAVE TO CHOOSE MY WORK!
ENOUGH!
NO MORE!

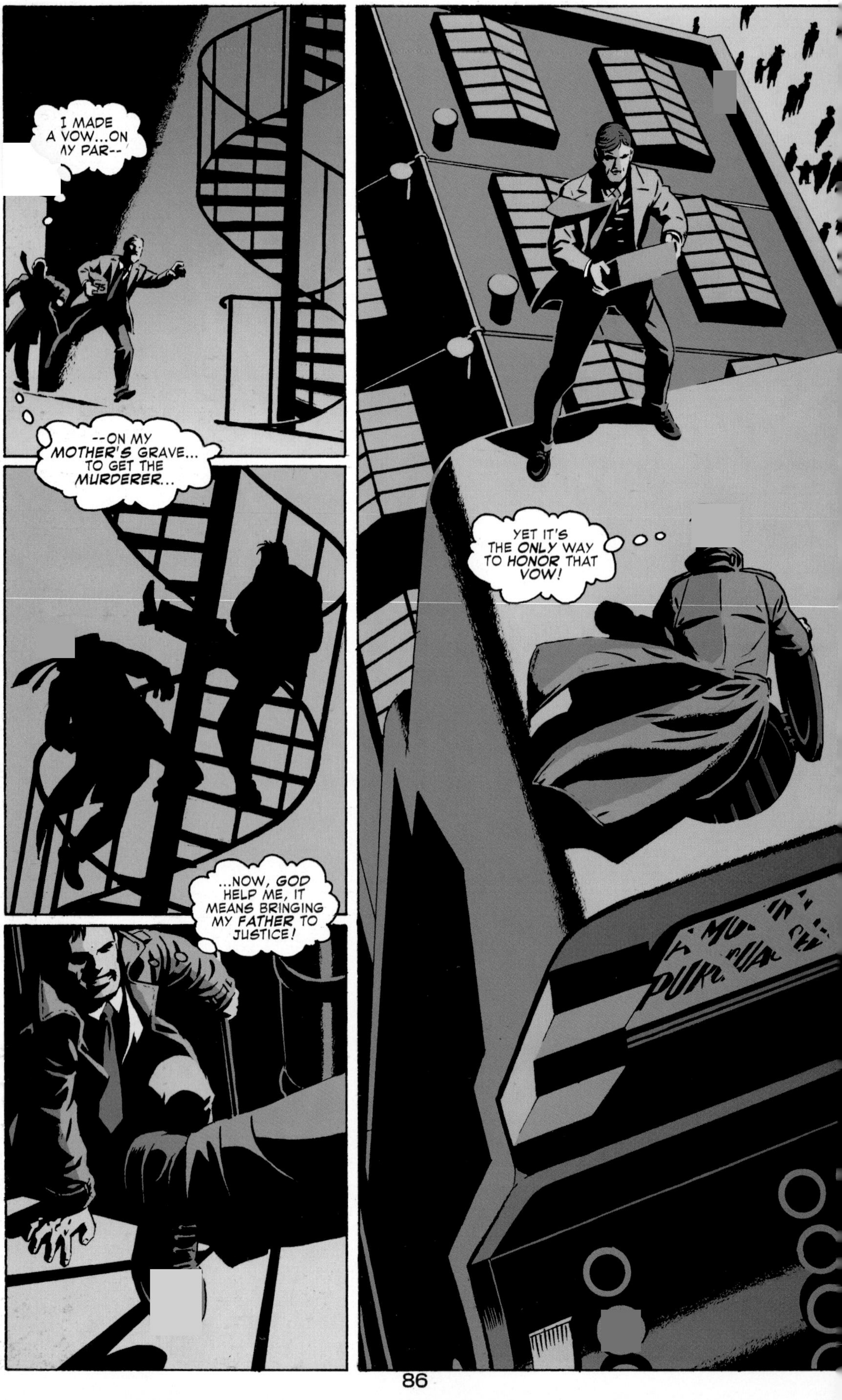

I MADE A VOW...ON MY PAR--
--ON MY MOTHER'S GRAVE... TO GET THE MURDERER...
...NOW, GOD HELP ME, IT MEANS BRINGING MY FATHER TO JUSTICE!
YET IT'S THE ONLY WAY TO HONOR THAT VOW!

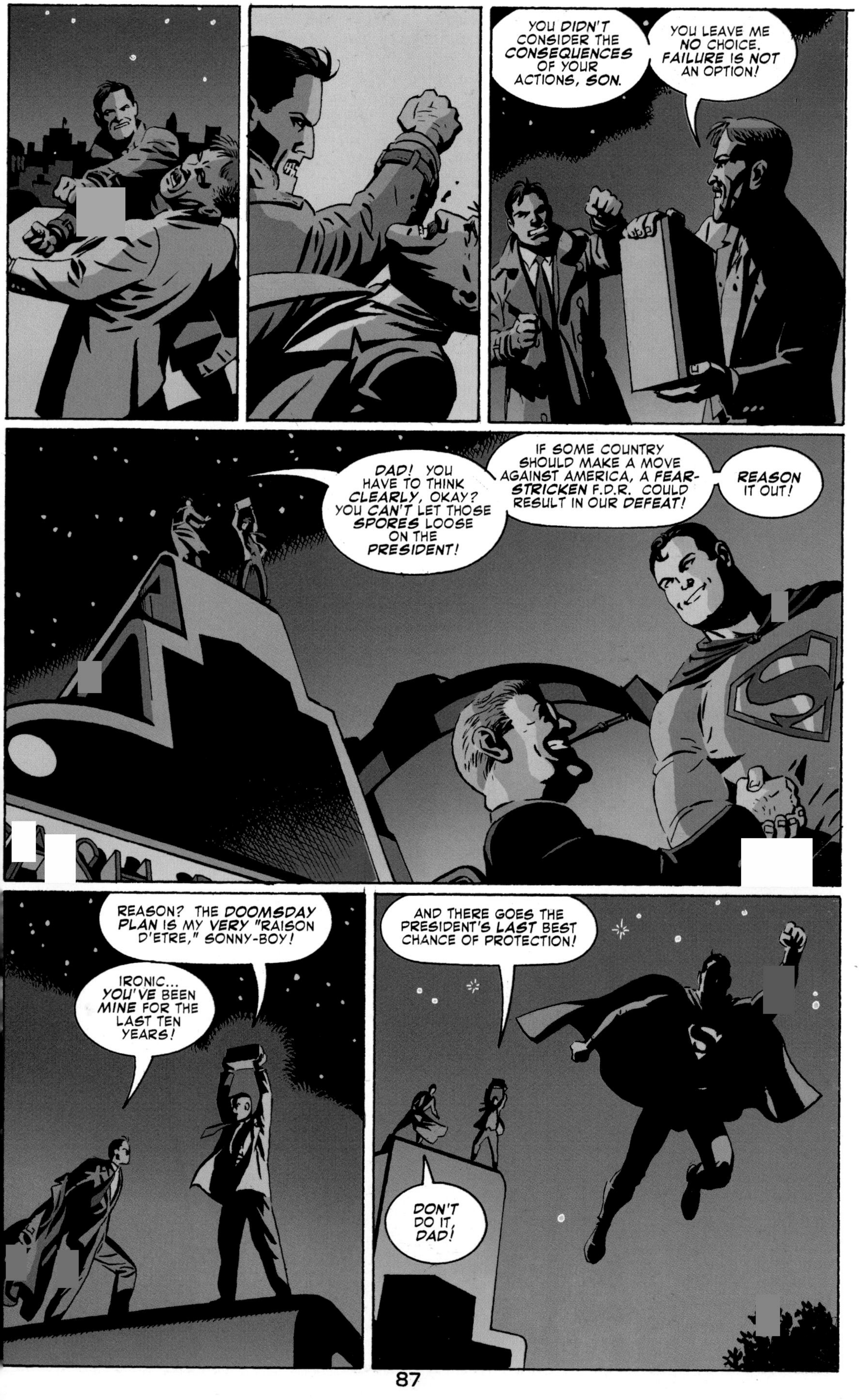
YOU DIDN'T CONSIDER THE CONSEQUENCES OF YOUR ACTIONS, SON.
YOU LEAVE ME NO CHOICE. FAILURE IS NOT AN OPTION!
DAD! YOU HAVE TO THINK CLEARLY, OKAY? YOU CAN'T LET THOSE SPORES LOOSE ON THE PRESIDENT!
IF SOME COUNTRY SHOULD MAKE A MOVE AGAINST AMERICA, A FEAR-STRICKEN F.D.R. COULD RESULT IN OUR DEFEAT!
REASON IT OUT!
REASON? THE DOOMSDAY PLAN IS MY VERY "RAISON D'ETRE," SONNY-BOY!
IRONIC... YOU'VE BEEN MINE FOR THE LAST TEN YEARS!
AND THERE GOES THE PRESIDENT'S LAST BEST CHANCE OF PROTECTION!
DON'T DO IT, DAD!

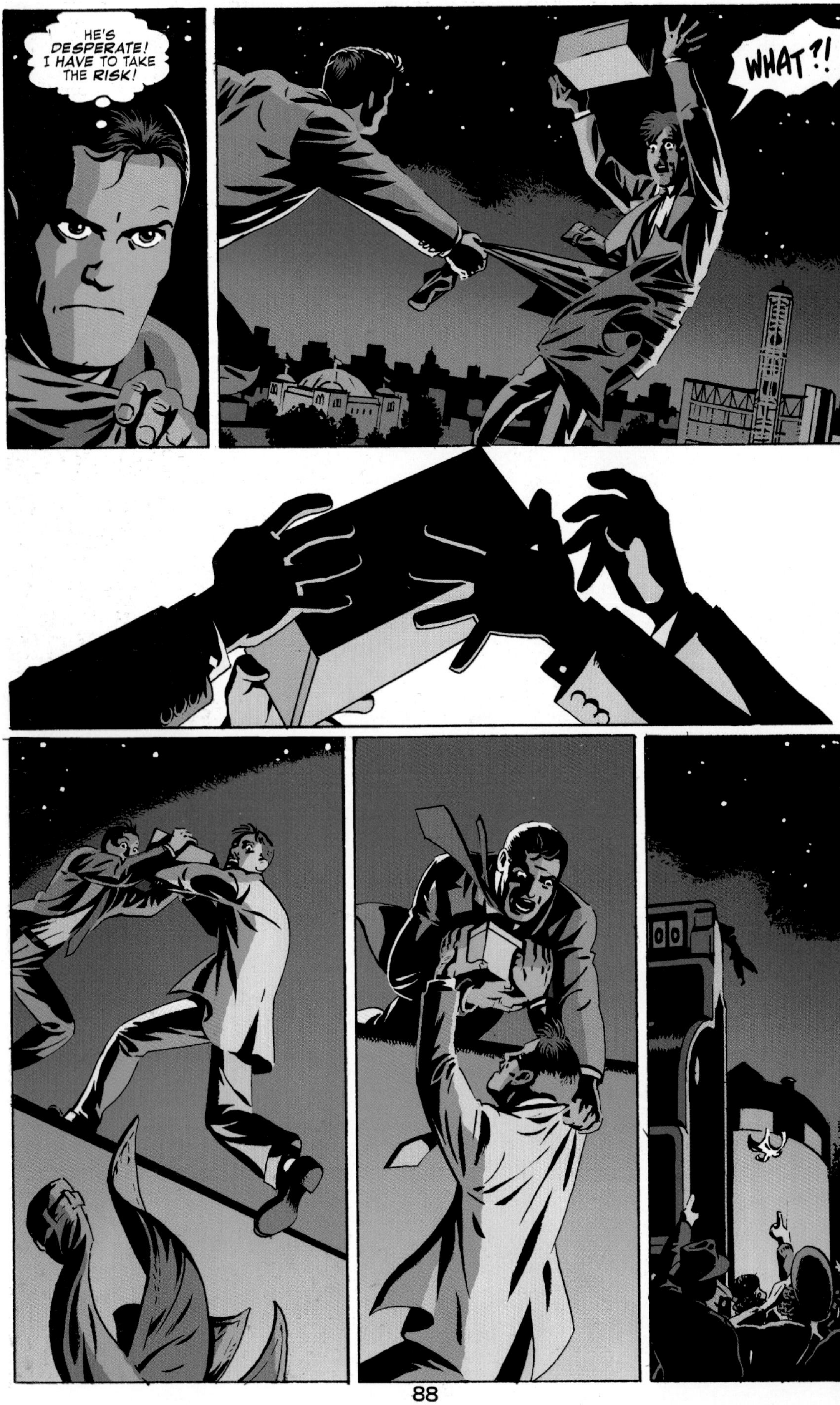
HE'S DESPERATE! I HAVE TO TAKE THE RISK!
WHAT?!

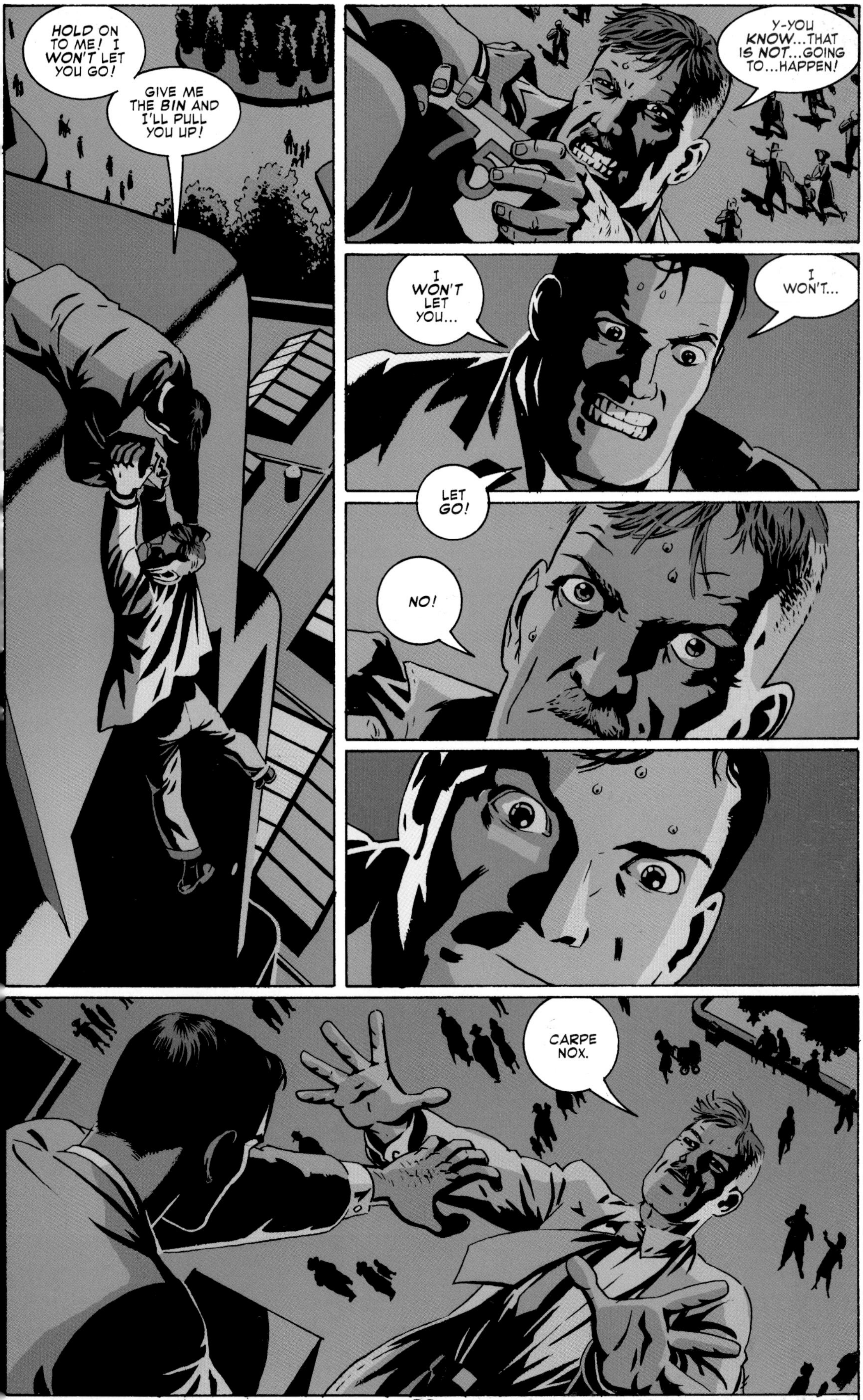
HOLD ON TO ME! I WON'T LET YOU GO!
GIVE ME THE BIN AND I'LL PULL YOU UP!
Y-YOU KNOW...THAT IS NOT...GOING TO...HAPPEN!
I WON'T LET YOU...
I WON'T...
LET GO!
NO!
CARPE NOX.

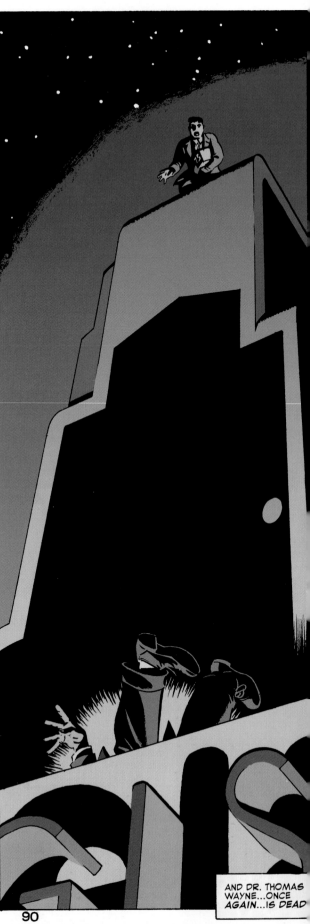

AND DR. THOMAS
WAYNE...ONCE
AGAIN...IS DEAD

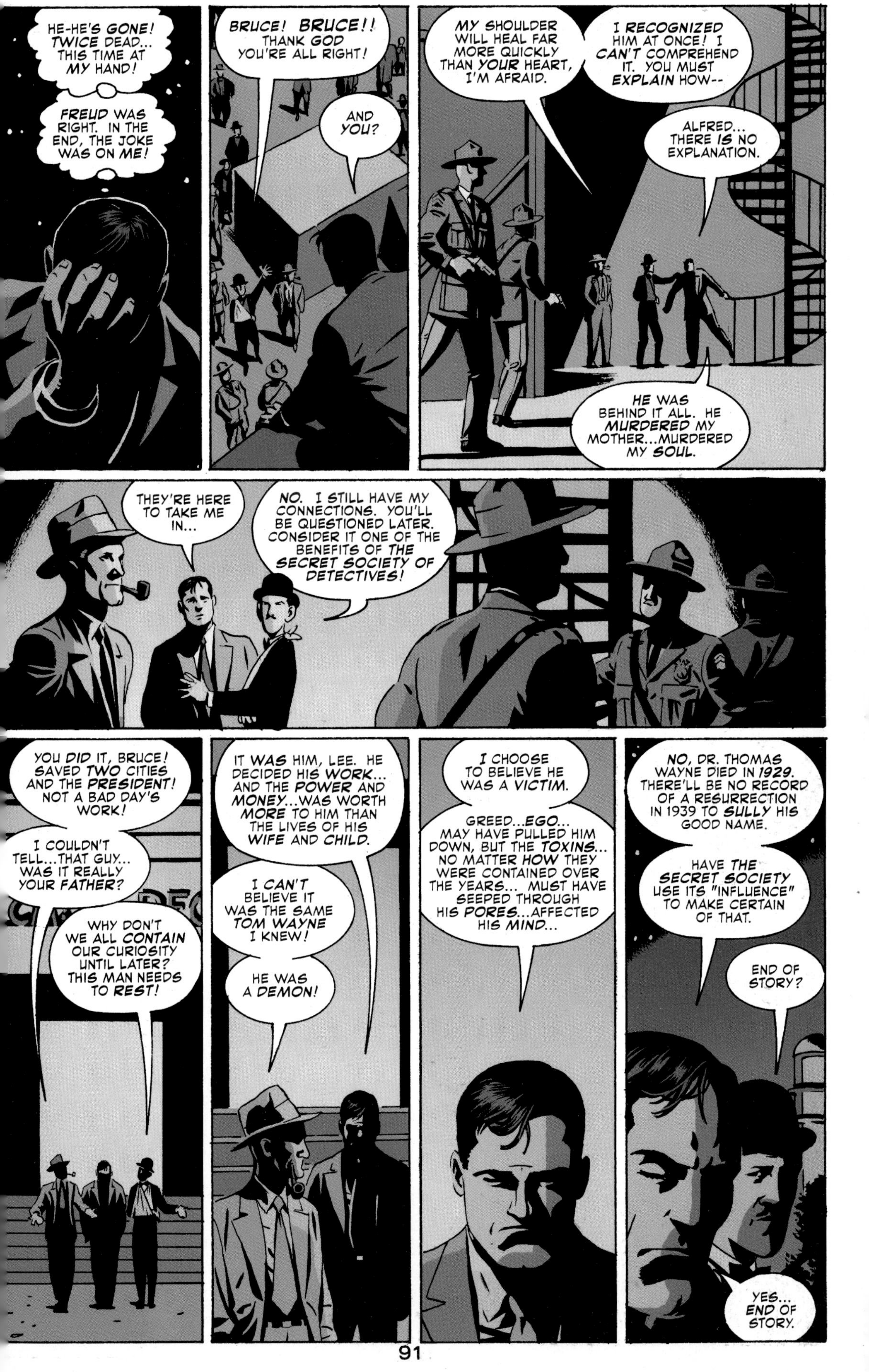
HE-HE'S GONE! TWICE DEAD... THIS TIME AT MY HAND!
FREUD WAS RIGHT. IN THE END, THE JOKE WAS ON ME!
BRUCE! BRUCE!! THANK GOD YOU'RE ALL RIGHT!
AND YOU?
MY SHOULDER WILL HEAL FAR MORE QUICKLY THAN YOUR HEART, I'M AFRAID.
I RECOGNIZED HIM AT ONCE! I CAN'T COMPREHEND IT. YOU MUST EXPLAIN HOW--
ALFRED... THERE IS NO EXPLANATION.
HE WAS BEHIND IT ALL. HE MURDERED MY MOTHER...MURDERED MY SOUL.
THEY'RE HERE TO TAKE ME IN...
NO. I STILL HAVE MY CONNECTIONS. YOU'LL BE QUESTIONED LATER. CONSIDER IT ONE OF THE BENEFITS OF THE SECRET SOCIETY OF DETECTIVES!
YOU DID IT, BRUCE! SAVED TWO CITIES AND THE PRESIDENT! NOT A BAD DAY'S WORK!
I COULDN'T TELL...THAT GUY... WAS IT REALLY YOUR FATHER?
WHY DON'T WE ALL CONTAIN OUR CURIOSITY UNTIL LATER? THIS MAN NEEDS TO REST!
IT WAS HIM, LEE. HE DECIDED HIS WORK... AND THE POWER AND MONEY...WAS WORTH MORE TO HIM THAN THE LIVES OF HIS WIFE AND CHILD.
I CAN'T BELIEVE IT WAS THE SAME TOM WAYNE I KNEW!
HE WAS A DEMON!
I CHOOSE TO BELIEVE HE WAS A VICTIM.
GREED...EGO... MAY HAVE PULLED HIM DOWN, BUT THE TOXINS... NO MATTER HOW THEY WERE CONTAINED OVER THE YEARS... MUST HAVE SEEPED THROUGH HIS PORES...AFFECTED HIS MIND...
NO, DR. THOMAS WAYNE DIED IN 1929. THERE'LL BE NO RECORD OF A RESURRECTION IN 1939 TO SULLY HIS GOOD NAME.
HAVE THE SECRET SOCIETY USE ITS "INFLUENCE" TO MAKE CERTAIN OF THAT.
END OF STORY?
YES... END OF STORY.

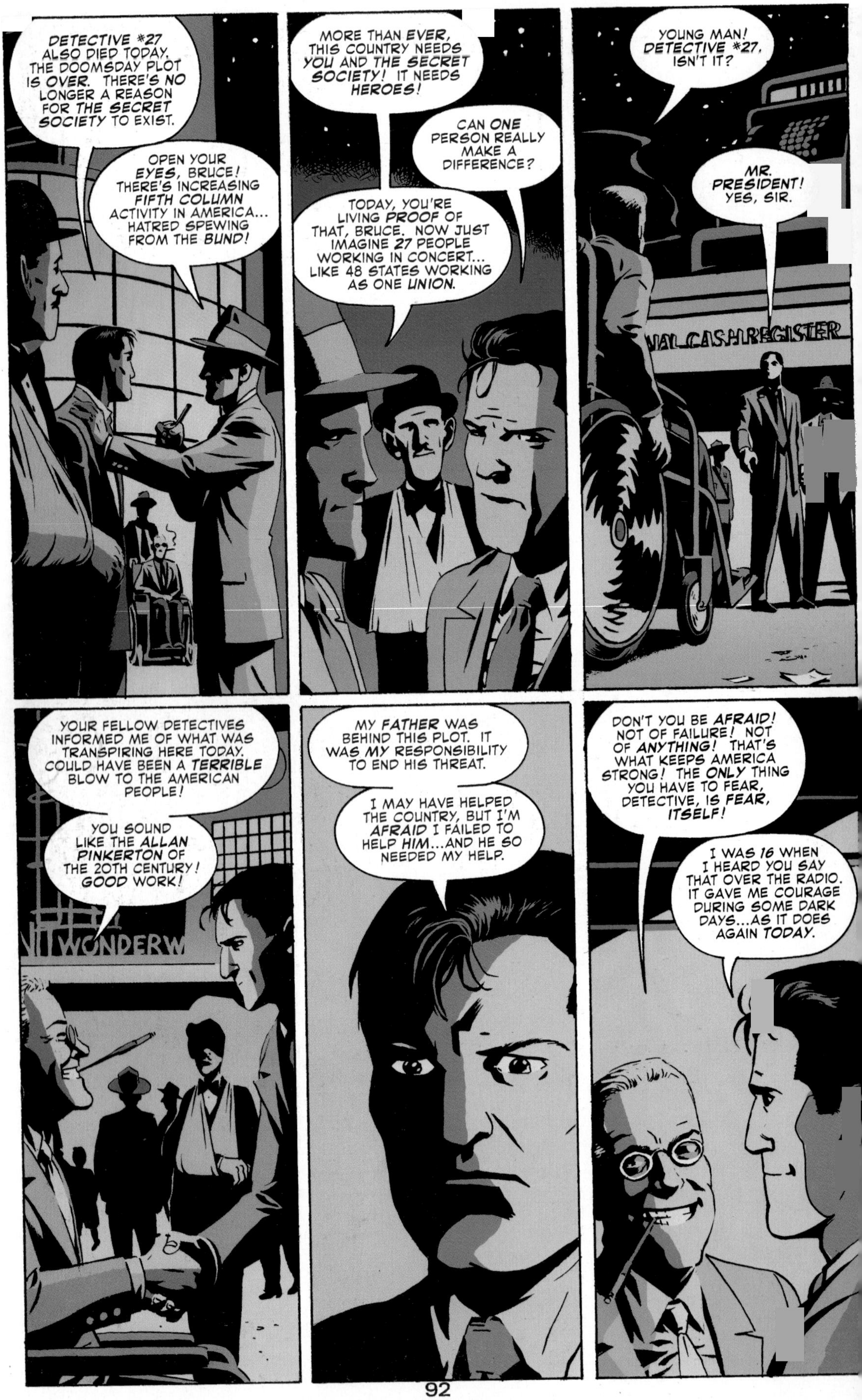
DETECTIVE #27 ALSO DIED TODAY. THE DOOMSDAY PLOT IS OVER. THERE'S NO LONGER A REASON FOR THE SECRET SOCIETY TO EXIST.
OPEN YOUR EYES, BRUCE! THERE'S INCREASING FIFTH COLUMN ACTIVITY IN AMERICA... HATRED SPEWING FROM THE BUND!
MORE THAN EVER, THIS COUNTRY NEEDS YOU AND THE SECRET SOCIETY! IT NEEDS HEROES!
CAN ONE PERSON REALLY MAKE A DIFFERENCE?
TODAY, YOU'RE LIVING PROOF OF THAT, BRUCE. NOW JUST IMAGINE 27 PEOPLE WORKING IN CONCERT... LIKE 48 STATES WORKING AS ONE UNION.
YOUNG MAN! DETECTIVE #27, ISN'T IT?
MR. PRESIDENT! YES, SIR.
NAL CASH REGISTER
YOUR FELLOW DETECTIVES INFORMED ME OF WHAT WAS TRANSPIRING HERE TODAY. COULD HAVE BEEN A TERRIBLE BLOW TO THE AMERICAN PEOPLE!
YOU SOUND LIKE THE ALLAN PINKERTON OF THE 20TH CENTURY! GOOD WORK!
WONDERW
MY FATHER WAS BEHIND THIS PLOT. IT WAS MY RESPONSIBILITY TO END HIS THREAT.
I MAY HAVE HELPED THE COUNTRY, BUT I'M AFRAID I FAILED TO HELP HIM...AND HE SO NEEDED MY HELP.
DON'T YOU BE AFRAID! NOT OF FAILURE! NOT OF ANYTHING! THAT'S WHAT KEEPS AMERICA STRONG! THE ONLY THING YOU HAVE TO FEAR, DETECTIVE, IS FEAR, ITSELF!
I WAS 16 WHEN I HEARD YOU SAY THAT OVER THE RADIO. IT GAVE ME COURAGE DURING SOME DARK DAYS...AS IT DOES AGAIN TODAY.

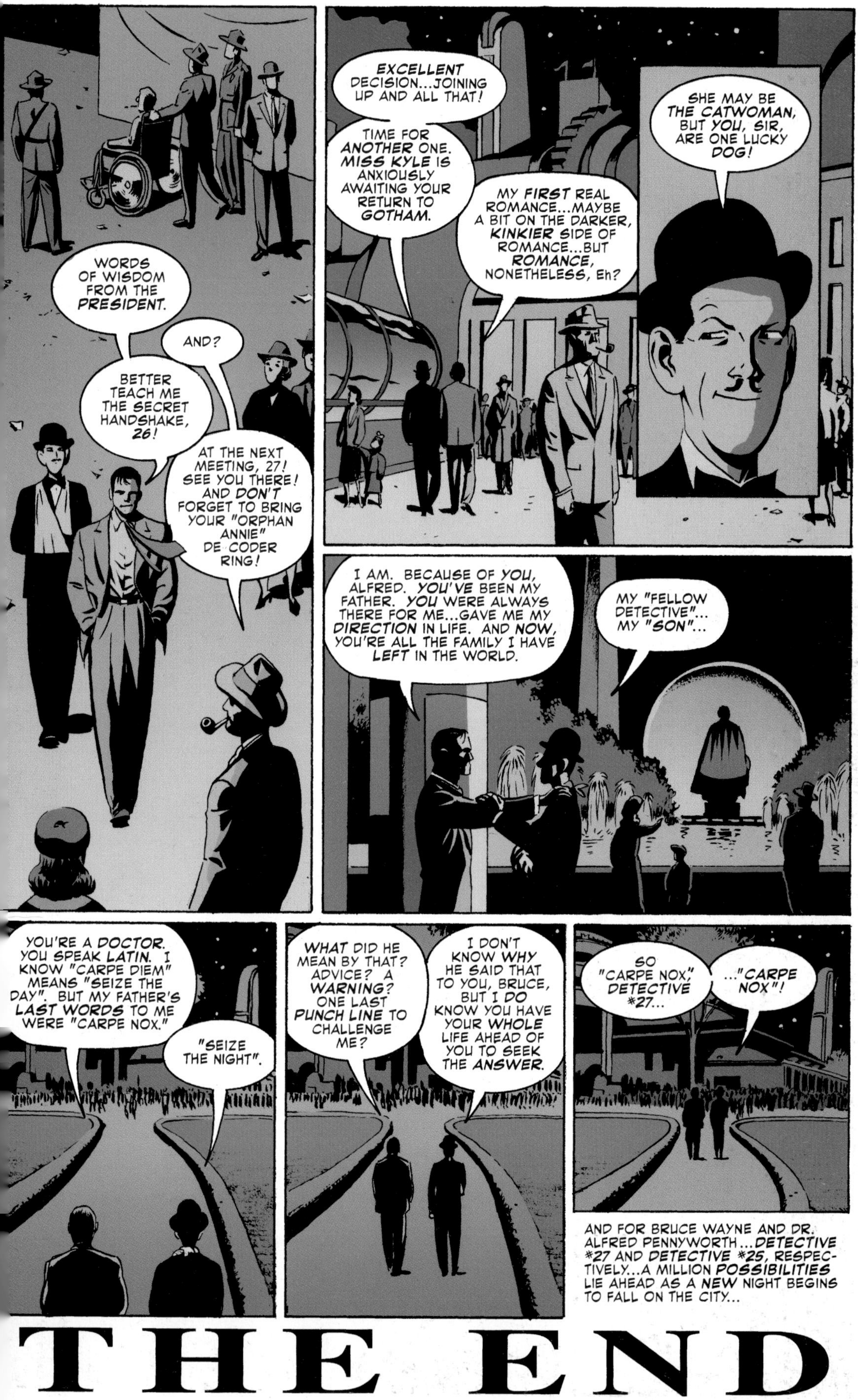
WORDS OF WISDOM FROM THE PRESIDENT.
AND?
BETTER TEACH ME THE SECRET HANDSHAKE, 26!
AT THE NEXT MEETING, 27! SEE YOU THERE! AND DON'T FORGET TO BRING YOUR "ORPHAN ANNIE" DE CODER RING!
EXCELLENT DECISION...JOINING UP AND ALL THAT!
TIME FOR ANOTHER ONE. MISS KYLE IS ANXIOUSLY AWAITING YOUR RETURN TO GOTHAM.
MY FIRST REAL ROMANCE...MAYBE A BIT ON THE DARKER, KINKIER SIDE OF ROMANCE...BUT ROMANCE, NONETHELESS, Eh?
SHE MAY BE THE CATWOMAN, BUT YOU, SIR, ARE ONE LUCKY DOG!
I AM. BECAUSE OF YOU, ALFRED. YOU'VE BEEN MY FATHER. YOU WERE ALWAYS THERE FOR ME...GAVE ME MY DIRECTION IN LIFE. AND NOW, YOU'RE ALL THE FAMILY I HAVE LEFT IN THE WORLD.
MY "FELLOW DETECTIVE"... MY "SON"...
YOU'RE A DOCTOR. YOU SPEAK LATIN. I KNOW "CARPE DIEM" MEANS "SEIZE THE DAY". BUT MY FATHER'S LAST WORDS TO ME WERE "CARPE NOX."
"SEIZE THE NIGHT".
WHAT DID HE MEAN BY THAT? ADVICE? A WARNING? ONE LAST PUNCH LINE TO CHALLENGE ME?
I DON'T KNOW WHY HE SAID THAT TO YOU, BRUCE, BUT I DO KNOW YOU HAVE YOUR WHOLE LIFE AHEAD OF YOU TO SEEK THE ANSWER.
SO "CARPE NOX," DETECTIVE #27...
..."CARPE NOX"!
AND FOR BRUCE WAYNE AND DR. ALFRED PENNYWORTH...DETECTIVE #27 AND DETECTIVE #25, RESPECTIVELY...A MILLION POSSIBILITIES LIE AHEAD AS A NEW NIGHT BEGINS TO FALL ON THE CITY...
THE END

FOOTNOTES TO HISTORY

DETECTIVE #27, LIKE *RAGTIME*, *THE ALIENIST*, *THE AMAZING ADVENTURES OF KAVALIER & CLAY*, AND *CARTER BEATS THE DEVIL*, IS ABOUT A FICTIONAL CHARACTER ENTWINED WITH REAL PEOPLE WHILE MINGLING IN REAL EVENTS OF HISTORY. HISTORY BUFFS, THEREFORE, MIGHT FIND THEIR READING OF THIS GRAPHIC NOVEL ENRICHED BY THE FOLLOWING NOTES AS TO WHO AND WHAT IN THIS TALE WERE BASED ON FACT. GET THE FULL, TRUE STORY BY EXPLORING EACH OF THE FOLLOWING ON THE INTERNET OR AT YOUR LOCAL LIBRARY:

PAGE 1. ABRAHAM LINCOLN (1809-1865)- 16TH PRESIDENT OF THE UNITED STATES.

PAGE 1. ALLAN PINKERTON (1819-1884)- FOUNDER OF THE PINKERTON DETECTIVE AGENCY AND THE U.S. SECRET SERVICE. FOUGHT THE KNIGHTS OF THE GOLDEN CIRCLE, SMASHING THEIR 1861 PLOT TO ASSASSINATE LINCOLN.

PAGE 1. "THE PRESIDENT'S HOUSE"- A COMMON PHRASE USED TO DESCRIBE 1600 PENNSYLVANIA AVENUE UNTIL TEDDY ROOSEVELT IN 1901 OFFICIALLY CHRISTENED IT "THE WHITE HOUSE."

PAGE 1. MARY TODD LINCOLN (1818-1882)- VOLATILE WIFE OF ABRAHAM LINCOLN.

PAGE 1. MAJOR HENRY RATHBONE (1837-1911) AND MISS CLARA HARRIS (1834-1883)- THE ENGAGED COUPLE INVITED TO JOIN THE LINCOLNS IN THE PRESIDENTIAL BOX AT FORD'S THEATRE. HE FAILED TO STOP OR CAPTURE JOHN WILKES BOOTH AND SLOWLY DESCENDED INTO MADNESS. HE MARRIED CLARA, HAD A FAMILY WITH HER, AND BRUTALLY MURDERED HER IN 1883.

PAGE 2. CONSTABLE JOHN PARKER'S THIRST, COUPLED WITH THE LACK OF JURIS- DICTION OF THE NEW U.S. SECRET SERVICE IN WASHINGTON DC, DID LEAD TO THE SUCCESSFUL ASSASSINATION OF ABRAHAM LINCOLN BY JOHN WILKES BOOTH AT FORD'S THEATRE ON APRIL 14, 1865.

PAGE 4. THE ROCKING CHAIR IN WHICH LINCOLN WAS SITTING WHEN HE WAS ASSASSINATED WAS PURCHASED BY HENRY FORD AT AUCTION IN 1929 AND MAY BE FOUND TODAY AT THE HENRY FORD MUSEUM IN DEARBORN, MICHIGAN.

PAGE 7. IN 1929, THE S.S. MAURITANIA OF THE CUNARD LINE WAS SAILING BETWEEN NEW YORK CITY AND LIVERPOOL.

PAGE 8. THE KNIGHTS OF THE GOLDEN CIRCLE- AN EXTREMIST ORGANIZATION OF SOUTHERN SECESSIONISTS INFILTRATED BY PINKERTON'S "PINKS," WHO FOILED ITS 1861 PLOT TO ASSASSINATE LINCOLN AS WELL AS ITS OTHER ESPIONAGE ACTIVITIES.

PAGE 9. "EXPERIMENTS IN PLANT HYBRIDIZATION" BY GREGOR MENDEL (1822-1884) WOULD LEAD TO A NEW WORLD UNDERSTANDING OF GENETICS. MENDEL'S WORK WAS FINALLY PUBLISHED IN 1866 BUT RECEIVED NO ATTEN- TION UNTIL 1900.

PAGE 9. JOE MILLER'S JOKE BOOK- OFTEN MENTIONED AS ABE LINCOLN'S FAVORITE BOOK. THIS WAS THE FIRST ENGLISH LANGUAGE JOKE BOOK, ORIGINALLY PUBLISHED AFTER MILLER'S DEATH, IN 1738.

PAGE 12. CHARLES DARWIN (1809-1882)- THIS NATURALIST STUDIED PLANTS AND ANIMALS, LEADING HIM TO ADVANCE THE THEORY OF EVOLUTION AND THE PROCESS HE CALLED "NATURAL SELECTION."

PAGE 14. KATE WARNE – MRS. WARNE JOINED THE PINKERTON DETECTIVE AGENCY IN 1856, BECOMING THE FIRST FEMALE DETECTIVE IN THE U.S. SHE MOVED ON TO THE U.S. SECRET SERVICE FORMED BY PINKERTON AND WORKED UNDERCOVER, POSING AS A SOUTHERN BELLE TO GAIN INFORMATION ON CONFEDERATE TROOP MOVEMENTS.

PAGE 14. WILLIAM PINKERTON- SON OF ALLAN PINKERTON, RECRUITED AT AGE 16 TO JOIN HIS FATHER'S DETECTIVE AGENCY AND SECRET SERVICE, WAS AN EFFECTIVE UNDERCOVER OPERATIVE, SPY, AND FIELD AGENT. AFTER HIS FATHER'S DEATH, HE AND HIS BROTHER ROBERT RAN THE AGENCY.

PAGE 19. THE PENNSYLVANIA LIMITED- ONE OF SEVERAL TRAINS CONNECTING CHICAGO AND NEW YORK CITY IN THE 1880s.

PAGE 19. THEODORE ROOSEVELT (1858-1919)- 26TH PRESIDENT OF THE U.S. WHO, IN 1884, WAS THE 26-YEAR-OLD MEMBER OF THE N.Y. STATE ASSEMBLY AND CHAIRMAN OF THE COMMITTEE ON CITIES. HIS FIRST CHILD HAD BEEN BORN ON FEBRUARY 12TH AND HIS WIFE AND MOTHER HAD BOTH DIED ON FEBRUARY 14TH OF THAT SAME YEAR.

PAGE 20. IN AN ATTEMPT TO RAISE SUFFICIENT FUNDS TO ERECT AND MAINTAIN FRANCE'S GIFT OF A STATUE OF "LIBERTY ENLIGHTENING THE WORLD," JUST THE HAND HOLDING THE TORCH WAS SENT AHEAD TO NEW YORK CITY WHERE IT WAS PLACED ON DISPLAY IN MADISON SQUARE. PASSERSBY COULD CLIMB INSIDE IT AS A PREVIEW OF THE FULL STATUE TO COME. IN FUTURE YEARS, ITS NAME WAS COMMONLY SHORTENED TO "THE STATUE OF LIBERTY."

PAGE 20. IN 1884, POLO WAS OUT AND BASEBALL WAS IN AT THE ORIGINAL POLO GROUNDS IN CENTRAL PARK BETWEEN 5TH AVENUE AND 6TH AVENUE AT 110TH STREET TO 112TH STREET. THE N.Y. METROPOLITANS PLAYED ON THE SOUTHWEST FIELD, WHILE THE NEW YORKS (EVENTUALLY CALLED THE GIANTS) PLAYED ON THE SOUTHEAST FIELD.

PAGE 20. "OLD SLEUTH" WAS A HUGELY POPULAR DIME NOVEL DETECTIVE BEGINNING IN 1872 IN "FIRESIDE COMPANION" AND "OLD SLEUTH LIBRARY."

PAGE 22. THE CELTIC, ONE OF THE GREAT SHIPS OF THE WHITE STAR LINE CON- NECTING LIVERPOOL WITH NEW YORK CITY, WOULD BE INVOLVED IN 1887 IN AN INFAMOUS COLLISION WITH ANOTHER WHITE STAR SHIP, THE BRITANNIC, 300 MILES OFF THE COAST OF SANDY HOOK, NJ.

PAGE 22. TEDDY ROOSEVELT WOULD, IN FACT, BE APPOINTED POLICE COMMISSIONER OF NEW YORK CITY BY MAYOR STRONG IN 1895.

PAGE 24. ROBERT FROST (1874-1963)- AUTHOR OF THE POEM "THE ROAD NOT TAKEN."

PAGE 29. DELMONICO'S RESTAURANT WAS TEDDY ROOSEVELT'S FAVORITE, LOCATED ON 5TH AVENUE AND 26TH STREET ON MADISON SQUARE. OWNER CHARLES DELMONICO'S DEATH — IN 1884, AS WELL — WAS REPORTED AS "UNEXPECTED AND VERY ODD."

PAGE 29. "LOBSTER WENBERG" WAS CREATED IN 1876 BY BEN WENBERG AND SERVED EXCLUSIVELY AT DELMONICO'S UNTIL HE GOT INTO AN ARGUMENT WITH CHARLES DELMONICO SOME MONTHS LATER. AN ANGRY CHARLES, DETERMINED TO STRIP BEN OF CREDIT, REVERSED THE LETTERS "W" AND "N" IN "WENBERG" AND THUS, "LOBSTER NEWBERG" WAS BORN.

PAGE 29. DATURA- VERY DANGEROUS, VERY POWERFUL, VERY BEAUTIFUL PLANT CAPABLE OF INDUCING HALLUCINATIONS AND NIGHTMARES AND, IN SUFFICIENT DOSAGE, PERMANENT INSANITY OR DEATH. SEE ALSO EMEX SPINOSA POLYGONACEAE/DEVIL'S THORN/DEVIL'S BACKBONE/THORN APPLE.

PAGE 30. THE DAKOTA- THE FIRST GRAND APARTMENT BUILDING ON NEW YORK CITY'S UPPER WEST SIDE OPENED ITS DOORS IN 1884 ON 72ND STREET OVERLOOKING CENTRAL PARK.

PAGE 32. CARL SANDBURG (1878-1967)- AUTHOR OF THE POEM "THEY WILL SAY."

PAGE 39. "GINGER SNAP" WAS A COMIC PAGE CREATED BY BOB KANE WHICH ACTUALLY DEBUTED IN MORE FUN COMICS #36 (OCTOBER 1938) AND APPEARED IN NEW YORK WORLD'S FAIR COMICS 1939.

PAGE 50. 1934 BROUGHT THE WORLD THE PULP MAGAZINE, "OPERATOR #5" BY CURTIS STEELE (REAL NAME: FREDERICK DAVIS), AND THE COMIC STRIP "SECRET AGENT X-9" BY FORMER PINKERTON DETECTIVE DASHIELL HAMMETT AND ARTIST ALEX RAYMOND.

PAGE 52. THAT "PAPER-HANGER IN BERLIN" EVENTUALLY BECAME DER FUEHRER, ADOLF HITLER.

PAGE 54. "THREE ESSAYS ON THE THEORY OF SEXUALITY, JOKES AND THEIR RELATION TO THE UNCONSCIOUS" BY SIGMUND FREUD WAS PUBLISHED IN 1905 AND CONSIDERED BY DR. FREUD TO BE HIS MOST IMPORTANT WORK NEXT TO "THE INTERPRETATION OF DREAMS." FREUD DIED IN 1939.

PAGE 59. BABE RUTH, "THE SULTAN OF SWAT," PLAYED IN MAJOR LEAGUE BASEBALL'S FIRST ALL-STAR GAME IN 1933. HIS UNIFORM NUMBER WAS "3". THE 1939 ALL-STAR GAME WAS PLAYED AT YANKEE STADIUM.

PAGE 73. THE HOTEL ASTOR- IN TIMES SQUARE, IT WAS A PALACE FOR THE ELITE. THE ASTOR BAR WAS A FAMOUS HANGOUT FOR CELEBRITIES, POLITI- CIANS, AND POWERFUL MEN IN BIG BUSINESS.

PAGE 74. THE NEW YORK WORLD'S FAIR OF 1939 AND '40 TOOK PLACE WHERE THE 1964-65 WORLD'S FAIR, SHEA STADIUM, THE NATIONAL TENNIS CENTER, AND FLUSHING MEADOWS PARK HAVE SINCE TAKEN ROOT. WHILE THERE WAS A NATIONAL CASH REGISTER PAVILION AT THE '39 FAIR, IT WAS NOT IN THE SHAPE OF A GIANT CASH REGISTER. THAT PARTICULAR BUILDING WAS ACTUALLY THE NATIONAL CASH REGISTER PAVILION AT THE SAN FRANCISCO WORLD'S FAIR OF 1939. "SUPERMAN DAY" AT THE NEW YORK WORLD'S FAIR IN 1939 WAS PART OF A PROMOTIONAL TIE-IN TO DC COMICS' PUBLICATION OF NEW YORK WORLD'S FAIR COMICS 1939, WHICH FEATURED SUPERMAN, BATMAN, AND OTHER DC HEROES. RAY MIDDLETON WAS THE ACTOR PORTRAYING THE MAN OF STEEL THAT DAY. "SUPERMAN DAY" WAS REPEATED ON JULY 3, 1940 IN CONNECTION WITH DC'S PUBLICATION OF NEW YORK WORLD'S FAIR COMICS 1940.

PAGE 74. MAYOR FIORELLO LAGUARDIA (1882-1947)- MAYOR OF NEW YORK CITY DURING THE 1939-'40 WORLD'S FAIR,

PAGE 74. FRANKLIN DELANO ROOSEVELT (1882-1945)- 32ND PRESIDENT OF THE UNITED STATES WHO, IN 1941, WOULD MAKE A LEGENDARY SPEECH ABOUT THE "FOUR FREEDOMS," WHICH WOULD INCLUDE "THE FREEDOM FROM FEAR."

PAGE 74. TOD BROWNING- MOVIE DIRECTOR OF "FREAKS" AND THE ORIGINAL "DRACULA."

PAGE 93. THANKS TO OVALTINE, KIDS COULD ORDER A "LITTLE ORPHAN ANNIE DECODER RING TO DECIPHER SECRET MESSAGES BROADCAST DURING EACH EPISODE OF HER RADIO ADVENTURES.